Merry Christmas!
Whoda thought Canadians
could be so damned funny—
even when they weren't
trying to be!
Love,
Roxane.

THE GREAT BIG BOOK OF CANADIAN HUMOUR

THE GREAT BIG BOOK OF CANADIAN HUMOUR eh?

ALLAN GOULD, EDITOR

MACMILLAN CANADA
TORONTO

Canadian Cataloguing in Publication Data

Main entry under title:

The Great big book of Canadian humour

ISBN 0-7715-9180-2

1. Canadian wit and humour (English).* I. Gould, Allan, 1944-

PS8375.G73 1992   C818'.5402   C92-094312-8
PR9197.8.G73 1992

1 2 3 4 5 WC 96 95 94 93 92

Cover and text design by Matthews Communications Design

Macmillan Canada
A Division of Canada Publishing Corporation
Toronto, Ontario, Canada

Printed in Canada

*To my beloved wife of nearly a quarter-century,
Merle, who has (usually) laughed at my own work,
and (nearly always) laughed at the superb humour
of the many gifted women and men in this book.
And to our brilliant children, Judah and Elisheva,
who have (often) brought us more laughter than
tears.*

CONTENTS

Acknowledgements

To the awesomely talented humorists of Canada, who—with rare exception—opened their libraries, their hearts, and their minds to the project, choosing their best to stand with the best of others. May their wise and witty choices bring as many hours of pleasure and laughter to readers of this collection as they did to myself and to my fine editor, Jackie Rothstein.

The Great Collector John Robert Colombo wrote to me early in my research, "I don't know *why* previous collections of Canadian humour have always ignored what we Canadians are particularly good at: TV and radio sketch comedy." How right he was. And how determined I was, to track down the best.

I was also assisted by another (great) anthologizer, Alberto Manguel, who made numerous invaluable suggestions; by Urjo Kareda, the superb artistic director at the Tarragon Theatre, regarding stage comedy; and Mark Breslin of Yuk Yuk's fame, who recommended several marvelous Canadian comedians who were unknown to me.

An Anthologizer's Comments About Our Comically Gifted Countrypersons

Are Canadians funny?

Do Quebecois speak French? Do Albertans feel alienated? Can the country that gave the world William Lyon Mackenzie King (and then kept re-electing him for a third of a century), Meech Lake and William Vander Zalm *not* be funny?

Which leads us, as both Prufrock and your grade-seven homeroom teacher used to say, to an important question: Why should a northern country with a smaller population than the state of California (where some one million Canadians are living, by the way—"If you're that good...") produce such an astonishing array of comedic genii?

Canadians? Hockey players, sure. Cold fronts, *sans doubt*. But humour? Why on earth humour? What makes a witty Atwood, a caustic Richler, a folksy Harron, a satiric Second City, a hip Kids in the Hall, a devastating Aislin and Gable, an intellectual-yet-childlike Wayne and Shuster, a just-plain-uproarious Nicol, or Ritter or Broadfoot?

I have one theory, although I sense that there are others that would be even better: one of the frequent reasons given for the impressive impact of Jews (and later, Blacks, Catholics, gays, women, and others not part of the White Protestant Male Power System) upon American comedy is that they were (at least back at the turn of the century when the Jews were pouring in to the lower east side of Manhattan) *outsiders*. They could see—and comment upon—"where it was at" precisely because they were *not* "where it was at."

In other words a George Burns, a Jack Benny, (and later) a Lenny Bruce, a Mort Sahl, a Mel Brooks, a Woody Allen, could poke fun at American fables and foibles and foolishness around them because they were not allowed to be part of it. Or, at the very least, because they did not *feel* part of it. As a renowned Canadian named Marshall McLuhan once noted about the media—I may be paraphrasing here— "We don't know who discovered water, but it certainly wasn't a fish." Translation: fish are too busy swimming about in water to realize what they are swimming in. And so are white Protestants in a white Protestant society (usually—there are no hard-and-fast rules to comic inspiration). But the Jews—and, more and more, other "outsiders"— were truly like fish out of water, free to look down into that water and mock the hell out of the feel-right-at-home, complacent, well-adjusted bourgeois fish happily swimming about below.

Canadian humour is also like classic Jewish humour in that it is often self-deprecating; it pokes fun at Jews themselves and by doing so, magically comes out on top. Many people think that self-deprecation implies self-hatred. On the contrary. More often than not it says something far more complex: "I am only human; I have flaws," it declares; "I am willing to admit this." By poking fun at their own failings, self-deprecating comedians (whether Jew, Canadian, woman—or WASP, for that matter) end up in far better shape than the Other to whom they are admitting their weaknesses.

You can probably already see the Canadian connection to this argument: The United States is this huge, vulgar, wealthy, dangerous, irresistible country to the south. And here we are, the citizens of the country to the north, who can look down (both geographically and—often unfairly—morally) upon the polluted waters of American society and poke fun to our hearts' content.

In short there are great, and often, comic advantages to being an outsider. And in the political, social, economic scheme of things we Canadians are very much outsiders to where it really does all happen: the United States.

We Canadians also tend to take ourselves far less seriously than Americans, which also helps. After all, *we* are not at the centre of the world; *we* are not the world's policeman; *we* are merely a friendly, disarming (and usually unarmed) peacekeeper in Cyprus—or Sarajevo.

Not that my little theory explains why there is so much quality comic talent in this country, especially when much of that humour is not necessarily about the United States, or even about being an outsider. Does his nationality explain Stephen Leacock's hilarious parody of nineteenth-century Romantic literature, "Gertrude the Governess," or his wicked study of the personal life stories of those famous men of math, "A, B, and C"?

Does one need to be Canadian, as are the writers and performers of the Montreal-based comedy troupe Radio Free Vestibule, to write a crushing attack of the Disney corporation's propensity to sue anyone who dares infringe upon their copyright?

Would not a talented essayist such as Ed Hailwood be talented in any country? Or Susan Musgrave? Or Ray Guy?

Indeed, though we Canadians are so often labelled with that terribly descriptive adjective, "nice," how many Americans are aware that their funnybones have been molded by a much larger number of (scathing) Canadians than any other people. From Frank Peppiatt and John Aylesworth's "Hee Haw" to Lorne Michael's "Saturday Night Live," to Andrew Alexander's "SCTV," to the wildly successful on cable, and as-of-1992-picked-up-by-CBS "Kids in the Hall," to David Steinberg, John Candy, Catherine O'Hara, Martin Short, Mike Myers, Howie Mandel, and a stunningly large number of other major comedy writers and performers of this half-century, who have been "that good" that they "made it in the States." (And I won't even mention the several Canadian comedy writers who wrote a great deal of Johnny Carson's material over three decades, if only because I can't remember their names. But you get the point.)

To be honest I have no idea why Canada has produced such a staggeringly high number of inspired comedians, comic essayists, political satirists, parodists, editorial cartoonists, sketchwriters, and more.

What I do know—and what every reader of this book shall soon discover—is that this country has produced some of the richest lodes of comedy in the world, and that it is about time that a goodly selection be found in one place.

In collecting the best of over one hundred Canadian men and women I found it important to include a large number whose names (if not whose selections) will undoubtedly be familiar to many: Richler, Atwood, Gallant, Fotheringham, Quarrington, Slinger, Zolf, Carrier, Guy, Torgov, Tremblay. But there will be many, probably even dozens, whose names will be new to you, and whose comedic gifts are awesome.

I am particularly proud of the cartoonists included, ranging from the fine daily (Lynn Johnston of "For Better or For Worse," Warren Clements of "Nestlings," Jim Unger of "Herman") to the world-class editorial (Peterson, Dewar, Gable, Mayes, to name a few). I am also proud of the quite extraordinary stage, radio, and TV sketches which were so generously shared with me—and now with you—from such major artists as Johnny Wayne and Frank Shuster, The Royal Canadian Air Farce, Second City, Kids in the Hall, CODCO, the Frantics, Double Exposure, Smith and Smith, and, yes, several more.

Here is where I should share a (possibly important) fact with you, the reader: I wrote to over 150 Canadian authors, essayists, cartoonists, poets, comedians, playwrights, et al, asking them to suggest their best. Fully 90 percent did so (the several deceased notwithstanding). Why did I do this? you ask. Because I am of the firm belief that *writers know what works best*—what got the most laughs in their readings, their performances, their stand-up routines. And, with the *very* rare exception, they were "right." What they sent me, or recommended to me, was usually uproarious—and often not "available" to the public before now. To paraphrase Hamlet, "for this release, much thanks."

This is one very funny book. Open to any page—you dirty it, you buy it—and see what I mean. It's got plenty of cartoons for those who have had a rough day but deserve better than what's on TV, especially if the show was written by some talentless non-Canadian from south of the border. And even *more* especially if what's on TV is a discussion about the Canadian constitution.

As my late grandmothers—Russian-born, inarticulate in every official language except Yiddish—would say, "Enjoy."

HOCKEY TO HOOKEY

GROWING UP AND GETTING EDUCATED IN CANADA

FROM *KING LEARY*

Paul Quarrington

One day Clay Clinton informed me that the two of us had to defend the honour of his sister, Horseface. I never did learn the exact nature of the insult to Olivia, but I was more than willing to help. Clay told me that revenge had to be exacted.

This is how he was talking, revenge had to be exacted, satisfaction given, recompense had for the besmirchment of the family name. I said fair enough. So, Clay told me, go get a bag full of dog dirt. Well, a lifelong problem has been this inability of mine to think things through, but a bag full of dog dirt made as much sense as anything else back then. My next-door neighbour was an old widow woman named Mrs. Dougherty, and she had a dog. Her dog was a particularly gruesome thing, one of those wrinkled little brutes that God dropped on its face two or three times before setting onto the earth. This dog—I can even remember its name, Rex—spent all of its waking hours rooting in Mrs. Dougherty's vegetable garden. The beast was inordinately fond of radishes, so Mrs. Dougherty, having no one else to fuss over and being a motherly sort, grew the dog a whole backyard full of the little red things. Rex was out in the garden most of the time, chewing on radishes and passing them, and it was not a matter of much difficulty to go over into the yard and gather up a big sack full of shit.

Then, at night, after I was supposed to be asleep, I snuck out my bedroom window and carried this bag over to the house of Clay Clinton. The first thing Clay did—and mind you, this is absolutely typical—is go on about how much I smelt. What the Jesus did he expect? First he tells me to get shit, then he's mad because the stuff stinks. He made me walk ten paces behind him. We walked straight

Lorne Elliott
Comedian

We used to go to this place called Club Debris. It was a great place for underage-drinking; the bouncer couldn't read to check your I.D. We walked in; we were 15 years old. We tried to look cool: went to the bar; ordered beer on the rocks. The clientele in this place looked like an insult to Darwin. Guys in there could have traced their family tree back two generations and hit the invertebrates...I asked this girl for a date. "I wouldn't. My husband is big, jealous, and he's just come in."

I turn, and there's this knee. On top of this knee there's this guy the size of a dumpster—and easily as intelligent. *Definite* light came into his eyes when *both* neurons fired at once. I don't know what he did for a living, but judging by his face, he was a kick-boxer who never had the rules completely explained to him. He saw me with his girl. Picked a fight.

I handled myself pretty well. Had him scared....He thought he'd killed me.

---

downtown, across Rideau Street and into the market, just the place you want to be when you're carting a three-pounder of dog do. Then we went into a little residential area—poor people, I saw, but not as poor as my family, and certainly nowhere near eel-poor—and Clay Clinton stopped and told me, "His name is Humphries."

"Whose name is Humphries?" I wanted to know. It hadn't occurred to me that any specific person had insulted Horseface's honour. I sort of figured it was something that just happened.

"He lives," Clay went on, "right over there."

Clay pointed to a tiny wooden house with a rickety porch. There was a chicken tied up in the front yard.

Clinton produced a box of Eddy matches. It all became clear. This was how Clinton intended to avenge his sister, the old light-the-bag-of-dog-shit caper. Clay did his best to laugh ghoulishly. Even as a boy he was concerned mostly with style. Clinton pressed the matches into my hand and whispered, "Percival, the honour is yours."

"Horseface is your sister!" I argued.

"She's your betrothed, isn't she?" News to me. "You watched her take a bath."

I couldn't quarrel there. If watching a girl bathe meant you and she were betrothed, well, that's the way the world rolls. I took the matches and the bag of dog dirt up onto the little front porch.

The way the stunt works, of course, is: you light the bag aflame, knock on the door, and then scamper to a hiding place with a view. The victim opens the door and naturally starts stomping on the fire. He ends up with dog shit all over his foot. It ain't the people's choice for defending the honour of a young maiden, and maybe Clay hadn't put as much thought into the whole affair as he might have. It's all historical, anyway.

I set a match to the brown paper, knocked on the door, screamed, "This is for Horseface!" and then hightailed it to where Clay was hiding. Naturally enough, Humphries wasn't home. He was likely out insulting someone else's honour. This might have been the best thing that could have happened. The paper bag might have burned and left behind a pile of smouldering manure and that would have been the end of it, were it not for Rex's strange diet. The ugly little beast ate nothing but radishes, and they rendered his shit volatile. All of a sudden there was a series of pops and fizzles coming from the front porch, and the air filled with a thick gray smoke. Great licks of flame started shooting from the bag. Then, with an enormous boom, the little porch exploded.

Clay Clinton said, with uncommon understatement, "Shit."

I ran for the porch, thinking that I might somehow be able to put the fire out. The house, however, was old and wooden, and the air was dry and hot, and it didn't take but a few seconds before the place was gone. I stood there and waved my hands, and about all I really accomplished was pointing out to all the neighbours that I was the one who had started the fire.

I didn't even bother looking for Clay. I knew he'd be long gone.

THE HALF OF IT

John Krizanc

(Lights up slowly. The curtain is still closed, but in front of it stands JILLSON ASHE, an interesting-looking woman in her early thirties in a black dress. There is a blackboard behind her. On it are written several phrases: "Mind/Body," "Nature vs. Reason," and "Dead or Alive?" She is moving her lips, but we still can't hear what she's saying until the lights are fully up.)

JILL: ...and it wasn't once upon a time, but at a specific time not so long ago, when we still looked upon the world and saw everything in it as equal to ourselves, because everything was alive. If we needed branches for our shelter we would ask the tree's forgiveness before cutting it down. And if a rock didn't move, it wasn't because it was dead but because it was sleeping. Occasionally we met bad spirits in the forest, but we always knew a good spirit we could call on to protect us.

Now, as individuals formed themselves into tribes it was inevitable that hierarchies should develop and that our view of nature should change to reflect this...that the tribal chief should make an offering to the chief of all deer spirits, whatever. Thousands of years pass and eventually all these spirits are reduced to one life force—God—and this is called...anyone? *(Pause.)* Monotheism.

Now, if this guy—and it's interesting that we usually think God is masculine and the earth is feminine—if this God is up there somewhere, the life force is up there somewhere, then the earth is dead. It's no longer a source of magic and

—GABLE

Harland Williams
Comedian

———

My little brother has an ant farm. The other night my father came home drunk and irrigated it. Now it's just kind of an ant *Poseidon Adventure* type of thing.

———

wonderment. We no longer have to thank the tree for its branch because we have it from God, the God that *we* invented, that all this stuff, his nature stuff, is here for the taking. This was like—the biggest real-estate deal in history—the whole world. And the great thing about it was that it made it okay to cut down all the trees because really—they were dead already. You didn't have to feel guilty now, unlike before, when the earth was your mother. You never would have done such nasty things to your mother, would you? I heard that, Becky...

Anyway, we got this thing from God—the whole earth— it's a present from God. So, remember when you were a kid—what's the first thing you do with a present? (*Points.*) Ann? Play with it—a good answer. Unfortunately it may be the reason girls are discouraged by science. Do you have a brother? What would he do with his present? Find out how it works. How? Take it apart? Right. Now, when it comes to the world, the system that was developed for this purpose was called science.

Science was supposed to reveal the mysteries of creation and thereby bring us closer to God. Unfortunately He or She didn't want anything to do with us...maybe it was our breath? The trouble began when it became apparent to the scientists that what they were finding didn't jive with what the church was telling them they were supposed to find. This hurt their pride. They started to have doubts. They started thinking their own senses were deceiving them. Had God pulled the old cosmic wool over their eyes?

Determined to get to the bottom of this, a fun guy named Francis Bacon suggested scientists should tie nature to the rack and torture her secrets from her...The boys started playing for keeps. They wanted to find the truth, a truth which was experimentally verifiable and quantifiable, a one-plus-one-always-equals-two kind of truth. You'll notice I said the truth, because for most scientists how something works is equal to its truth.

In what became traditional science you and I are reduced to nothing but valves and pumps. Yet surely we have a uniqueness beyond the mechanisms which give us life.

This term, we'll delve into that question by exploring some of the ways in which recent science has realized the limitations of traditional reductionism.

Kimberly? (*Beat.*) No. I said at the beginning none of this is in your textbook. Like it or not, our knowledge is always evolving, and since science has come to be the way through which we interpret the world, it's important that we keep up with new developments, or else the way we see the world will be a little out of focus.

A concept like the survival of the fittest may have been indispensable for the success of the industrial revolution, but you only have to breathe the air to know it's been devastating for the environment. And yet it's an idea which has gone from fact to myth, and been bastardized into clichés like "dog eat dog," and no one ever stops to say, "I've never seen a dog eat a dog!" Corky?...Absolutely. There are lots of predators— but they wouldn't survive if they ate all their prey. Nor will we if we use up all nature's resources. The point is balance— it's moving away from the idea of self-interest to mutual interest. Nature is filled with co-operation and harmony, yet we prefer not to see it. We prefer to see only what allows us to justify our own self-interest.

Even your parents' decision to send you here to Grace can be seen as a Darwinian attempt to consolidate advantage by keeping you out of touch with an inferior gene pool. My parents certainly saw it like that.

By the way, if you hate the place as much as I did, just tell your mother you're thinking of becoming a lesbian.

Now, where was—(*A school bell rings.*). Okay, tomorrow we'll start to look at the collapse of objectivity in contemporary physics. (*Sound of students closing books, she has to talk over the noise.*) Right. Homework. When you go home I want you to ask your parents..."What is reality, and how much does it cost?"

Lorne Elliott

In grade nine, I had a school teacher come in and tell me, "Today is the first day of the rest of your life." Now, that certainly made it easier to explain why I could *not*, therefore, *possibly* have yesterday's homework done.

A, B and C—The Human Element in Mathematics

Stephen Leacock

The student of arithmetic who has mastered the first four rules of his art, and successfully striven with money sums and fractions, finds himself confronted by an unbroken expanse of questions known as problems. These are short stories of adventure and industry with the end omitted, and though betraying a strong family resemblance, are not without a certain element of romance.

The characters in the plot of a problem are three people called A, B and C. The form of the question is generally of this sort:

"A, B and C do a certain piece of work. A can do as much work in one hour as B in two, or C in four. Find how long they work at it."

Or thus:

"A, B and C are employed to dig a ditch. A can dig as much in one hour as B can dig in two, and B can dig twice as fast as C. Find how long, etc., etc."

Or after this wise:

"A lays a wager that he can walk faster than B or C. A can walk half as fast again as B and C is only an indifferent walker. Find how far, and so forth."

The occupations of A, B and C are many and varied. In the older arithmetics they contented themselves with doing "a certain piece of

Stevie Ray Fromstein
Comedian

————

I moved to Vancouver where I worked with juvenile delinquents for a year—until we got caught.

work." This statement of the case, however, was found too sly and mysterious, or possibly lacking in romantic charm. It became the fashion to define the job more clearly and to set them at walking-matches, ditch-digging, regattas, and piling cord wood. At times they became commercial and entered into partnership, having with their old mystery a "certain" capital. Above all they revel in motion. When they tire of walking-matches—A rides on horseback, or borrows a bicycle and competes with his weaker-minded associates on foot. Now they race on locomotives; now they row; or again they become historical and engage stage-coaches; or at times they are aquatic and swim. If their occupation is actual work they prefer to pump water into cisterns, two of which leak through holes in the bottom and one of which is watertight. A, of course, has the good one; he also takes the bicycle, and the best locomotive, and the right of swimming with the current. Whatever they do they put money on it, being all three sports. A always wins.

In the early chapters of the arithmetic, their identity is concealed under the names John, William and Henry, and they wrangle over the division of marbles. In algebra they are often called X, Y and Z. But these are only their Christian names, and they are really the same people.

Now to one who has followed the history of these men through countless pages of problems, watched them in their leisure hours dallying with cord wood, and seen their panting sides heave in the full frenzy of filling a cistern with a leak in it, they become something more than mere symbols. They appear as creatures of flesh and blood, living men with their own passions, ambitions and aspirations like the rest of us. Let us view them in turn. A is a full-blooded blustering fellow, of energetic temperment, hot-headed and strong-willed. It is he who proposes everything, challenges B to work, makes the bets and bends the others to his will. He is a man of great physical strength and phenomenal endurance. He has been known to walk forty-eight hours at a stretch, and to pump ninety-six. His life is arduous and full of peril. A mistake in the working of a sum may keep him digging a fortnight without sleep. A repeating decimal in the answer might kill him.

B is a quiet, easy-going fellow, afraid of A and bullied by him, but very gentle and brotherly to little C, the weakling. He is quite in A's power, having lost all his money in bets.

Poor C is an undersized, frail man, with a plaintive face. Constant walking, digging and pumping has broken his health and ruined his nervous system. His joyless life has driven him to drink and smoke more than is good for him, and his hand often shakes as he digs ditches. He has not the strength to work as the others can, in fact, as Hamlin Smith has said, "A can do more work in one hour than C in four."

The first time that ever I saw these men was one evening after a regatta. They had all been rowing in it, and it had transpired that A could row as much in one hour as B in two, or C in four. B and C had come in dead fagged and C was coughing badly. "Never mind, old fellow," I heard B say, "I'll fix you up on the sofa and get you some hot tea." Just then A came blustering in and shouted, "I say, you fellows, Hamlin Smith has shown me three cisterns in his garden and he says we can pump them until tomorrow night. I bet I can beat you both. Come on. You can pump in your rowing things, you know. Your cistern leaks a little, I think, C." I heard B growl that it was a dirty shame and that C was used up now, but they went, and presently I could tell from the sound of the water that A was pumping four times as fast as C.

For years after that I used to see them constantly about town and always busy. I never heard of any of them eating or sleeping. Then owing to a long absence from home, I lost sight of them. On my return I was surprised to no longer find A, B and C at their accustomed tasks; on inquiry I heard that work in this line was now done by N, M and O, and that some people were employing for algebraical jobs four foreigners called Alpha, Beta, Gamma and Delta.

Now it chanced one day that I stumbled upon old D, in the little garden in front of his cottage, hoeing in the sun. D is an aged labouring man who used occasionally to be called in to help A, B and C. "Did I know 'em, sir?" he answered. "Why, I knowed 'em ever since they was little fellows in brackets. Master A, he were a fine lad, sir, though I always said, give me Master B for kind-heartedness-like. Many's the job as we've been on together, sir, though I never did no racing nor aught of that, but just the plain labour, as you might say. I'm getting a bit too old and stiff for it nowadays, sir—just scratch about in the garden here and grow a bit of a logarithm, or raise a common denominator or two. But Mr. Euclid he use me still for them propositions, he do."

From the garrulous old man I learned the melancholy end of my former acquaintances. Soon after I left town, he told me, C had been taken ill. It seems that A and B had been rowing on the river for a wager, and C had been running on the bank and then sat in a draught. Of course the bank had refused the draught and C was taken ill. A and B came home and found C lying helpless in bed. A shook him roughly and said, "Get up, C, we're going to pile wood." C looked so worn and pitiful that B said, "Look here, A, I won't stand this, he isn't fit to pile wood to-night." C smiled feebly and said, "Perhaps I might pile a little if I sat up in bed." Then B, thoroughly alarmed, said, "See here, A, I'm going to fetch a doctor; he's dying."A flared up and answered, "You've no money to fetch a doctor." "I'll reduce him to his lowest terms," B said firmly, "that'll fetch him." C's life might even then have been saved but they made a mistake about the medicine. It stood at the head of the bed on a bracket, and the nurse accidently removed it from the bracket without changing the sign. After the fatal blunder C seems to have sunk rapidly. On the evening of the next day, as the shadows deepened in the little room, it was clear to all that the end was near. I think that even A was affected at the last as he stood with bowed head, aimlessly offering to bet the doctor on C's laboured breathing. "A,"whispered C, "I think I'm going fast." "How fast do you think you'll go, old man?" murmured A. "I don't know," said C, "but I'm going at any rate."

Harland Williams

You ever notice on "The Flintstones," you never see a car with a wheelchair sticker on it?

The end came soon after that. C rallied for a moment and asked for a certain piece of work that he had left downstairs. A put it in his arms and he expired. As his soul sped heaven-ward A watched its flight with melancholy admiration. B burst into a passionate flood of tears and sobbed, "Put away his little cistern and the rowing clothes he used to wear. I feel as if I could hardly ever dig again."—The funeral was plain and unostentatious. It differed in nothing from the ordinary, except that out of deference to sporting men and mathematicians, A engaged two hearses. Both vehicles started at the same time, B driving the one which bore the sable parallelopiped containing the last remains of his ill-fated friend. A on the box of the empty hearse generously consented to a handicap of a hundred yards, but arrived first at the cemetery by driving four times as fast as B. (Find the distance to the cemetery.) As the sarcophagus was lowered, the grave was surrounded by the broken figures of the first book of Euclid.—It was noticed that after the death of C, A became a changed man. He lost interest in racing with B, and dug but languidly. He finally gave up his work and settled down to live on the interest of his bets.—B never recovered from the shock of C's death; his grief preyed upon his intellect and it became deranged. He grew moody and spoke only in monosyllables. His disease became rapidly aggravated, and he presently spoke only in words whose spelling was regular and which presented no difficulty to the beginner. Realizing his precarious condition he voluntarily submitted to be *incarcerated* in an asylum, where he abjured mathematics and devoted himself to writing the History of the Swiss Family Robinson in words of one syllable.

—CLEMENTS

THE DONKLESS HERO

Norman Ward

"Say, pappy," a six-year-old blood relative, still sweating from a day's toil in grade one, asked me, "what does 'donkless' mean?"

It took me back. This was no simple confusion arising from a failure to catch the words of a standard song appointed to be sung in schools, but a family tradition. That six-year-old's father and, if I remember correctly, his grandfather before him, had been similarly baffled by the donklessness of an otherwise highly touted character, the only real black mark against whom, in my set, was that he would rather have written a certain dull poem than shinny up the river bank near Quebec to trim the wick of one Montcalm. What red-blooded Canadian boy cannot recall when

>In days of yore, from Britain's shore,
>
>Wolfe, the donkless hero, came?

At that, Wolfe's donkless condition did not cause so much discussion in my time as his singular act of planting

>...firmbra Tanya's flag
>
>On Canada's fair domain.

Wolfe, with or without donk, we could take; but Tanya, a fleshy child with whom I shared a pegboard in kindergarten, was never able to give a satisfactory explanation of how she got into the song at all. As for that firmbra business, I don't recall that any of us gave it a second thought. Of course that was before women's magazines, with their copiously illustrated scenarios of bras of all degrees and separations, had filled in the picture for any literate four-year-old.

Donkless was cleared up for me at a relatively early period, through the researches of a fellow patriot. Naturally it never occurred to any of us in school to ask the teacher what it meant. Miss Newby was amiable, but in her testier moments could turn blue litmus red without even going down the hall to the older kids' chemistry room. We had no way of knowing whether asking about Wolfe's donkless situation might not light one of those fuses that seemed to send so many of our public-school teachers soaring toward the ceiling, whistling like a jet. Fortunately we never had to ask her; one day in church, under excellent auspices, an older boy happened to come to "The Maple Leaf Forever" in a songbook somebody had left in the rack.

On Sundays it was the custom for the older boys, having exuded every drop of piety earlier at Sunday School—where they variously ran the magic lantern, took up and counted the collection, or performed any other little office calculated to keep them out of the classrooms—to sit in the back rows of the gallery during the regular church service. There they were very quiet, and their modest demeanour, marked by downcast eyes, was frequently praised from the pulpit as a shining example to one and all. As a special treat, smaller boys were often permitted by their parents to sit with the older ones in the gallery. And it *was* a treat, because what we all did up there (a shade closer to heaven than the rest of the congregation, as one sentimental visiting preacher put it) was read the week's supply of penny dreadfuls. It was on an occasion when the supply of papers gave out, in the face of an unconscionably long sermon, that one of the boys, having in sheer desperation flipped through everything in the book rack, turned up for me the word dauntless.

At first it made me little wiser, for a dauntless Wolfe presented no clearer picture than a donkless one. But dauntless kept popping up in the penny dreadfuls, and thanks to several weeks of assiduous

Northrop Frye
FROM *THE EDUCATED IMAGINATION*

To see these resemblances in structure will not, by itself, give any sense of comparative value, any notion why Shakespeare is better than the television movie. In my opinion value-judgements should not be hurried. It does a student little good to be told that A is better than B, especially if he prefers B at the time. He has to feel values for himself, and should follow his individual rhythm in doing so. In the meantime, he can read almost anything in any order, just as he can eat mixtures of food that would have his elders reaching for the baking soda. A sensible teacher or librarian can soon learn how to give guidance to a youth's reading that allows for undeveloped taste and still doesn't turn him into a gourmet or a dyspeptic before his time.

FROM *ZINGER AND ME*

Jack MacLeod

Dear Mrs. Thornton,

Recently I took a speed-reading course. I can now read more than ten or fifteen words per minute. One of the things I like to read is pornography. My question is, if I speed-read pornography, will this cause premature ejaculation?

Mr. L.R. (Age 13)

Dear Mr. L.R.,

Yes. Definitely. Recent studies by Professor Schnellspritzer at Arkansas University confirm the suspicion, long held by serious students of the subject, that speed-reading of pornographic material does indeed cause premature ejaculation. Also pimples. You must try to restrain yourself. Stay off the uppers, and tell your friendly neighbourhood pusher that you want to stick with the downers (the little purple ones). The traditional remedy of cold showers may help, but even better will be a rigorous regime of reading pornography more slowly, moving your index finger at a deliberate pace under each word, and preferably moving your lips as you read. This will have the added advantage of leaving your Ovaltine or biting your fingernails. For a short period (say, six years), you should avoid reading altogether and just look at the pictures.

church-going, backed up by sufficient respectability to win me permission to sit with the older boys fairly frequently, its meaning began to sink in. The whole episode, from first to last, has often appealed to me as a convincing demonstration of the value of the church habit, though I have not yet figured out a way of using it against my own children. However, I am still in a strong strategic position to handle donkless.

The same cannot be said for another word that has been turning up lately, not in songs but in newspaper headlines. Every once in a while a headline spins past my eyeballs and causes them to thrum in an unwonted manner, usually because it leads me to read the accompanying story for what is surely the wrong reason: viz., to decipher the rubric at the top. In fact it has become a game in our household for the non-commissioned ranks, who somehow got wind of their senior's frequent helplessness when clutching the average newspaper, and who long ago settled the question of who gets the evening paper first by unfairly arriving home first, to read me out a headline. Then they challenge old dad, weary from long hours over a cold typewriter, to guess what the headline means, and to outline the tale that goes with it.

For some time now the compositors have been putting together with regrettable regularity a word which will probably stay with us as long as capitalism does. It is "jobless," and I staved it off for some time by pretending not to know its meaning. When asked, "What does 'Jobless Up' mean?" by a pre-citizen whose reading capacity had only recently moved onwards and upwards from certain carefully selected four-letter words, I used to paw through a dictionary, Fowler's *English Usage*, and *Roget's Thesaurus*, and come up with some weighty pronouncement like this: "'Jobless Up' means that unsuccessful small wholesalers, or jobbers, are leaving the ground."

It never worked. I knew jobless meant unemployed, and the rank and file knew I knew. They also knew I despised the word. They fell into a dirty habit of looking through the paper for it on purpose, taxing me with such code phrases as "Jobless Rise" (which made me see hundreds of brawling artisans engaged in civil insurrection in the banking belts of Toronto and Montreal); "Jobless Drop" (I'd see them all flat on the ground); and "Jobless Increase" (and I'd hear the patter of millions of tiny out-of-work feet). When they read out "Jobless Up 200 Last Week," I didn't know which way to turn.

At that, my skirmishes with the jobless have—as befits an ordinary jobful person like myself—found me coming off rather better than with other headlines that get into the news columns from time to time. It may be that I have lived a peculiarly sheltered life, but headlines keep cropping up that throw me for a ten-yard loss or more. When you get right down to it, how does a well-meaning father, with or without the help of reference works, start from scratch to explain to the innocent such banners as:

TWO AFFAIRS ARRANGED FOR MRS. HUTCHISON

or

SHEEP BREEDERS SEEN IN IMPROVED POSITION

or

SIGHT RESTORED WOMAN BY BANG

What would Freud (or Jung, for that matter) have done with:

TRAVEL-WORTHY TARTS IDEAL FOR PICNICS

One of the chief problems of being startled day after day by having headlines like those read out to me (and the examples above are all real, edited only enough to get them past the censors) is that the more I satisfactorily explain, the more the youngsters can interpret for themselves. The result is that the headlines referred to me are becoming increasingly abstruse and esoteric, and my batting average is dropping steadily. Gone are the days when headline-explaining was a sinecure, with such easy ones—for a father of several children—as

LOADED PANTS LIKELY BURNED

Now we have the days when father loses two falls out of three with headlines, and his prestige is going down proportionately.

Paradoxically, it is not that I do not know enough to interpret the headlines. The game has taught me plenty, but I still know too much.

FROM *THE HOPE SLIDE*

Joan MacLeod

FIFTEEN-YEAR-OLD IRENE TALKS TO HER TRUANT OFFICER.

IRENE: I like your hair. I believe women should have long hair, another one of my theories. In pre-prehistoric times our hair was long so that babies, our babies, could hold on while we ran through the trees being chased by God knows what. Babies are born knowing how to hold but now have lost it and they have to be taught. No. They come out knowing but then they forget and have to be taught. I don't know. But something has happened with regard to babies and their ability to hold on in this century.

I don't mean I don't ever think about sex. I think about it often. Perhaps constantly. Not the actual act of sex, which is as yet unknown to me, but I do think of my policies regarding sex, i.e.—do everything but, you know, as many times as you want with whoever you want just KEEP YOUR HYMEN INTACT. When I first learned of my hymen and the importance of keeping it untouched, in place, I imagined it this big shield I could hold out front and ward off guys with, rather like a Viking would have. It's a great word hymen—hymn and amen and hyena all rolled into one. This big bouncy kangaroo thing that laughs its guts out. I mean I know it isn't that and I know it isn't something that you carry with a spear but I used to also worry that my time will come, I will meet

Susan Ryan
Comedian

———

Everything I Need To Know I Learned in Kindergarten?
The cheese stands alone.

A Word for the Young People #8 Rebelling

The Red Green Show

Red wanders around outside the lodge as he has a heart to heart talk with the young people of today.

RED: I know that alot of you teenagers out there are rebelling and you don't know why. Maybe you're questioning your parents or torching school buses or knocking over variety stores. It doesn't matter. What does matter is that this is a normal part of the maturing process. Everyone does it. I'm sure Queen Elizabeth stole her share of motorcycles when she was seventeen. It's your way of saying "I am not the same as my parents. I'm me." And if that means taking a flame thrower to the Mall then so be it. I guess what I'm trying to say is that if you have to be rebellious, do it with a sense of fun. And imagination. Anyone can steal a car. But who could drive it down a subway track? Show imagination: employers look for that sort of thing. They say the teenage years are the best years and

HIM and it will be perfect and holy and wild but...what if my hymen didn't break? What if guys just sort of bounced off it? This tough old piece of skin pulled tight as a drum, a bongo drum barring the way to heaven.

What if it leaves men in pain, pain is something they cannot bear nearly as well as us. They also have a great deal of trouble touching their own eyes.

Don't write that down! Just write down stuff like I am knuckling under. I love that kind of crap. I am knuckling under. I know, I know. Our time is up. Tell me about it.

BLYTHE LLEWELLYN CHAFTIT
FROM *TRUE CONFECTIONS*

Sondra Gotlieb

Mother had done the best anyone could do for a daughter; but after my sweet sixteen party and my failure with Kenny, a mood of weltschmertz pressed in upon me. I idled about in the cemetery looking at the gravestones; I never replied when my father spoke to me; and when I opened the refrigerator at 4 o'clock, as was my custom, I was bored by the brisket, revolted by the ribs, found the chocolate cake mundane and loathed all the soups. I opened the cookie tins and found them filled with tedious almond crescents and dry nothings (their true name, called so because they were made of mazola oil, eggs, sugar and little else) that stuck to the top of the mouth, if you were unwise enough to eat them without a cup of tea.

I was lovesick and jealous. Since the party, Kenny had gone with Norma Bled to a lecture given by W.H. Auden who had spent a night in Winnipeg. Popular Carol had been seen giving Kenny rides in her father's Caddie. But their friendship was platonic, she said, because of the Harvard man. She still wore her pin and fondled her Saturday rose. Kenny, a milkman's son who wasn't getting such good marks at school, despite his interest in great books, could not be considered a rival.

It was impossible to confide in mother about my feelings for Kenny. If she told father he would try to be tactful with unbearable remarks like, "I saw that Kenny yesterday. He's got a bad slouch. If I were a girl, I wouldn't waste time worrying over a boy who can't stand up straight."

I refused to eat mother's food and looked for someone to blame for my misery besides Kenny. That's when I thought of Culinary Rut. "You only think of Daddy when you cook. We can't even eat hot dogs." Father, as a young man, had worked in Burns Meat Packing plant and said ever since, "I won't repeat in mixed company what goes in those wieners."

I had to express my bitterness somehow. If I was unable to talk about my failure in love I could be nasty to my mother about the next most important thing in my life, her cooking.

so remember that and enjoy them. Enjoy being twelve to twenty, because who knows, after that you may be serving twelve to twenty.

The only interesting time of the week was reading *Life* magazine on Wednesday. I would beat my brother home from school in order to be the first to sink into its pages. Close-ups of dead-eyed miners' wives waiting at the pits for broken bones that used to be their husbands. And on the next page an engrossing account of the way the Compte de Paris really lives, complete with hidden camera shots of his wife at Cap Ferrat.

One week *Life* published a five-page article on how to set a duck afire in your own home, with the help of a lighting fluid called cognac. There was a technicolor picture of a golden bird, high up on a silver chafing dish, and two hands, male but manicured, doing something with a liquid that was transformed into a bonfire. Long coils of orange peel and water lilies carved, as the caption explained, from white turnips, surrounded this phoenix.

Like one of Plato's chained men living in a cave, who took shadows of artificial things for reality, I had believed that my mother's cooking was the best. But *Life* broke my bonds and dragged me up the steep way out of the cave into the sun. I realized there was an excellence above and beyond the petty world of brisket and blintzes, a light that shone clearer and brighter than anything I encountered before: Flaming Duck, "Canard à l'Orange Flambée." I was determined to descend into the cave once more and expose to my fettered folk their mistaken assumptions.

Mother was in the kitchen folding egg whites for a sponge cake and I thrust the article under her nose.

"Why don't you ever cook this way?"

Mother had never seen anyone set fire to a perfectly good duck before and she thought that it was some kind of practical joke. I explained about the brandy and she sat down and scrutinized the recipe.

My parents were not teetotallers but their enthusiasm for drinking was limited to having a bottle of Seagrams V.O. and one of South African sherry that normally would lie about the house for two or three years without being consumed. A business acquaintance would occasionally send father a basket of fruit with a bottle or two tucked in between the hothouse grapes and the woody apples. Once in a while, after a vexatious day, my father would go to the kitchen cupboard for his *ketchickle* or little glass, a miniature german beer mug which looked like part of a doll's bar equipment. He would pour half a finger into it and, standing up, drink it in a gulp. On great occasions—a birthday, an anniversary—he'd pour mother the same amount of sherry in another kitchen glass (the good crystal was for ice water) and tell her to drink.

Mother had never heard of food being drenched with alcohol. I'm not sure she had even seen a bottle of brandy before although she had read about what brandy does in *The Brothers Karamazov*. While she never let on, I think the whole flambée affair was as repugnant to her as frying beetles.

But since I had told her my life was flat, stale and unprofitable on account of her cooking, she promised me that she'd make father buy brandy at the government liquor store. The only women who went there, according to father, were unmarried and reeling at midday. "No man would have them." He never made it clear if their alcoholism was a result of their unmarried state or whether their sluttish ways had turned away possible courtiers.

Another reason why mother was intrigued was because of the chafing dish. Relatives in California were always sending us care packages—Hawaiian shirts with palm trees for father, loose fuschia-colored muu-muus for mother (to make her look younger, they wrote) and occasionally boxes of dried-out dates for my brother and me. The last package had contained a copper chafing dish, apparently an indispensable item in La Jolla, which was placed unused along with everything else, including the dates, in the linen closet.

Nothing would ever have got my mother into a muu-muu, but the La Jolla relatives had thrown down the gastronomic gauntlet with the chafing dish. She had avoided the showdown for a year but now the time had come.

Just at the point when mother was seriously thinking about making Flaming Duck, Ida Bled called with a problem. The synagogue regularly invited internationally famous intellectuals to come on Friday nights and give the congregation a piece of their minds, for a fee. Would mother ask the latest lion for dinner before the lecture? Usually mother did not entertain strangers but, with Flaming Duck for dinner, she felt there was some kind of divine coincidence in Ida Bled's request and consented.

His name was Blythe Llewellyn Chaftit (all the lecturers used treble names) and no one had ever heard of him. Ida thought he had something to do with Ayn Rand or Welsh miners. "One of the two. In New York or Cardiff he's famous, so who are we to judge?"...

Blythe Llewellyn Chaftit.

I imagined him to be a grownup successful Kenny who travelled around the world enlightening ignorant girls like myself on the latest in great thoughts. B.L. Chaftit lived in England and presumably hung around with true thinkers like Bertrand Russell instead of the questionable ones I knew, like Harvey Stone. Despite Kenny's belief in Harvey's genius, I could not put him in the same category as Russell or Einstein. Chaftit must know the writers Kenny admired, like T.S. Eliot. Without doubt, Chaftit had read "The Wasteland," even advised Eliot on metaphors and similes. Here was a man to take me away from Winnipeg, a weightier Kenny who was too mature to be distracted by vacuous girls like Popular Carol, or skinny ones like Norma Bled.

Blythe Llewellyn Chaftit was my chance to make something of myself. When he saw and spoke to me at the dinner he might think, "Only sixteen and she knows what the S. stands for in T.S. Eliot and eats Flaming Duck!"

If my father kept quiet and let him talk, Chaftit might even help me forget Kenny.

But Zora was a worry.

"Who's going to flame the duck," I asked, knowing her incompetence in these matters.

"Your mother. I'll set the chafing dish with the duck in it, in front of her. All she has to do is strike the match. It will give graciousness to the whole dinner. Chaftit will think you eat that way every day."

Mother started cooking for the dinner four days in advance. She always made sure that her meals would please everyone by having two main courses. If the pièce de résistance was roast beef, there would be a pan of stewed chicken, because, she said, "you never know." She felt that with the duck, Spanish tongue, cut in slices, covered with tomato sauce and onions, would be a suitably exotic accompaniment. We were also to have two kinds of soup and chocolate and strawberry shortcake for dessert along with dainties.

The day of the dinner, Zora came early, in full regalia rented from Malabars Costumes. Black dress, lace apron and cap; the white gloves were her own. She bounced in full of confidence.

"Don't worry, Fanny, as long as the others don't give me away, it will be a night to remember."

Ida and Harry Bled were to pick up B.L. Chaftit at the airport and, to add class, mother had asked Emelia Stone, Harvey's mother, considered by everyone "a lady" because she spoke in low tones and never mentioned her money.

I dressed in a way that I felt brought out my most attractive aspects and reduced the least appealing. Mother said that I had good shoulders; they were more fleshed out than on other girls. I wore a black (to make me look older) off-the-shoulder blouse with white fringes and an elastic cinch belt that squeezed in my waist at least two inches. *Seventeen* claimed that vertical stripes were a must for plumper teens so mother made me a red, black and white striped skirt with a flounce on the bottom. I didn't think Chaftit would look all the way down to my feet and wore my usual saddle shoes and socks.

Blythe Llewellyn Chaftit's appearance was not spectacular. He was small and sand-colored all over, hair, complexion, suit, and shoes. He kept fooling around with his moustache—"Like a monkey looking for a louse," father said afterwards—and hardly spoke. I realized long after that he needed a drink badly but such a thought would never occur to father. It was not his habit to serve cocktails before dinner. That entailed meaningless activity: making sure there was ice, finding glasses, measuring out the right amount of rye and even buying soda and ginger ale. If mother had wanted to organize the drinks herself, he would not have objected. But she was peeling oranges in the kitchen for Flaming Duck.

The Bleds, my brother and myself, father and Emelia Stone stood around Chaftit in the living room, wondering how to pursue the kind of sophisticated conversation that the man must be used to. I felt that a literary topic was in order and asked if he had reread Thomas Wolfe lately. Chaftit obviously read everything and I was too worldly to insult him by assuming that he had not read Thomas Wolfe years ago.

"Thomas Wolfe is for adolescents. Hysterical adolescents."

I pursued my questioning, notwithstanding my feeling that I was the number one example of the type he just mentioned.

"You must know T.S. Eliot, Mr. Chaftit. What is he really like?"

Harland Williams
————

My friends asked me to babysit their kids, so I bought a bottle of Sani-Flush, went over to the house, the water turned blue in the toilet, then I hid their Smurfs.

Stevie Ray Fromstein

A woman came up to me recently, and she said, "I want you to be the father of my children."

So I said, "Great."

You know what happened?

Two weeks later, she's gone and I'm stuck with these two kids.

"A foul piece of shit."

My father spoke up.

"Watch your language, mister. We don't talk like that in my house."

I was embarrassed for my father. Chaftit was his guest and he talked to him as if he were a delivery man.

"In what way," I asked, as lightly as possible, "is T.S. Eliot a shit?"

Emelia Stone stared at me, Ida Bled gasped, and Chaftit smiled nastily.

"If I were to tell you, little girl, your father would call the police."

Zora came in then to announce dinner and when we sat down father did his best to eradicate his rudeness.

"What do you think of Winnipeg, Professor?"

Father did not know if Chaftit had even been to university but he thought it best to flatter his guest, especially after the previous conversation. It was thirty below outside and B.L. Chaftit had been in the city about an hour. We heard from under the moustache kind of a mumbling, in which we understood the words "dark" and "cold."

"Winnipeg is the most boring city in the world," I contributed. "There's nothing of interest for a man like you, Mr. Chaftit."

Chaftit didn't answer, but my father said, "Boring, boring. That's all you ever say. If you had to go out and work for a living it wouldn't be so boring."

Zora, her eyes bulging, warning us all to keep her secret, was passing soup around.

"Chicken or bean and barley?" she hissed in our ears.

But there was a space problem. The dining room was too small for her to squeeze behind the chairs of the Bleds, who were sitting along the side of the table, and get to the end where Chaftit sat. In order for Zora to serve him, she had to retrace her steps past my mother, disappear into the kitchen, and unseen by everyone in the dining room, go out the back door that led off from the kitchen. She rushed round to the front door in the snow, with a bowl of soup in each hand and eventually reappeared, this time at Chaftit's end of the table. After serving him, she'd disappear again, running out the front door and returning to the kitchen, via the sidewalk that my brother had reluctantly shoveled a few hours before.

Zora's sudden appearance at each end of the table (as well as the endless wait for cold soup) was disturbing and inexplicable to a stranger like Chaftit, who couldn't tell how she was able to pop up at each end of the table without passing through the dining room itself. He became so fascinated with her eerie appearances that he gave up on conversation.

I was mortified. The man was used to dining in vast ancient halls where butlers passed tureens of turtle soup, and then hovered about attentively, in case a guest wanted a second helping.

I tried to take B.L. Chaftit's mind off Zora.

"Have you ever met T.S. Eliot's wife?"

Chaftit looked at me.

"Wives of famous men are never interesting."

Eagerly hoping I had started a meaningful discussion, I asked why. But he didn't answer because a current of below zero air hit the table.

Zora had found it a nuisance to open the front door in the hall each time she came in with a bowl of soup so she left it ajar for the remainder of the meal. No one said anything, but B.L. Chaftit was shuffling his feet, as if he wanted to get the circulation back into them.

We all looked to the end of the table where mother sat. Zora brought out the chafing dish containing the duck, decorated with lots of orange peels. Some matches and the bottle of brandy, just like in *Life*, were set before mother, whose face was screwed up with tension. The time had come to flame the duck.

The duck was my last chance to impress Chaftit. Perhaps he would suddenly realize that I was a cultivated young woman amidst friends and family of obvious refinement. I whispered to him, so that no one else would hear.

"We have flambée duck every Friday. It's sort of a family tradition."

Father had a smug look on his face, like a lesser prophet when one of his forecasts of disaster was about to come true. Chaftit had his eyes closed. Mother struck a match and with a frightened gesture threw it at the duck, it sizzled, snuffed out and floated around like a little boat in the sauce. Zora, blank-faced as an adjutant corporal, watching the major misfire at a regimental shooting drill, handed mother a second match which failed. Father was looking, "I told you so." Mother repeated her action until there was a flotilla of fourteen matches floating in the orange sauce.

"You've poisoned the gravy, Fanny," father announced with satisfaction. "I knew it wouldn't work. Throw it out and bring in something decent to eat."

I protested and said I didn't care if it wasn't flaming I wanted to eat it anyhow.

"You will die of sulfur poisoning and the Professor could sue us."

Mother didn't hesitate. She told Zora to bring in the Spanish tongue.

Chaftit, at last, sat up and opened his eyes.

"Tongue," he said. "Tongue. I never eat anything that has been in another's mouth."

Zora said that Blythe Llewellyn Chaftit was a real fraud.

"When I gave him his soup, he pinched my bum. Would a really famous person do a thing like that?"

Obviously, B.L. Chaftit was not going to be my older substitute for Kenny. Anyone who pinched Zora's bum and didn't like tongue was unsuitable even though he lectured internationally. And like the rest of the boys and men I knew, it was pretty clear that he wasn't interested in me.

I was disillusioned and feared that my love for Kenny was becoming an obsession. I knew I had to put him out of my mind with someone, anyone else. I lowered my ambitions and tested a market that was cheap enough for me.

—CLEMENTS

IT'S A GIRL! (FATHER EXPECTED TO LIVE)

FROM *ARTHUR! ARTHUR!*

Arthur Black

I have before me a report in the *Canadian Journal of Anaesthesia* suggesting that fathers should think twice before venturing into the delivery room to get "personally involved" in the birth of their children.

I have several responses to a proposal such as that—two of which are: "No kidding," and "*Now* they tell me."

Where were these experts when I needed them—in the delivery room of Port Arthur General Hospital when my daughter was being born? This, of course, was several years ago. Back in the Age of Mariposa and Woodstock—a Caring, Sharing, Involved and Happening Era when friends in bandanas and denim would say, "Naturally you'll be attending the birth with your wife." "Yup," you would reply. "Oh, sure. You bet. Wouldn't have it any other way."

But of course you would share the sacred birth process. Wasn't that what Life Was All About?

Well, yes. Yes, it is. But, friends. . .

It's messy.

It's more than messy—it's mortifying.

Thoreau once said: "Beware of any enterprise that requires new clothes." Black's corollary reads: "Be extra leery of any enterprise that requires paper slippers and a surgical mask." That's what they dress maternity room Dad voyeurs in—paper slippers and a surgical mask. Then they ask you if you'd mind if a class of student nurses watches the birth.

Now think about this: you are in a room with your wife who is naked and in some considerable distress. The two of you are poised uneasily on the cusp of one of the biggest days of your life. The authorities want to know if you'd mind if a herd of strangers takes notes. If it happened in your living room, at your office, on the street—anywhere that was even close to your own turf, you would tell the authorities to go pound Sifto, but you are in a strange room full of

Richard J. Needham
Journalist

An effective form of birth control would be to have the father look after the kid for the first month.

sundry stainless steel mysteries not to mention tubes and dials and you are wearing paper slippers and a surgical mask. Cowlike, you nod your assent.

Cheer up—this is only the first assault on your dignity. Soon the doctor comes. You can tell he's the doctor because the maternity room staff defers to him. Besides, he's got the rubber gloves on and his surgical mask is regular-issue cloth, not cheap paper like yours.

It's good that you have these clues to the doctor's identity because you'd never figure out who he was from his conversation. He talks like your garage mechanic. He chats about the weather and the Blue Jays and his golf game. He offers his analysis of the current stock market slump. He crows about the gas mileage he gets with his BMW.

And as he talks, this doctor—this *stranger!*—is doing unspeakable things with his hands to your soulmate. But casually! Offhandedly, as it were, like a butcher rearranging the cold cuts in his display cooler.

This is an outrage! A flagrant flouting of everything you hold dear! Are you just gonna stand there like a schnook and allow this to go on? Aren't you going to roar like a bull, rage like a tiger and put those interlopers in their place with your icy, rapier wit?

Wearing paper slippers and a surgical mask? Get serious.

In any case, it will soon get worse. The birthing process is moving along briskly. Your wife is howling and panting and perspiring, pausing only briefly to denounce you, at the top of her lungs, as the source of all pain and evil in the world. You ask her to remember the breathing exercises.

She asks you to perform something that is both dexterously demanding and impossible to repeat in a gentle, family-oriented volume such as this.

And now the doctor is brandishing a. . .what is that thing, anyway? A fencing sword? A jackhammer? A jousting lance? No. It is a needle. And he is going to give it to your wife. Oh, my God!!!!

That's all I remember. They tell me I hit my head at quite a clip on the stirrup on the way to the floor.

Did I mention that we had a beautiful baby girl?

My wife told me all about it in the recovery room.

Mine, not hers.

RICHARD SPEAKS!

FROM *TAKE MY FAMILY...PLEASE!*

Gary Lautens

Our Richard is thirteen and I've come to a landmark decision: He's now old enough to talk directly to clerks in stores.

As any parent will immediately realize, it's another watershed in our lives.

Up till last Saturday, the "baby" in our family always conversed with salespersons through his mother or father.

Of course there's nothing wrong with his voice and he does have a tongue.

But traditionally that's how it's done. In the presence of a parent, children and clerks never speak to each other.

On the weekend, however, I took Richard to the neighbourhood department store for a pair of slippers: We went straight to the shoe section.

"Yes?" the clerk asked.

"My son needs a pair of slippers," I informed the clerk.

"What size?" he asked me.

"What size do you take?" I asked Richard, who was standing right beside me.

"I think about an eight," Richard stated.

I looked at the clerk. "About an eight."

"What colour slipper would you like?" was his next question.

"What colour, Richard?" I inquired.

"Blue," Richard answered smartly.

"Blue," I told the clerk.

"Any particular style?" the clerk asked me.

"Any particular style?" I demanded of my son.

"No, just as long as they don't have slippery soles and won't mark the floor," Richard said.

"No," I responded to the clerk, "just as long as they don't have slippery soles and won't mark the floor."

The clerk nodded and went into the back room, returning in a moment or two with several boxes of slippers. He slipped one on Richard's foot.

"How is that for fit?" he asked.

"How is that for fit?" I relayed to Richard.

"It's a little tight," Richard commented.

"It's a little tight," I informed the salesman.

The clerk slipped it off. "Will he be wearing socks with the slippers? Those are pretty heavy socks he has on," he commented.

"Will you be wearing socks with the slippers? Those are pretty heavy socks you have on," I passed on to Richard.

"I like heavy socks," Richard stated.

"He likes heavy socks," I repeated.

"We'll try a half-size larger," the clerk suggested. "How's this?" he asked me after putting one on Richard's foot.

"How's..."

I broke in mid-sentence. I looked at Richard—128 pounds, taller than his mother at five feet, six inches—and I made the breakthrough.

"Richard, you tell the clerk," I said. "You two can talk to each other."

Richard was taken aback but he looked at the clerk and said, "Fine."

"Better try the other one," the clerk advised Richard directly.

Within five minutes it was all over, and it didn't sound as if the sale were taking place in an echo chamber.

It's the end of an era, I guess.

Next time we're at a restaurant, I'll even have to let Richard give his own order to the waiter. That's the ultimate.

I just hope he takes the hint if, when he orders the $22.95 filet, he feels a kick under the table.

–JOHNSTON

THE UNEAGER BEAVER

John Gray

Anyone puzzling his way through the minefield of late 20th-century parenting welcomes any insight, however painfully acquired. With that in mind, we learned two things from the Beaver Sleepover of March 31: to a child who has not experienced it, squalor is an adventure; and there are parents out there who would walk on white-hot coals, would jump in a pond of cold vomit, if doing so would provide their child with an experience.

Zack, six, came home very excited one evening. For only $30, he and I could spend the night on the floor of B.C. Place Stadium with up to 7,000 other beavers and their parents in the "world's biggest sleepover," a kind of grade one Woodstock.

You should have seen him, standing there in his brown beaver vest and his sky-blue beaver hat and scarf. "Brodie's going," he said, referring to his best friend. "His dad is taking him."

"It's something you could do together," cooed my Significant Other, always quick with the guilt-inducing non sequitur.

A feeling of weariness came over me. Couldn't we just impale ourselves with sharp sticks instead?

The beavers are not toothy furbearers, but an organization created by Scouts Canada for five- to seven-year-old boys. After beavers they become cubs, then scouts, then rovers, then Prime Minister of Canada.

Beavers were invented in Winnipeg 15 years ago. Their promise is "Love God and take care of the world;" their motto: "Sharing! Sharing!" Pure United Church Canadiana. Zack loves it.

My enthusiasm is restrained... At cubs, you learn that people can be nasty to you for no reason at all. Cub camp was reef knots by day, hell by night; a sadistic rite called blackballing involved shoe polish. ... Dream On '89, as the beaver sleepover was called, sounded to me like cub camp in a parking garage. Zack saw it as the greatest adventure of his life.

When Innocence meets Experience, Experience always backs down.

6 p.m., March 31. We stuff sleeping bags, foamies and a change of clothing into Brodie's dad's battered blue Volvo. It is quiet in the front seat, while in the rear Zack and Brodie are in uniform and in top form, Zack having skipped supper with the excitement of it.

We arrive at B.C. Place Stadium, Gate A, where at least 4,000 beavers and their escorts stand in six lines that do not appear to be moving. Everyone is searching for someone they are unable to find. We are supposed to join our group at the Terry Fox Memorial just outside Gate A, and receive instructions from Our Leader, code-named Malek. Unfortunately, that's what everyone else was told to do.

Everyone carries some kind of equipment. A few have proper knapsacks and sleeping bags, but most have stuffed their belongings into green garbage bags—foamies and sleeping bags, mainly, but I did notice several complete sets of bedding, including bedspreads. Out of each garbage bag peers a battered stuffed animal.

This does not look at all like cub camp—more like a population fleeing a natural disaster. The throng fills Beatty caps of the style you normally see in Irish tweed. They take tickets, and check those mysterious, numbered yellow hospital bracelets everyone else seems to be wearing.

I have crossed borders into unfriendly Communist countries with greater dispatch. The queues move with such agonizing slowness, there seems no point in lining up at all. The Georgia Court hotel across the street is starting to look awfully snug to me, but I can't interest Brodie's dad, even though I think I could get us a corporate rate.

Brodie's dad goes off to find out what we are to do. We want to know about those strange numbered bracelets. I am to watch our gear and the boys, whom I can just make out in the distance, spinning around a streetlamp.

Time passes. The queue moves not. Now Zack and Brodie are jumping up and down on their knapsacks, possibly crushing tubes of toothpaste. It is nearly dark now, and the streetlamps cast an eerie glow over the steadily growing mob and their garbage bags. Zack is complaining of hunger pangs. Brodie wants his dad. They are calm, but it's only a matter of time. Brodie's dad returns to report the following conversation with an official-looking person. Brodie's dad: "How do we find our group and get our yellow bracelets?" Official person: "You should have thought of that before you left Chilliwack."

... 8 p.m., March 31. We are inside Gate A now, the stout, red-hatted guards having given up the body searches or whatever they were doing for the last hour and a half. We stand in a crush while a high-level meeting of officials in scarves and goggles takes place on the other side of a glass door. We adults exchange curses sotto voce, not to disillusion the beavers, whose energy has not flagged. In fact, the decibel level has gone up several notches.

Sixteen hours to go. Courage.

At last, we pass through the door and down what appears to be an enormous heating duct to Gate 16, which leads to the stands. We are told to deposit our gear in the seats, then to head to another part of the stadium for the show. This we do with difficulty, for there is a bottleneck getting on and off the stands. By the time we reach the "entertainment area," it is 8:30. Zack's normal bedtime is 8 p.m. Parents will know what that means.

To an adult it is not easy to adjust to the scale of B.C. Place Stadium; to a beaver it must look like another planet. An enormous, dirty blimp hangs over a vast gray concrete surface where we are to, for want of a better word, sleep. They have removed the astroturf, so there is not even the pretense of nature.

In this immensity, the world's largest sleepover has been dwarfed: thousands of beavers occupy only a tiny number of the seats facing a stage containing children's performer Norman Foote, who is doing well even though a half-mile of concrete separates him from his audience. The rest of the stadium is occupied by nothing but a blaze of white light. At the far end is a huge screen containing a happy face in a beaver hat, a kind of disembodied Big Sister symbol named Brownie whose voice cajoles and flatters us over every speaker in the place: "Are we having fun, beeeeavers? And it's only getting started! Give yourselves a biiiiiig hand!"

9 p.m., March 31. Norman Foote says goodnight. Zack is nearly hysterical with hunger, so we retire to the concession stand for a hot dog, which involves a 20-minute lineup. By the time we return, opening ceremonies are already under way. Several thousand Beavers have assumed the "chopping position" for a clapping ritual called Tailslap (I'm not making this up), after which they launch into the beaver yell:

Beavers! Beavers! Beavers! Sharing! Sharing! Biiglflagl paaaaawww!...

The roar of echo obscures the rest, which has something to do with working hard and helping family and friends—another Canadian invitation to niceness and unrelenting toil. Then everyone sings "O Canada." As usual, we are unable to agree on the lyrics.

Meanwhile, on the concrete floor of the stadium, uniformed adults roll along red carpets into a grid pattern. Large garbage cans are placed at intervals beside the carpet. Theoretically, beavers can walk to the washrooms and back without stepping on the heads of other beavers. This is our bedroom. Courage.

9:40 p.m., March 31. We are into the official part of the ceremony, clapping and cheering when ordered to by the merciless Brownie.

Mayor Gordon Campbell gives a welcoming speech, informing us that beavers are here from as far away as Saskatoon. (Imagine all this in addition to a two-day busride!) Our appreciation of his presence is mitigated by the knowledge that the mayor will be spending tonight in a warm, soft bed somewhere in the Point Grey area.

A Word for the Young People #11 Leaving Home

The Red Green Show

Red wanders around outside the lodge as he has a heart to heart talk with the young people of today.

RED: Maybe we have a few teenagers watching tonight because the cable's on the fritz and this is the only channel you can get. But I want to take this opportunity to talk to you young people about leaving home. I know there's a lot of appeal to having your own place where your parents can't hassle you about your knives. Where you can get some privacy and not have to explain where you're going, or how you got forty-three television sets, your own home to paint and decorate and have divorcees over on P.D. days. But when you sit down and figure out what it's costing your parents to have you live with them and how miserable it makes their lives, it all kind've works out. I'm not saying you have to talk to them, or like them, or be nice to them. Just treat them the way they treat each other. Stay in there. Because as your parents get older they start losing it and eventually they end up willing everything to the kid who stayed home the longest. Make sure it's you. Your parents worked hard for what they have; don't make the same mistake.

Then Hystar, the hovercraft from Expo'86, arises in a puff of stage smoke, and we watch it hover. For 10 minutes. From her perch somewhere above us, Brownie chimes in, "Three cheers for Hystar! Oh come on, beavers, you can do better than that!" It's even starting to get to Zack. "Why doesn't she shut up?" he asks.

At last, we are told to go to bed. We line up once again in a concrete cavern, where—in a ritual called "mug-up"—we are given brown paper bags containing a snack. We gather our foamies and sleeping bags, and stagger onto the landing strip that is to be our bed.

10:30 p.m., March 31. We lay out our sleeping bags in neat rows on the concrete between the red carpets, under those Orwellian lights. The stadium as refugee camp. Everyone digs hungrily into his snack, which consists of a large, chocolate-covered cookie-and-marshmallow thing, a container of Kool-Aid, a bag of candy, a piece of fruit leather, a piece of cheese and four crackers.

A tad heavy on the sugar, you might say, and the beaver pancreas reacts accordingly. Suddenly, beavers are racing madly up and down the red carpets, chattering like squirrels, then bursting unaccountably into tears. Other beavers quietly upchuck into those conveniently located garbage cans, their foreheads held by wan, expressionless parents. The disembodied voice of Brownie shrills, "Only 15 minutes to showtime!"

—JOHNSTON

Unbelievably, there is to be a movie on the big screen. But by 11 p.m., Brownie is still chanting "15 minutes to showtime." Time has passed slowly so far. Evidently, it has now stopped altogether.

11:30 p.m., March 31. Is this some sort of sleep-deprivation experiment? At least those ferocious lights have been turned down as we watch the NFB film *The Cat Came Back*. Now, Brownie tells us all how sleepy we are. You got it, Brownie. By midnight, adults squirm, sweating, in their sleeping bags, trying to undress with decorum. By 12:30 a.m., most have already passed out from tension and fatigue.

At 3:15 a.m. I awake with a shriek, thanks to a nasty stomp on the calf by a beaver on his way to the washroom. It is quiet now, with only a few beavers running around madly in the shadows. I fall back into my feverish slumber, giving my head a bad crack.

6 a.m., April 1. "Wake up, beavers! Rise and shine!" It's the howl of our tormentor, the hated Brownie.

Bent over double, stupefied with fatigue, adults gather up their sleeping gear and redeposit it in the stands while beavers run about, yelling hysterically. We line up for breakfast: a cake muffin, some canned fruit and a bowl of Sugar Frosted Flakes. We eat in silence, crouched like rats in a dimly lit hallway.

The breakfast sugar energizes the beavers further. Their parents have the haunted look I have seen on the faces of immigrants whose papers have been held up indefinitely.

7 a.m., April 1. Brownie tells us to sit in the entertainment section again. We adults shuffle along like something out of a Russian novel, beavers spinning around us like Sufis. We wait a long time, watching safety films between rounds of inane cheering.

More ceremony. A uniformed person leads a prayer of thankfulness, with much tail slapping and chanting, while more uniformed people set up tables for the games, science projects, singsongs and creative activities that are to make up the rest of the morning. Compared to what we have been through already, this is a piece of cake. Zack makes himself a hat, gets his face painted. He and Brodie proclaim it the best time they have had in their whole lives.

11:30 a.m. We never did find out what the yellow bracelets are for, but we are still wearing them when we file out of the stadium, at last. I am filled with a sense of wonder. Parents, some of them single mothers, after a full week of work, endured this ordeal solely to be with their kids while they experienced something to remember. As a test of utter selflessness, it boggles the mind.

The Beaver Sleepover. So Canadian: improbable, nonsensical, damned uncomfortable, boring as anything, corny, saccharine enough to make you gag. And yet, in this age of the Yuppie, the fitness club and the Perrier lunch, in a strange, perverse way it gives you hope for the human race. Then again...

Ozzie, Harriet, David and Monique

Canadian Homelife

My Father's Pyjamas

Joey Slinger

My father's pyjamas moved in with me. My father came and stayed one night and after he left I found his pyjamas hanging on a hook on the back of the bathroom door. They are white pyjamas with a blue paisley design. They didn't seem in any hurry to leave.

Mine is a one-bedroom apartment in a building inhabited mainly by young people who spend most of their time in Old Vienna beer commercials. I would have thought my father's pyjamas would find their ways frivolous and noisy. Some of these young people are not great respecters of their parents' pyjamas. "They don't even wear pyjamas of their own," I told my father's pyjamas.

But they just hung there, unfazed by the suggestion that they were out of their element. I put them in the laundry. I thought of the philosophical irony: the child is father to the father's pyjamas. I took them out of the dryer, folded them, and put them in a drawer. And then I started to feel just awful.

-JOHNSTON

"Comes a time in a life—" I debated with myself. "Comes a time in a life when pyjamas aren't much use to anybody any more. That's when, as it may be, they just get washed and folded and put away in a drawer.

"Oh, sometimes they get a bit of extra use as a duster or as a rag to polish shoes. But I couldn't let that happen to my father's pyjamas. The family wardrobe always had its pride. Even at its most threadbare, it was too proud to go into a rummage sale. It could always fend for itself. At the very least I have some responsibility for caring for my father's pajamas.

"After all, flannelette is thicker than water."

I took them out of the drawer and put them on the couch beside me and we watched the news. I had to switch from the CBC news to Global, though, because my father's pyjamas are accustomed to watching Global. "That's all right," I said. "News is news."

When it was over, I spread my father's pyjamas out on the couch and went into the bedroom and climbed into bed.

I lay awake for ages. Sleep wouldn't come. All I could think of was my father's pyjamas on that narrow, lumpy couch. Finally I got up, took the pyjamas off the couch, put them in my bed, and tucked them in. "It's all right," I said. "You need a rest. A little discomfort doesn't bother me at all." I went and lay down on the couch.

Until my father's pyjamas came I hadn't realized how small the apartment was. Now it seemed that everywhere I turned they were there. Spread over a chair with the paper on their lap. Draped over the shower rail when I was in a rush to shower and get to the office. Listening to the radio when I wanted to play a record. Knotting and unknotting their ties disapprovingly while I explained why I was late getting home.

When in need of warm companionship it was my habit to drop by an Old Vienna beer commercial, sweet-talk a waif, and invite her back to my apartment for a little hanky-panky.

"What's that?" the waif hissed as we came in one night.

My father's pyjamas were seated at the table, a game of solitaire spread out before them. "Just my father's pyjamas," I explained. "Pay no attention to them."

In any case, I took them and hung them in the bathroom. It did no good. My whining entreaties were as much use as a candle trying to boil an iceberg. "I'm sorry," she said. "I just don't feel right, knowing your father's pyjamas are in there."

I sent her back to the beer commercial in a cab and brought my father's pyjamas out and settled them beside me. Together we watched Global news. "It's all right," I said. "Having my father's pyjamas is company enough. What need have I of transient, insincere relationships with women?"

But despite my best intentions, my father's pyjamas started to get on my nerves. I would raise my voice when I spoke to them. Sometimes when I went off to work I left them in a heap. Soon I wasn't coming home for meals. I stayed in bars until all hours and rolled home full of abuse for the lint they left everywhere.

Harland Williams

My father is a slow guy. The war amps asked him to make a donation. He sent them his legs.

He's the type of guy who gets confused by Licorice Allsorts.

One day I came home to find the Goodwill truck in front of the building and the Goodwill man coming out of my apartment with my father's pyjamas over his arm. "Ingrate," sneered the Goodwill man.

My father's pyjamas didn't look back as they left.

NEW AGE BUZZWORDS

Tony Molesworth

My tarot reader's on vacation, my channeler has a cold
　　My spirit guide is spacy, don't trust my horror-scope

I tried pendants, crystals and a dowsing tool
　　All give me conflicting answers, guess fortune cookies'll do

I act thru intuition, spirit directs my every move
　　I've transcended anger, except when I'm pissed at you

I'm making my own tarot deck, with perfect New Age hook
　　My smiling face is on every card, and it comes with auto-graphed book

I eat white sugar but I add organic bran
　　Every conversation starts with "I'm a vegetarian"

I'm macro-neurotic, I eat brown rice, soya sauce
　　For dessert I pig out on chocolate Haagen-daz

'Cause I'm not a man or woman, I'm a person: Hear me roar
　　I'm a New Age Mom and Dad and I own a health food store

I compost my old clothing, I'm health food hip
　　I put garlic in my protein shake, with tofu rice cream whip

Got my herbal toothpaste spread on my whole wheat bread
　　Sucking back cactus jam–that's what the instructions said

I put aloe vera juice on my face
　　Shirley MacLaine got the recipe direct from outer space

I'm enviro-mentally friendly, I re-use my pesticides
　　Buy vegetarian rat poison—OK, I compromise

I snort epsom salts & herbs to de-tox
　　Bathe in cold distilled water sitting in my Blue Box

I re-cycle my bicycle everytime I ride
　　No preservatives in my whole wheat bread, it committed moldy suicide

'Cause I'm not a man or woman, I'm a person: Hear me roar
　　My guru is omnipresent—Even more than yours

I traveled in India with my Yuppi begging bowl
　　I meditated on my hot tub. Boy those caves are cold

My guru Swami Veranda, a Swedish enlightened saint
  He's on welfare, while he meditates—He has to pay his rent

I study Sanskrit as I lie in my float tank
  Visualize my radiant soul and abundant cash in the bank

I love all races, have no prejudice traits
  I gotta Chinese and Indian friend—It's me I still hate

Everyone's my child, no kids of my own
  God's compassion in my voice, as I talk through my
  speakerphone

My girl friend doesn't love me, it's just a Tantric fling
  Our relationship has no romance; we're just networking

She calls me a Yuppi, whatever that means
  One hundred dollars jeans and fifty more for ripped knees

I'm just a meek guy with an inheritance on my way
  Me and my meek friends are promised the earth some day

I'm not a man or woman I am a person: Hear me roar
  I'm a New Age Mom and Dad, and I can blind you with my soul

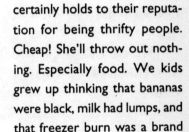

Gord Paynter
Comedian

My Mom is Scottish and she certainly holds to their reputation for being thrifty people. Cheap! She'll throw out nothing. Especially food. We kids grew up thinking that bananas were black, milk had lumps, and that freezer burn was a brand name.

I'M BABBLING

FROM *MOMNIPOTENT—SONGS FOR WEARY PARENTS*

Nancy White

Excuse me if I'm babbling,
It's something I do more now.
I think it is because I have
two children under four now.
I have to speak in fragments
so I speak a little faster
and pitch my voice at volume
levels of a ghetto blaster.

I try to keep in touch
so I tune in to CBC.
Of course I can't quite hear it
'cause of voices calling me!
Now was it our Ben Johnson who
assaulted dear old Zsa Zsa?
I missed part of the story
because baby wanted ba ba.

I know I talk too much
but I'm excited as can be.

Simon Rakoff
Comedian

———

I'm of the Jewish persuasion—I was eight days old when they persuaded me.

Being Jewish, I have a lot of relatives from Eastern Europe—old people who don't speak English. Don't get me wrong. They speak all the English words, they just don't know what order to put them in. You have to listen to the whole sentence or you might miss the point entirely. I hear things like, "Would somebody please do me a favour, and pick me up, and throw me over the balcony...my sweater." I killed six of them; they just never got to the end. They also like to say everything twice but backwards the second time. An old guy'll come up to me at a family gathering (*elderly European accent*): "You look so good. So good you look." Or I'll be in a restaurant with my Aunt (*old Jewish lady voice*): "I'll have the chicken. The chicken I'll have." She wonders why her long distance phone bill is twice as much as anyone else's.

So glad that Patrick Watson's
heading up the NDP.
I didn't catch the details
but I know I heard his name,
'cause that was just the moment
when the diaper service came.

I'm babbling!—there I go again
I'm babbling!—clucking like a hen.
People see me coming and they run away.
Please stay!

Our older daughter burst into
a loud and piercing song
as I listened to the story
'bout those brothers from Hong Kong
who got their landed status
'cause of jobs that they can give here,
though neither brother kind-of-sort-of
seems to really live here!

I know that's too preposterous,
it simply can't be true.
Our government would never let
such con artists get through,
I'll have to shut the kids up
and listen carefully,
'cause if it's true I think I might
withhold my G.S.T.

Forgive me if I'm blubbering,
so many tears I've cried.
I felt so sad to hear
Fernando Marcos finally died.
His wife, Yolanda,
must be going through such hell,
I guess that she'll go back to P.T.L.

I'm babbling!—morning, noon, and night.
I'm babbling!—not a pretty sight.
I see your eyes glaze over but I just can't help it.
So help me.

Bear with me if I seem to be
a little out of touch.
But lately I don't get to talk to

adults very much.
Except for other mothers
at the daycare and the park,
I don't see many grownups after dark
(except my companero, but he always
has headphones on, I can't imagine why).

I have so much to say, I fear
there's something I have missed,
I guess, like Peter Worthington,
I ought to make a list.
I know that I'm on shakey ground
when I express my views,
If only "Sesame Street" would run
a little more hard news.

I'm babbling! la la la la la,
I'm babbling! blah blah blah blah blah
Babbling, la la la la la
I'm babbling.

GUYS: She's babbling, isn't it a shame.
She's babbling, what a dizzy dame.
Babbling: there she goes again.
Babbling: clucking like a hen.

VINTAGE MISERY

CODCO

NAMES OF SPEAKERS REFER TO CODCO PERFORMERS

*(Interior: old ladies' living room. Four ladies are sitting around playing
bridge. Mom sits in the corner "waiting to die.")*

MARY: My God, it's so cold. The weather is really after
turning.

TOM: Yes, but it was a gorgeous summer. We can't complain.

(They all look a little depressed at the thought of not complaining.)

GREG: No, I s'pose we can't. What's trump?

CATHY: Clubs. Doesn't feel like trumps when it's clubs. You
want something sensible, like hearts.

GREG: Oh my god, don't mention hearts. Poor old Merce Dwyer
died of a heart attack last Tuesday!

TOM: Go on! Sure, he was only a young man, too.

Mary: God love him. That's the three Dwyers gone now.

Cathy: No. Sure, he's got a brother living in the States.

Tom: Had a brother.

Cathy: You don't mean it.

Tom: Yeah, kidney failure. Tried for three weeks to get a transplant but they had to give it up. Went toxic at the end.

(*They all cheer up noticeably at this bad news.*)

Mary: Are you hungry? I got a few crab things made but I s'pose your stomach is still acting up.

Greg: Sure, I got no stomach left. It's a wonder they even let me eat. I don't know where the food goes when I eats it.

Andy: I'll have a bite of something.

Mary: Now mom, you know you're going in for the X-ray in the morning.

Greg: God, she'll outlive us all. What are they testing her for now?

Mary: Well, her circulation is gone in her right leg. Hasn't been the same since they took her toes off and y'know they thought it was diabetes but now they're not sure so she's goin' in for more testing. Legs gone all black... show 'em your leg, mom.

Tom: Don't talk to me about testing. I've been in so many times they got me a special room. I'm a mystery to the medical profession. I got 'em stumped.

Cathy: How's May gettin' on? She must be killed over Walter?

Greg: Why, what happened to Walter?

Tom: He was out in Fort McMurray. Worked like a dog in the tar pits. Sent home every cent to May. Lived on nothing. May hadn't seen him in 10 years and he was comin' home for Christmas.

Mary: She thought the sun shone out of him. He'd been off alcohol for eight years. Had the antabuse implant. Took one drink on the plane.

Tom: Just a little drop of champagne to celebrate.

Mary: Had a heart attack. Arrived at Torbay Airport D.O.A. Merry Christmas!

All: Tsk, tsk, tsk. That's shockin'. My God! Green Christmas, full graveyard (etc.).

(*Cheering up considerably.*)

Cathy: I think I will have a little something.

Mary: I'll put the kettle on.

GREG: You never see the five signs of cancer anymore.

ANDY: I grew up cross-eyed looking for a change in the growth of a mole or wart.

GREG: That's right, Mrs. Kinsella. Used to be up on the mirror. A cut that refused to heal…

TOM: A sudden drop in body temperature.

GREG: No, that's death, Gert.

TOM: No, I'm having a sudden drop in body temperature. Since they took me off the chlogestetone and put me on the innocuall, I don't know whether I'm inside or out.

CATHY: The young crowd don't worry about cancer no more.

GREG: No, it's all condoms and body fluids. We don't have to worry about that.

TOM: Can I give you a hand with that?

(*They rise to go to the kitchen.*)

(*Dissolve to: tea cups and cookie trays. The cards have been cleared. The ladies are warming to their topic.*)

CATHY: He treated her like a queen. Took her to Europe. Had the house redecorated, did everything for her. He wouldn't let her lift a finger.

TOM: Sure, he wouldn't let her walk for God's sake. He carried her!

MARY: In a basket!

GREG: And she couldn't talk.

CATHY: She had to purr and he'd rub her fur. (*Pause.*) Sure, he treated her like a cat, for God's sake.

(*They all laugh.*)

MARY (*topping her*): Sure, Martin Slaney was only 29 years old. Handsome, my God. His mother thought the sun, moon and stars shone out of him. She loved him more than life itself. He was working nights and going to medical school. Graduated with a major in obstetrics.

(*They all look a little crestfallen.*)

Wait till I tell ya. Went up to the cabin for a break in June, a week before his wedding. His fiancé was in town picking out the dress. He went out for a spin in the boat and he drowned. They never found the body.

(*Pause—they all look at each other and laugh hysterically.*)

GREG: You heard about Abie Tilley? She was up in the Health Sciences.

Simon Rakoff

I'm just getting over my cold. I like that people say "Bless you" after a sneeze. A little religious moment in your day. I was trying to figure out what it is about a sneeze that's religious—I think it's that mist around you.

TOM: She couldn't take nothing, no excitement, no bad news or nothing like that. Wasn't even allowed to watch "The Price is Right."

GREG: So, we went up to see her with our masks of death on, and the flashlights, going oooooooh!

TOM: And aaaaaahhhhh!

GREG: But she was in a real deep sleep, like a cocoon or something.

TOM: I don't think she recognized us first or last.

GREG: Read her death notice in the paper three days later.

MARY: Sure, poor old Jose Tobin worked 29 years with Marine Atlantic. Got her pension. Bought the wardrobe. Felt a tickle in her throat. Better check it out.

(*The women are practically salivating.*)

Went in coughing. . . came out in a coffin!

(*They all clap for this story.*)

CATHY: There's no sense or reason to it.

TOM: No, my darling. All you can do is keep your wick trimmed.

GREG: Sure, you knows Gerard Morrisey, do you, Gert? Well, when his wife died I thought he was gonna buckle but he was good as gold with the youngsters. Then he found out he had six months to live.

ALL: Go on! There's no justice. I know what you're gonna say next.

GREG: He wanted to have a ride in Disneyland, once before he died. Took him five months to save the money!

TOM: One month left!

GREG: Three weeks to make the reservation.

MARY: One week left!

GREG: One day to travel, arrived in Tampa.

CATHY/TOM: Six days left!

GREG: No reservation at the motel.

MARY/CATHY/TOM: Five days left!

GREG: Four days rain.

ALL: One day left!!!

GREG: He arrived at Disneyland, six hours wait in the line-up.

ALL (*chanting*)**:**   Eighteen hours left!

Greg: Tilt-a-Whirl broke down. They called the mechanics. Seventeen hours to fix it.

All: One hour left!

Greg: His vision started to go in the line-up. Couldn't speak when they strapped him in. Three minutes left.

All: Died?

Greg: Died! Tilt-a-Whirl never left the ground.

(The ladies burst into applause. They flash cards: "5.9"; "5.9"; "5.9"; "5.9" Finally Mom, who gives it a perfect "6.0.")

(Freeze frame.)

YOUR RELATIONSHIPS

FROM *ZEN AND NOW*

Eve Drobot

As you approach 40 in the 1980s, you have to be married. Period. Being between marriages is acceptable, as long as it means you are tired of the empty single life you have led since your divorce and are now looking for a new, more meaningful commitment. Being gay is no excuse. However, if your first marriage broke up because you finally came to terms with your true sexual nature, you get bonus points. Now, of course, you've settled down with your one true love (of the sex of your choice) and only cruise on business trips. Promiscuity is still possible, but bouts of sexual gymnastics must be interrupted periodically for wedding ceremonies.

Magazine Cover Story of the Eighties

"The sexual revolution is over." (See *Esquire, Rolling Stone, New York, Mother Jones, Harper's, Glamour, Newsweek, Time* and *U.S. News and World Report.* Ignore *Cosmo*—it's all fiction anyway.)

Your First Wedding (Circa 1969)

Location: A cow pasture outside Canyon Creek, Montana, at dawn.

Guests: Your pottery teacher, your yoga teacher, your guru, your weaving instructor, your carpenter, members of the goat-farming collective, your Aunt Wilma who works as a legal secretary at the State House in nearby Helena, and your roommate from Choate.

Officiating: Sri Charwanbabarajgurdilip.

Readings: From Fritz Perls' "Gestalt Prayer," the "I Ching," bride and groom's own poetry.

Music: Inca flute and Sioux drums.

Richard J. Needham

The reason grandparents and grandchildren get along so well is that they both have the same enemy.

Dress:

The Bride: Hand-embroidered Afghani red polished cotton tribal wedding dress; Moroccan henna designs painted on hands and forehead; no shoes. Bouquet of black-eyed susans picked that morning.

The Groom: Clean work shirt, new jeans, old Kodiak boots.

Food: Picnic spread of vegetable curry, bulgur wheat salad, honey and yogurt in glazed pottery bowls, brown rice, dates, oatmeal and hash wedding muffins. Home-pressed cider.

Honeymoon: Mountain climbing in Colorado.

Your Second Wedding (Circa 1985)
Location: St. Luke's Lutheran Church at 4:00 p.m. Reception following at Saddle Bridge Country Club.

Guests: Your parents, your first husband, your first wife, your former in-laws, your children from your first marriage (as bridesmaids, best man or ringbearer), three people from your department at the advertising agency, your bank manager, your lawyer, your squash partner, the couple you met on the wine-tasting tour of Burgundy last summer, and your roommate from Choate.

Officiating: The Rev. Robert Soames, B.A., M.Sc., Ph.D., D.Div.

Readings: Genesis (1:26-28, 31a), Gospel of St. John (3:18-24). The word "obey" is deleted from the exchange of vows.

Music: Mendelssohn's Wedding March, played on organ.

Dress:

The Bride: Ecru Alençon lace bodice over fitted ivory satin, Victorian neckline with a row of satin-covered buttons down the back and four satin-covered buttons at the wrist. Full train. Peau-de-soie ivory shoes with Swiss dot panty-hose by Christian Dior. Small drop-pearl tiara over tulle veil. Bouquet of white freesia, sweet-heart roses and baby's breath. Blue satin garter, grandmother's ivory cameo pin. Bridesmaids in mauve organza with peplum waists. Ensembles all by Pronuptia of Paris.

The Groom: Black, double-breasted tuxedo of goat's hair cashmere by Armani. Wing collar, black silk tie, patent leather slippers, boutonniere of white freesia.

Food: Sit-down dinner for 150. Mousseline of pike with radicchio salad, duck with Cointreau sauce and kiwi fruit, potatoes dauphin, shitake mushrooms. Four-tiered wedding cake with doily-wrapped individual servings for the groom's party. Veuve Cliquot champagne.

Honeymoon: Snorkelling in Aruba.

(Please note: the same scenario, on a smaller scale and later at night, may be repeated for gay couples, with varying degrees of legality—check your local laws. Officiating in such a case would be Martin

Overduin, B.A., M. Psych., D.Div., of The Loving Brethren Fellowship. Dress for both bride and groom would be black leather tuxedos.)

Your Family

HOW TO KNOW WHEN YOU'RE READY FOR PARENTHOOD

When you already own a micro-computer, Cuisinart, telephone answering machine, home video system (including camera and monitor), one or more futons, his-and-hers Universal Gyms, Jacuzzi attachment for the bath, an indoor herb garden, two or more dhurri rugs and a pasta machine, and you feel ready for an animate object.

WHAT A BABY WILL BRING INTO YOUR LIFE

An opportunity to buy an Appalachian Spring rock-maple crib, Aprica stroller, Fisher-Price crib mobile, two Snuglis (one denim, one corduroy), handwoven Provençal carrying basket, a collection of Gund Bears,
non-toxic and dishwasher-safe Beatrix Potter plates, life insurance and, most important of all, a Volvo.

BECOMING A MOTHER

Past the age of 30, it's not enough for a woman merely to get pregnant and have a baby. She must be prepared, both mentally and physically, for the most rigorous test of her adult life.

COMPETITIVE MATERNITY

Are you eligible for maternity leave?
Is the potential father's gene pool acceptable?
Will you have Lamaze or Leboyer?
How much do you really like herbal teas?
Is there a store near you that stocks navy-blue, pin-striped maternity smocks?
Can morning sickness be scheduled to occur before 8:30 a.m.?
Is there room in your apartment for a live-in nanny?
Does your health club provide day care while you work out?
Will childbirth classes interfere with after-hours work on your MBA?
Can you wear running shoes with Velcro closings to your office when your feet start to swell?
Will you be able to wear your Walkman during labour?
Will the hospital let you have the ultrasound pictures for your baby album?

TOPICS FOR DISCUSSION AT DINNER PARTIES

The advantages of breastfeeding.
The disadvantages of leaking through your nursing shields during job interviews.
The appropriate moment during labour for an epidural.
If you already have a child: how long you lasted without any medication at all.
If you are soon due to have a child: how long you intend to last

Richard J. Needham

As you grow old, you lose your interest in sex, your friends drift away, your children ignore you. There are many other advantages, of course, but these would seem to me the outstanding ones.

---

before having medication.
Sex positions in the second trimester.
Amniocentesis.
The role of the father during delivery (men are not expected to participate in the conversation at this point).
Episiotomies (not during dessert).

THE PROPER WORDING OF BIRTH ANNOUNCEMENTS

Zen

MacDonald: A new being has joined life on this planet! A Scorpio with Leo in the ascendant, in perfect sync with Capricorn father and Libra mother. Named Moonbeam Zacko Raindrop (a boy).

Now

Haskell/Rosenberg: Linda and Greg joyfully announce the safe arrival of 7 lb. 4 oz. Jennifer Lauren (or Alexander Michael) in a partially
unsedated delivery. Father assisted throughout while also recording the miraculous process on videotape. We'd especially like to thank Maggie, our midwife-companion who was most encouraging during the attempted home delivery, the ambulance crew who arrived at just the right moment, and Dr. Legree, who performed the Caesarian.

HOW TO BOND

Repeat these words often to your child, before and after it's born: treasury bonds, corporate bonds, stocks and bonds, bond issue, bonded securities, municipal bonds, bonded whiskey.

YOUR CHILD'S EARLY EDUCATION CAREER

Fluent in French and Spanish by age 2 (bilingual nanny).
Water Baby classes beginning at age 15 months.
Mother-infant developmental classes at age 2.
Two hours twice a week: playgroup for the kids; information and discussion sessions for Moms. (Only possible if Mother is running her own successful business and can delegate during that time period.)
Accelerated learning day care at age 3.
Flashcards and socialization through collective mudpie making.
French language preschool at age 4.
Montessori kindergarten at age 5.
Miss McKinnon's Elementary Day School, first through sixth grade. Traditional curriculum with emphasis on reading, writing, math, manners and our Judeo-Christian heritage. Annual fee: $4,700 per annum. Cost of uniforms not included.
Computer and tennis camp in New Hampshire at age 7.

FAMILY OPTIONS

Mommy, Daddy and Baby
Mommy, live-in Lover and Baby
Mommy (corporate lawyer), Nanny and Baby
Mommy, Child from her previous marriage, live-in Lover and Baby

Mommy, live-in-Lover, Child from his previous marriage, and Baby
Daddy (stockbroker), live-in Housekeeper, day Nanny and Baby

Rare:
Daddy, live-in Lover (female) and Baby
Mommy, Child from her previous marriage, live-in Lover (female)
and child from her previous marriage

Not yet, but soon:
Daddy, live-in Lover (male) and Baby

IS THERE LIFE OUTSIDE THE FAMILY?
Yes. It's called "work."

MATERNITY

Robert Service

There once was a Square, such a square little Square,
And he loved a trim Triangle;
But she was a flirt and around her skirt
Vainly she made him dangle.
Oh he wanted to wed and he had no dread
Of domestic woes and wrangles;
For he thought that his fate was to procreate
Cute little Squares and Triangles.

Now it happened one day in that geometric way
There swaggered a big bold Cube,
With a haughty stare and he made that Square
Have the air of a perfect boob;
To his solid spell the Triangle fell,
And she thrilled with love's sweet sickness,
For she took delight in his breadth and height—
But how she adored his thickness!

So that poor little Square just died of despair,
For his love he could not strangle;
While the bold Cube led to the bridal bed
That cute and acute Triangle.
The Square's sad lot she has long forgot,
And his passionate pretensions...
For she dotes on her kids—Oh such cute Pyramids
In a world of three dimensions.

APOSTLES' SONG

The Frantics

We're the saviour's twelve disciples
Read about us in this Bible
We face deadly persecution
As we build our institution

We got thrown out of our home
Now we're being killed in Rome
If you think we're happy, we are
Martyrdom is real great PR

We're the saviour's twelve amigos
We all go wherever he goes
Now he's gone we spread the blessing
Make up stuff where parts are missing

No more fear and superstition
No Olympus, no magicians
No more Zeus and all that trash
Now you're saved, give us your cash.

TOGETHERNESS

AN ECUMENICAL QUARTET FROM *SPRING THAW '61*

———

Mavor Moore

(A Roman Catholic Cardinal, an Anglican Archbishop, a United Church Moderator and a Greek Orthodox Patriarch.)

CHORUS: Togetherness! Togetherness!
        All praise to brotherly love!
        The churches will soon coalesce
        If we keep singing of
        Togetherness! Togetherness! Togetherness!

CARDINAL: You may find a prelate too much of a zealot:
        But the trouble with other religions has been
        That they will not concede that the Catholic creed
        Is the only escape from Original Sin!
        You may think the Vatican awf'ly dogmatic and
        Strict in its doctrine—well, maybe it is:
        But God allows others to go their own way
        While we are infallibly going in His.

CHORUS: But still we bless Togetherness!...etc.

ARCHBISHOP: An Archbishop mustn't relent—and he doesn't—
        In spreading the gospel within his own See,
        And that includes routing the Low Churches out
        And keeping the Monarchy still C. of E.!
        But High Church adherents are warned that our way
        Is dead against vulgar religious display:
        For God is a gentleman, through and through,
        And in all probability Anglican, too.

CHORUS: But still we bless Togetherness!...etc.

PATRIARCH: In Orthodox litany we can't admit any
        Further political woes than we have—
        So we avoid feuds by a rule that precludes
        A Greek or a Serb contradicting a Slav.
        It'd take hours to chronicle all the canonical
        Differences between us and the rest:
        But we'd have you recall that though God made us all
        He incontrovertibly made us the best!

CHORUS: But still we bless Togetherness!...etc.

MODERATOR: United Church pastors are always past-masters
Whenever a compromise needs to be found:
And frankly, who cares to split Biblical hairs
So long as one's morals are perfectly sound?
Our flocks are enormous, and all non-conformist:
Our virtuous conduct all others' excels.
We've God's guarantee that our conscience is free—
And we won't take our orders from anyone else!

CHORUS: But still we bless Togetherness!...etc.

Bob Edwards

About the only people who won't quarrel over religion are the people who haven't got any.

—*Summer Annual*, 1924.

—JOHNSTON

FROM *CAKE-WALK*

Colleen Curran

(LEIGH *is a nun in disguise—lay clothes. MARTHA is a former hippie married to a draft dodger; they own the Heaven on Earth Cafe. RUBY is wearing her "Akela get-up"—den mother uniform—to gain points and will do anything to win a baking contest.*)

RUBY (*points*):   She's friends with the judge! She probably speaks French.

MARTHA (*joking*):   Maybe she'll win the Celebrity prize then. It's Dinner for Two at Madame Benoit's house.

RUBY: I didn't enter this to eat with Jean Ben-what. I want that trip to France.

(MARTHA *and* LEIGH *both flinch.*)

I'm gonna win it for a second honeymoon for Buckey and me. We went to Las Vegas for the first one. Oh, you should see that Liberace Museum. It's hard to believe that one person could

Simon Rakoff

I just celebrated my fourth anniversary. Went out for a nice big dinner—because after four years, I really wanted dinner.

My wife is not a fabulous cook. Now, I'm not a chauvinist. I don't expect my wife to cook for me but, if she's going to, she should know how. She's taking a French Cooking course. She was supposed to make duck à l'orange. She couldn't do it.

She fed me chicken with Tang.

own so many beautiful things. When I told Buckey I wanted to win us a honeymoon in Paris he said, "Ruby, you don't need any Cake-Walk to get you to Paris..."

Leigh: That's nice.

Ruby: "You got a bathing suit," he said, "If you start swimming now you should get there by November." *(Laughs.)*

Martha: Leigh doesn't need a bathing suit. This Cleary Cheesecake is gonna do it for her.

Ruby *(looking at LEIGH's cake):* Patsy Cherubino makes a really good chocolate cake. It has icing this thick and cherries at the bottom. She won the lottery, too. She should be here. So should that cake.

Martha: So where is it?

Ruby: All over Tiger, her cat. She's got this Flying Siamese that dives off cupboards, you know? This morning he landed in her cake and dashed her hopes of Paris or $500. All Patsy can do now is enter him in the Pet Show. Last year they dressed him like a little John Wayne? Had a good chance for Best Dressed 'til he bit the judge. And if that isn't bad enough, her husband looks like a mass murderer.

Martha: What?!

Ruby: The Psycho-kind. Like he'd do terrible things to you even if he didn't know you. It's a wonder I can sleep nights knowing he's loose.

Martha: What an awful thing to say. Pasquale Cherubino is a lovely man!

Ruby: Think what you like. But you've got to admit he looks like a mass murderer with his hair all stuck up like this. Be honest.

Martha: Yes. A little like one. But he is one of the nicest customers we've ever had at Heaven on Earth. We call him "Compliments to the Chef."

Ruby: Some people don't care how immoral their chefs are as long as they can feed their faces.

Martha: Who are immoral chefs?

Ruby: Well if you don't know...

Martha: I don't know.

Ruby: I'm not one to point a finger.

Martha: I think you've pointed all of them. Do you mean Jake and me?

Ruby: You can't expect people not to speak up about it. Living with him.

MARTHA: You live with your husband, don't you?

RUBY: Yes, I live with my husband. And I can call him that because we're legal.

LEIGH: So...are they.

(MARTHA *shows her wedding ring hand.*)

RUBY: How come you got different last names then?

MARTHA: You're not my father-in-law, all right?

RUBY: I'll bet he had plenty to say.

MARTHA: We were born with different last names and chose to keep it that way.

RUBY: You were born with no clothes on, too. I see you changed that. Barely.

MARTHA (*without realizing it, tries to make her shorts longer by pulling them*): I didn't get married to change my name.

RUBY: Why'd you get married then?

MARTHA: Because we were ready to start our famil—(*almost crying*) Why do you care?

RUBY: Seems to me the least you can do is take his name. The least I did for Buckey was that. Everyone in town thinks it's strange.

MARTHA: Oh, that was the latest Gallup poll was it?

RUBY: It would be a great deal easier if you'd take your husband's name.

MARTHA: Yes it sure would! Then I'd be Martha Danner and I'd be in the D-E-F Room away from you!

RUBY: Well! (*Pause.*) The D-E-F Room has drapes and a TV.

MARTHA: What were you doing there?

RUBY: You're mighty interested in other people's business aren't you?

MARTHA (*walks away from her*): Yarggghh. (*Sees the chocolate bars* LEIGH *left on a counter.*) Oh, whose are these?

LEIGH: Mine, everyone's.

MARTHA: They for your kids?

LEIGH: No.

RUBY: You've got kids?

LEIGH: Yes.

RUBY: But you're not married.

MARTHA: She's a teacher.

Bob Edwards

———

When Solomon said there was a time and a place for everything he had not encountered the problem of parking his automobile.

—*Eye-Opener*, July 1, 1922

RUBY: Oh, that's all right then.

MARTHA: Can I have one?

LEIGH (*shocked*): You want junk food?

MARTHA: Yes. Is that so strange?

LEIGH: Yes! Sure, please do.

MARTHA: I need calories right now.

RUBY: Be honest with yourself. You need caffeine. The way I see it there's your three basic caffeine groups: Coca-Cola, coffee and chocolate. I read this story about this woman in the *Enquirer*, you know? She said, "I gave up caffeine and it saved my life." So I'm doin' that too. You don't see me all jumpy and jittery.

(LEIGH *gets too close to the Pepsi cooler.*)

Stay away from there! After I kicked the habit I began to read what goes into those things.

MARTHA (*reads*): "Milk chocolate, sugar, soya lecithin, ethyl vanillin..."

RUBY: You could die right now and imagine what the doctor might find in your stomach linings. I read where they found a 9000-years-old skeleton woman and they could tell her last meal had been a rat. Can you imagine a 9000-year-old rat in your mouth?

MARTHA: Leigh, please, make her stop.

RUBY: I feel everyone should be alerted to the dangers of caffeine. That and jogging. I read where a woman—about your age—was jogging and her uterus fell out, right there on the street. (*Pause.*) So whose names are your kids gonna get, yours or his?

MARTHA: We don't have any kids...yet.

RUBY: Well you better hurry up. Loretta Lynn was a grandmother by your age.

FROM *LES BELLES SOEURS*

———

Michel Tremblay

A FRENCH-CANADIAN WOMAN HAS WON A MILLION CONSUMER STAMPS IN A CONTEST; HER NEIGHBOURS COME TOGETHER TO HELP STICK THEM INTO BOOKS.

MARIE-ANGE: You won't catch me winning something like that. Not in a million years. I live in shit and that's where I'll be till the day I die. A million stamps! Jesus, a whole house. If I don't stop thinking about it I'm gonna go nuts. It's always the way.

The ones with all the luck deserve it the least. What's she ever done, Mme. Lauzon, to deserve all this? Nothing! Not a goddamn thing. She's no better looking than me. In fact, she's no better period. These contests shouldn't be allowed. The priest the other day was right. They ought to be abolished. Why should she win a million stamps and not me? Why? It's not fair. Me, too, I got kids to keep clean and I work as hard as she does wiping their asses all day long. In fact, my kids are a lot cleaner than hers. What do you think I'm all skin and bones for? 'Cause I work like a carthorse. That's why. But look at her. She's fat as a pig. And now I gotta live across the hall from her and listen to her bragging about her brand new home. I tell you, I can't stand it. Oh, there'll be no end to her smart-ass comments. She's just the type, the loud-mouthed bitch. It's all I'll be hearing for the next five years. "I got this with my stamps, I got that with my stamps." It's enough to make you puke! Believe me, I'm not gonna spend my life in this shit while Madam Fatso here goes swimming in velvet. It's not fair and I'm sick of it. I'm sick of killing myself for nothing. My life is nothing. A big fat nothing. I haven't got a cent to my name. I'm sick to death, I tell you. I'm sick to death of this stupid, rotten life!

(During the monologue, GABRIELLE JODOIN, ROSE OUIMET, YVETTE LONGPRÉ *and* LISETTE DE COURVAL *have entered. They take their places in the kitchen without paying attention to* MARIE-ANGE. *The five women get up and turn to the audience.)*

THE FIVE WOMEN (*together*):   This stupid, rotten life! Monday!

LISETTE: When the sun with his rays starts caressing the little flowers in the fields and the little birds open wide their little beaks to send forth their little cries to heaven...

THE OTHERS: I get up to fix breakfast. Toast, coffee, bacon, eggs. I nearly go nuts just getting the others out of bed. The kids leave for school. My husband goes to work.

MARIE-ANGE: Not mine. He's unemployed. He stays in bed.

THE FIVE WOMEN: Then I work. I work like a demon. I don't stop till noon. I wash...dresses, shirts, stockings, sweaters, pants, underpants, bras. The works. I scrub it. I wring it out. I scrub it again. I rinse it...My hands are chapped. My back is sore. I curse like hell. At noon, the kids come home. They eat like pigs. They mess up the house. They leave. In the afternoon, I hang out the wash, the biggest pain of all. When I finish with that, I start the supper. They all come home. They're tired and ratty. We all fight. But at night we watch TV. Tuesday.

LISETTE: When the sun with his rays...

THE OTHERS: I get up to fix breakfast. The same goddamn thing. Toast, coffee, bacon, eggs. I get them out of bed and kick them out the door. Then it's the ironing. I work, I work, I work and I

"If you want the Pope press one. If you want God, press two. If you want Peter, John, Mark, Luke..."

—WICKS

Simon Rakoff

I'm glad that Hallowe'en is finally over. It's my least favourite time of year. When I was a little kid, my mom hated me. Every Hallowe'en she would dress me up as a diabetic—I wouldn't get anything.

work. It's noon before I know it and the kids are mad because lunch isn't ready. I make baloney sandwiches. I work all afternoon. Suppertime comes. We all fight. But at night we watch TV. Wednesday...Shopping day. I walk all day long. I break my back carrying parcels this big. I come home beat and I've got to make supper. When the others get home I look like I'm dead. I am. My husband bitches. The kids scream. We all fight. But at night we watch TV. Thursday and Friday...same thing. I work. I slave. I kill myself for a pack of morons. Then Saturday, to top it all off, I've got the kids on my back and we all fight. But at night, we watch TV. Sunday I take the family, climb on the bus and go for supper with the mother-in-law. I watch the kids like a hawk, laugh at the old man's jokes, eat the old lady's food, which everyone says is better than mine...At night, we watch TV. I'm sick of this stupid, rotten life! This stupid, rotten life! This stupid, rotten life. This stup...

(They sit down suddenly.)

LISETTE: On my last trip to Europe...

ROSE: There she goes with her Europe again. Get her going on that and she's good for the whole night.

(DES-NEIGES VERRETTE comes in. Discreet little greetings are heard.)

LISETTE: I only wished to say that in Europe they don't have stamps. I mean, they have stamps, but not this kind. Only letter stamping stamps.

DES-NEIGES: No kidding! You mean you don't get presents like you do here? Boy, that Europe sounds like a pretty dull place.

LISETTE: Oh no, it's very nice in spite of that...

MARIE-ANGE: I'm not against stamps, mind you. They're very convenient. If it weren't for the stamps, I'd still be waiting for that thing to grind my meat with. What I don't like is the contests.

LISETTE: But why? They can make a whole family happy.

MARIE-ANGE: Maybe so. But they're a pain in the ass for the people next door.

BACK BENCH

–HARROP

FROM *ROSES ARE DIFFICULT HERE*

W.O. Mitchell

Well into the dirty thirties Canon Midford had taken over his Shelby parish. These were the desert years, when mid-America thirsted. Hot and constant winds siphoned wells and creeks and sloughs and hold-up ponds, blistered and cracked the prairie and the foothills skin, smoked up topsoil to smudge the sky, blot the sun. Light the lamp at noon.

Okie time had come. Grain elevators paid ten cents a bushel for wheat, three for oats and barley, but only if farmers were able to harvest a crop. No price offered for tumbleweed or Russian thistle or wild oats. Never, since Shelby's frontier birth or throughout her rural career, had there been hard times like these, when drifted land and blind homes must be abandoned. Dust to dust; dust to dust. Head north for the parklands and just possible rain in the Peace River country.

Canon Midford had come by Pullman coach to the new Sahara; many others travelled by freight, human flies on boxcars and flatcars and tenders, rolling East and rolling West. Most were looking for a chance to make a living, but some of the young were not seeking work: the scenery hogs, who had left the East to see the West, or the West to see the East. There was of course an older group, bindlestiffs or lump bums, the hobo professionals who long before any depression had been non-paying railway passengers. These had their own jungle jargon for the people you encountered: the hard tails, johns, harness bulls, gazoonas, gazeenas, gazoots, and gazats, or the canned-heat, vanilla, and after-shave-lotion artists, winos or McGoof hounds, wolves and their young proosians. The dinos were those who went into cafés and ordered four-course meals, said they were broke, hadn't eaten for three days, and were willing to wash dishes to pay for the meal. This dangerous stratagem could land them in the bucket for thirty days on charges of vagrancy and obtaining food under false pretences, though odds against that were much better if the restaurant were Greek or Chinese. When the snow flew, it was the Winter Christians who hit for the nearest Sally Ann drum to promise the rest of their life to Jerusalem Slim so they could confess sin, sing hymns, and do Bible studies to get bed and three until the meadowlark would announce the spring. City downtown street corners had the dingbats, dinging passersby for the price of a cup of coffee or a night in the scratch-house.

In Shelby district as in most other Western rural communities Bennett buggies—cars pulled by real horsepower—showed up, plagiarizing the Hoover buggies south of the Forty-ninth, where teams were also being hitched up to car bumpers. On both sides of the border, Thanksgiving and Christmas were soon tainted with irony. Celebration by gift was difficult on a twenty-five-dollar-a-month relief cheque. His third Christmas in Shelby, Canon Midford decided to do something about that...

JiCi Lauzon
Comedian

You know, they say that when you give a present to somebody, it's as nice for the person who gives it as for the person who receives it. Well, I can confirm this. Because today, I gave *myself* a really nice present. And this gave me as much pleasure to give it to myself, as to receive it. But I didn't give it to myself *immediately*. I made myself *wait* a little. I was there, and I *could* give it to myself immediately, I thought—or, well, finally I decided to give myself a surprise. I gave it to myself at a moment when I *wasn't* expecting it *at all*.

Howie Mandel

I was in Montana and they put me in a hotel. They put me in a hotel because they didn't want me outside. So anyway, I never saw this before: there was a TV in the bathroom. So, I was in the bathroom watching TV for about half-an-hour, and then a commercial came on, so I went in the other room and pissed on the bed.

He approached Mayor Oliver and the town council with the suggestion that they have Santa Claus visit Shelby Christmas morning with presents for every child in the district. His Worship and a unanimous council approved. The thing took off like prairie fire. A "Santa Visits Shelby and Greater Shelby District Committee" was formed, to be chaired by Canon Midford. Since the RCMP handed out the monthly relief cheques and had a list of the vulnerable needy, Corporal Broadfoot was named vice-chairman. Nettie Fitzgerald would perform her usual committee role: chief shit-disturber. ...

Corporal Broadfoot had plotted out the strategy for "Santa Visits Shelby and Greater Shelby District" in careful detail. From his position up on the town square platform he would be in charge of tactics. Santa must make his entrance from the north, of course. In the sleigh loaded and hung with toys he and his driver helper must take off well before daybreak under cover of darkness, go up the hill slope north of town, over and down as far as McNally's cottonwood bluff at the bottom of the down slope, a distance of roughly half a mile. They would take cover there, but keep a sharp lookout at all times for wave signals to be given by Canon Midford, who would take his position on top of the hill, approximately halfway into town. It was a fitting coincidence that this very hill had been used by the first RCMP under Colonel Macleod, as a lookout in the old Blackfoot Crossing days, when they had put the run on the whiskey traders in 1874, Corporal Broadfoot explained. Charlie Bolton said that sounded like bullshit to him, but Corporal Bolton said he could show it to him in a history of the RCMP book. "Just proves it," Charlie said. "History books is bullshit too."

From his vantage point Midford would have a clear view of the Corporal on the platform, so he could receive and relay signals to alert Rory. At twenty-minute intervals, Walter Oliver, who had been cast as Santa's messenger, would come out of the depot across the square,

–RAESIDE

in Boy Scout uniform with staff and blue knees, waving a yellow telegram he would then hand up to his father. The following year Walter at seventeen would make it to King Scout and attend the Jamboree in England, then in 1939, at nineteen, to Spitfire pilot in the RAF, and in 1941 to death in the Battle of London.

It turned out to be a very white Christmas. And cold. Twenty below. Rory had been over-optimistic about breaking the young team to tandem harness; even without the elk-antler bridles in place they were difficult. It took four hostellers to ear them down while Rory and Art in costume got up and into the bobsleigh. Santa crouched to the rear in a nest of his toys; Rory up front, with a firm grip on the lines, his feet braced against the buckboard and the team facing north, gave the signal. The hostellers released the horses' ears and jumped free. Belly to the ground, the whites of their eyeballs rolled up, the team lit out in the direction of the North Pole. Because both had got the bit clamped between their teeth, it took Rory almost two miles to cool them down and get control. Only then was he able to turn them round and head back for McNally's bluff. The three-foot fall into the barrow pit gave him some trouble, but finally they made it into the shelter of the cottonwoods, where they uncorked a jug of Rory's Undiluted Best Number One Hard to fortify themselves against the chill as they waited for Canon Midford to give them the signal.

In spite of the weather, the turnout was great. The town square soon filled with young and old, behind the wide alley roped off along the front of the platform. Trucks and cars and rigs were parked outside the square for two blocks in every direction. The dignitaries came out of the community centre and took their positions on the platform. Mayor Oliver gave his welcoming address. Walter Oliver came out of the depot and handed the first telegram up to his father, who read it out:

SANTA CLAUS LEFT NORTH POLE 12:06 A.M. ARCTIC DAYLIGHT SAVING TIME STOP WITH REINDEER RIG AND SLEIGH LOAD OF TOYS STOP JUST CROSSED ARCTIC CIRCLE AND ENTERED YUKON STOP HEADED FOR SHELBY STOP MAKING GOOD TIME STOP

Walter Oliver's next telegram read:

SANTA CLAUS AGAIN STOP WELL INTO NORTH-WEST TERRITORIES STOP HEADED FOR GRAND PRAIRIE AND PEACE RIVER STOP MERRY CHRISTMAS STOP HO HO HO STOP

And the next one:

STILL COMING WITH EDMONTON NEXT STOP STOP BLIZZARD CONDITIONS UP HERE SO SPEED REDUCED STOP AFTER EDMONTON RED DEER STOP THEN SHELBY STOP

And the next:

WEATHER CLEARED STOP RED DEER BEHIND STOP SHELBY NEXT STOP STOP COMING FAST STOP

This would be the last telegram. Corporal Broadfoot waved to Canon Midford, who in turn signalled Rory, who began to fit the

Susan Ryan

In the old days, God was always talking to people. Like Abraham. Abraham was going to axe-murder his own son—because God told him to. Fortunately at the last minute God told him not to.

Borderline psychopath or what? And this man is the *model* of Judeo-Christian faith. What would *bad* people do? Eat their young?

Oh, I know—they'd use birth control.

Lorne Elliott

When Hare Krishnas ask me for money I just tell them "Screw off. I gave in a previous life."

elk-horn bridles over the horses' heads. No problem; they were quite subdued by two hours of standing still in the biting cold. Rory climbed back up in the bobsleigh, loosed the lines, slapped them and yelled: "Hi-yahhhhh! Senator! Duke! Get your lazy arses out of it now!"

Both responded, and did well till they hit the barrow pit, where Senator, the lead horse, made a couple of rump bucks to get up and out onto the road. That caused the reindeer bridle Willie MacCrimmon had made for him to slide down and over Senator's nose to form an elk-horn necklace that bumped alarmingly against his chest. Duke's followed suit. That did it. Even Rory could not hold back the team urged on by the antlers rapping them into a full gallop. At least they were headed in the right direction, but much too fast for Canon Midford, who was to have hitched a ride to the edge of town, but who had to leap clear into a snowbank to get out of the way. Santa crouched, clinging to the sleigh side with both hands, his tasselled toque down over his rosy cheeks and cherry nose, his driver helper standing upright and leaning back with all his might against the lines to no avail, as they entered Shelby town limits.

Down Lafayette Avenue they flew, then Marmot Crescent, which would become Bison and in five blocks Main, which arrowed right through the town square. It was Rory's best option, if only he could keep the reindeer team on course. He succeeded. Never in his entire rodeo career had he ever faced a greater challenge. Wild-eyed, goitre antlers bouncing, manes and tails flying, harness bells a-jingle, snort clouds of steam from their nostrils, bits welded between their teeth, they hit the town square of Shelby, Alberta, Canada. Not Pamplona. No amateur toreadors waiting for them here. As they passed the platform, Santa, now with tinsel and a hoop round his neck, forgot to deliver his ho-ho-ho lines, nor did his driver helper call out: "A merry, merry Christmas morn to one and all!" Instead: "Hold up goddamit! Whoa, you bay bastards! Whoaaaa-hup!"

They cleared the square, crossed the railway tracks, and kept right on out of town.

Back in the stunned square children were crying; parents were comforting. One tearful voice was heard: "Jesus Murphy! It looks like Santy ain't stoppin' in Shelby this Christmas!"

By following the toy spoor, Corporal Broadfoot and others were able to track down Santa and his helper. Both were trapped in drunken darkness beneath the upturned sleigh. The horses were gone. Three days later they were found ten miles south of town in an abandoned barn, where they had taken shelter from blizzard winds.

It could have been much worse; there had been no casualties. By the next Christmas, Rory had the bays well broken, and Santa's visit to Shelby went on to become an established annual event, ending the year after war was declared. The rains came; wheat and oats and barley and beef, eggs and milk and butter and chickens, went up. In or out of the army there were suddenly jobs for all. Canon Midford and Father McNulty, and all parsons, ministers, town clerks and magistrates, were inundated with marriages that had been delayed till better times. No more flies on freight cars. Looked like war wasn't so bad after all.

Happy days were here again.

CANADIAN PLAY

SECOND CITY
**(by John Candy, Joe Flaherty, Eugene Levy,
Rosemary Radcliffe, Gilda Radner)**

Intro

Identity, identity, identity. Now how many times have we heard that tiresome word?

(Yelled out: three times!)

Thank you, thank you very much. Nevertheless, the problem of the Canadian identity has been the concern of many Canadians—filmmakers, authors and playwrights—for a long time now, and we at the Second City were fortunate enough to find behind a filing cabinet in a Toronto underground theatre, a manuscript of a play which we believe will be the Great Canadian Play. And tonight we would like to present that play to you, entitled, "You're Going to be Alright, You Creep, Leaving Home and All, Eh?"

(General hubbub.)

ANGUS: OK, shut up. I want some peace and quiet at my table. After all, today is a very special day, Johnny's coming home from hockey camp. Colleen, stop slurping your soup. And don't bang Johnny on the beaner like that, you dumb retard. Leonard, what are you doing down there—you reading again? How many times have I told you not to read at the table?

LEONARD: Well, I'm sorry Father, but I'm a poet, okay? It's my occupation to read at all possible times.

ANGUS: You and your damn poetry. You make me want to puke.

BEATRICE: Oh, Angus, don't talk to Leonard like that. Leonard's my pride and joy.

ANGUS: I know well he's your pride and joy. It's your mollycoddling that's made him the way he is.

BEA: Oh.

ANGUS: Aye, you're turning him into a damn pansy. *(Hubbub.)* Sit down!

BEA: Angus, Leonard's the only one of mine that has a sense of occasion and he's written a little poem on Johnny's homecoming, haven't you, darling?

LEONARD: Perhaps I have.

BEA: Would you like to read it for us, honey?

LEONARD: I don't know.

BEA: Come on.

Howie Mandel

Did you ever do this?— I got up in the middle of the night to stub my toe, but I slipped, and went to the bathroom.

JOHNNY: Come on, come on, Leonard, read it for your brother.

LEONARD: OK, Johnny, just for you. It's entitled, "Johnny's Home."

Skate, skate, skate Johnny,
Skate down the arena,
The hot steel thrashing,
Against the frozen water,
Swish, there goes Johnny
He shoots, he scores
One, two, three,
A hat-trick for Johnny McV.
And now he's back home
With his family.

ANGUS: That's a crock of shit, if ever I've heard one.

(Hubbub.)

(BEATRICE stands during soliloquy.)

–JOHNSTON

BEA: Oh, I wish today had been a little happier. I've been cooking and cleaning and getting ready for Johnny's homecoming and still it seems that we're always fighting. You know Angus is always a little hard on us when he gets to drinking. Still I know he loves me, eight times a day sometimes. You know he's nearly fifty and he's as frisky as a little piglet. Still I wish his standards for the children weren't quite so high, he's never been happy with Leonard and he's always been a little disappointed in Colleen. He says she's not right in the head. I say she's just a little socially withdrawn.

(Hubbub.)

ANGUS: Shut up and sit down.

BEA: Angus, Colleen has learned something today.

ANGUS: Ohhh, so the wee lump has learned something today.

BEA: Tell Daddy what you've learned today, Colleen.

COLLEEN: To take out the kitty litter!

ANGUS: And where do you put it?

COLLEEN: On Daddy's pillow.

ANGUS: On my pillow! What the hell do you want to do that for, you retard? Oh, Colleen, you make me want to puke. Johnny, pass the vegetable there. Sit down, sit down. *(Hubbub.)* That's a right funny joke, John. You know I love it when you pick on your sister like that. You're right too, lad, you know. Look at her sitting there like a damn brussels sprout. Colleen, Colleen. You're not my daughter. Leonard's my daughter. *(Hubbub.)* Aye, it's true, look at him sitting there like a pansy.

LEONARD *(disgusted)***:**   Oh, sorry.

ANGUS: Oh, yeah, right, yeah, there's only one man in the family besides me. That's Johnny here, right John? You're going to be a hockey-playing fool, aren't you, lad? Aye, I worked my fingers to the bone to send this boy to hockey camp, driving that damn linen truck—up Bloor, down Bloor, over to Spadina, down Spadina to Queen, Queen all the way over to Pape, Pape up to Don Mills, Don Mills to Eglinton and across over to Leslie and then all the way up Leslie to Lawrence and all the way along Lawrence to Yonge, and then straight down Yonge to College, and all the way along College to Lansdowne, up Lansdowne to St. Clair, across St. Clair to Bathurst and down Bathurst to Dupont which turns magically into Davenport and all the way down Davenport to Church, across Church and Adelaide to Jarvis and up Jarvis in the outside lane in my wee linen truck, passing all the cars 'cause I got three lanes going for me, till I'm back up on Bloor again, driving up and down Bloor, up and down Bloor...

Stevie Ray Fromstein

———

I'm very health conscious. I'm not in good shape, but I'm very aware of it.

———

JOHNNY: Will you shut up!

ANGUS: Well, I'm sorry, John.

JOHNNY: I don't care.

ANGUS: You don't give a hoot about my route?

JOHNNY: No. Sit down, Dad.

ANGUS: Alright, lad.

JOHNNY: I've got something to say.

ANGUS: OK.

BEA: What is it, sweetheart?

LEONARD: What is it, Johnny, what is it?

JOHNNY: Dad, I got kicked out of hockey camp.

ANGUS: What the hell for?

JOHNNY: Well, because I didn't go to any of the practices. I hate hockey. I've always hated hockey, you know that, Dad. I can't even skate, my ankles keep bending, and I'm never going back to hockey camp and you can't make me—I'm through.

LEONARD: You selfish son-of-a-bitch! You mean to say that Mommy gave up all her bingo winnings to send you to hockey camp and you didn't even go?

(Hubbub.)

ANGUS: What are you doing, John, you know he's frail.

WOMEN: Stop it, stop it!

JOHNNY: It wasn't always like this. Once we were happy. Once we were a family till Dad got that linen route and he started drinking...

ANGUS: Come on, Johnny...

JOHNNY: ...picked up that accent somewhere, and it hasn't been the same since. I wasn't born to be a hockey player.

ANGUS: Come on, John, back to the table now.

JOHNNY: In a minute, Dad.

ANGUS: Come on, John, finish your hot dogs and tea, lad.

JOHNNY: In a minute Dad, I'm doing my soliloquy. I should have been a . . .

ANGUS: Come back to the table, lad.

JOHNNY: Get off my back, Dad.

ANGUS: Come back to the table or get the hell out.

JOHNNY: Alright, alright, I will get the hell out and I'm going to take everyone with me. Come on, let's get out of here.

FAMILY: We're going to be alright, you creep, leaving home and all, Angus.

BEA: Come on, children.

ANGUS: Beatrice, Beatrice, no Beatrice, don't leave me. Beatrice? Oh, Beatrice. You wouldna leave me now, you couldna leave me now, oh you wouldna, couldna, shouldna leave me now. You remember me and you Beatrice in the old days in Scotland rollin in the heather, do you remember that? Eh, Colleen you've come back to your old Dad. Come, give us a wee kiss now, eh girl. What are you doing? What?

COLLEEN: You make me want to puke.

–KRIEGER

WAS IT GOOD FOR YOU?

THE BATTLE OF THE SEXES

Anthony Jenkins

Little Ms. Muffet,
Sat on the board of directors,
 Eating her curds and whey.
 Along came a spider
 Who sat down beside her
So she maced the creep
and transferred him to the
Anchorage office.

INVASION OF THE AIRLINE STEWARDESSES
FROM *URBAN SCRAWL*

Erika Ritter

Like a lot of people for whom the ability to remain in constant motion functions as a life-saving device—much like protective colouring in some animals—I take a lot of airplanes. And in the course of my travels I run into more than my share of stewardesses.

Not stewardesses. Excuse me. Flight attendants. "Flight attendant" is that kind of meaningless adjective-noun airline phrase ("smoking materials" being the quintessential example) that has been designed by commercial airlines for maximum ambiguity (read: minimum legal liability) aboard regularly scheduled flights.

I've learned a lot about modern communication from studying the language of commercial aviation—almost as much, in fact, as I've learned about food from studying puréed carrots. And I'm here to share with you what I've managed to pick up.

Actually, the most instructive language-learning session I've ever had at a cruising altitude of 37,000 feet came to me on one journey when I was dozing off, into that never-never world between meditation and deep coma, shortly after the termination of the meal service and prior to the commencement of the inflight entertainment...

Aw heck. No point in mincing words. You know the state I'm talking about. When you're completely ripped on the carafe of complimentary wine, too buzzed on chemically reconstituted chicken divan and apple charlotte to tune in to the flick, and consequently good for nothing but a sort of rapt and open-mouthed trance. Mine was that kind of haunting airborne dream that comes to you at such a moment.

In the dream, I had donned my complimentary headset specially designed to enhance my listening pleasure and had obediently tuned my armchair console (conveniently located within easy reach) to

Channel Two, upon which movie reception was rumoured to be about to commence in just a few moments' time.

Sure enough. Up came the ominous throb of the introductory chord; up came the opening title upon the viewing screen. *Invasion of the Airline Stewardesses!* was how the hysterical message read.

There was another suspenseful chord, then a tracking shot of a friendly middle-American midsummer street, followed by a sequence in which a young friendly middle-American midsummer man strode up the front walk of one of the middle-American houses to ring the doorbell in an open-hearted and purposeful way.

The door opened, and a young woman with a fringe of dark hair appeared, looking out with an expectant smile.

"Hi there, Mary Lou," said the young man. "Ready for our picnic?"

Whereupon the young woman opened the door wider and ushered him in, her smile decidedly mechanical now. "Good afternoon, Steve. Welcome to Number Seven-Forty-Seven Boeing Street. Our house temperature today is maintained at a moderate seventy-two degrees Fahren-"

"Pardon?" said Steve, with an uneasy grin.

"However," Mary Lou continued, "should you at any time during your visit today become uncomfortable, you will find a thermostat located within easy reach in the front hallway."

"Mary Lou," said Steve, kindly but firmly, "I'm here to take you to Lake Periphrastic for a picnic, remember?"

But Mary Lou appeared to take no notice as she led him to an armchair in the living room, plumping up the pillow before indicating he should sit. "For your added visiting pleasure a beverage service is available to you this afternoon. Should you—"

"Mary Lou!" Steve was snapping at her now. "Cut it out! It's Steve, your fiancé. Don't you know me?"

"Because of the short duration of your visit this afternoon, there will be no hot-meal service available."

His face ashen, Steve rose out of the armchair with an expression of unalloyed alarm. "Mary Lou, what in the consarned heck's happened to you?"

"Our visiting time this afternoon will be approximately—"

At that point, Steve cut her off. "Stay right where you are, Mary Lou! I'm going for help."

And then, with the soundtrack music pursuing him like the Furies, Steve hurries out of the house and down the front walk. In the next scene, we see him in the local police station, where the local police officer is sprawled complacently behind his desk, smiling with sceptical indulgence as Steve pours out his fervent tale.

"I swear to you, Joe," Steve is saying urgently, punching the officer's desk with his forefinger for emphasis, "It's not *Mary Lou!*"

The cop stretches and yawns pacifically. "Now there, Steve. Don't tell me you've been riding your tractor in the noonday sun without a hat again?"

Susan Ryan

When a man says in that special voice, "I'll do anything you want," should you say, "Marry me," or does it break the mood? I say, "Get down on your hands and knees and bark like a dog."

It breaks the mood, but it's a heck of a lot of fun.

Susan Ryan

What *don't* men want to hear?

Maybe where the big hand is on your biological clock. To me, it doesn't make sense to spend one quarter of one half of your adult life bleeding and have nothing to show for it. All that time pulling a squeegee behind you?

Steve rises to his full height, white-lipped, furious, dignified. "Listen to me. It looks like Mary Lou. It walks like Mary Lou. Shucks, it's even got her voice. But the things she's saying, Officer Dogma, I swear to you—" He looks around furtively, then lowers his voice to an ominous whisper. "They don't sound a bit like my girl."

"No?" The police officer smiles politely, but with a trace of mockery pulling at the corner of his mouth. "Who *does* she sound like, Steve?"

"Joe—Officer Dogma—I know this seems crazy, but...but she sounds like—like an airline stewardess!"

A close-up on Steve's face, terrified but convinced, followed by a close-up shot of Officer Dogma looking bemusedly stunned, as though someone had just struck him across the face with a frozen filet of lemon sole. Another thrill of nervous music, as the scene fades out.

Cut to a night-time shot of the officer still looking bemused and meditative as he drives his car up the driveway of a darkened bungalow, turns off the ignition, then pulls the emergency brake noisily before killing the headlights.

We follow him out of the car, up the front walk, then wait with him as he rummages in the moonlight to find his keys in the pocket of his uniform slacks. At last, he inserts the key in the lock.

Next we follow the same Officer Dogma surreptitiously making his way through the interior of the darkened house, then into the bedroom, where a single bedside lamp is burning.

In the bed, her attractive nightgown-clad shoulders protruding above the snowy boundary of the bed sheet, lies a pretty thirtyish woman reading a paperback. As Joe leans over the bed to kiss her cheek, she does not look up from her book, but flinches slightly and, almost imperceptibly, pulls away.

Joe notices, but pretends not to notice. He removes his uniform, hangs it up carefully on a coat hanger, then takes a crumpled pack of Lucky Strikes from the pocket of his shirt before hanging it up, and sets the cigarette pack down on his bedside table. Then, clad in his undershirt and shorts, he crawls into bed beside the woman, and regards her for a long moment before speaking.

Joe: Hey, Lizabeth, you sulking now? Put down that book, honey, and kill the light.

(*Before he can reach across her to extinguish the bedside lamp beside her, she strikes his arm away, still feigning absorption in her book.*)

Elizabeth (*flatly*):   I regret to inform you that, at this time, sexual overtures will not be encouraged.

Joe: Say what?

(*Startled, he pulls away, and looks at her from an alarmed distance.*)

"Currently in our marriage," recited Elizabeth, "we are experiencing some turbulence. For this reason, you are advised to remain on your side of the bed, with your undershorts securely fastened."

–KRIEGER

At this point, if I remember correctly, there was yet another chord of suspenseful music, as Joe regarded his wife with a replay of the same struck-by-a-lemon-sole expression he'd exhibited to Steve, back in the police station.

"Look," he said at last, cagily narrowing his eyes. "Let's *talk* about it, whatever it is." And he reached for the crumpled pack of Luckies on the end table beside him.

"At this time, you are requested to extinguish all smoking materials."

Quick as a shot, Joe's hand retracted, and he gave Elizabeth another look of horrified alarm as she continued her expressionless announcement.

"Once, however, your wife has switched off her bedside lamp and has achieved her sleeping state, cigarette smoking will be permitted. Except, of course, in those parts of the house specifically designated as no-smoking areas, including the furnace room and the children's sleeping quarters."

At this point, without warning, Elizabeth throws back the cover and gets out of the bed, padding purposefully across the room on bare feet to the clothes closet.

Susan Ryan

Condoms for women. What do you...how do you...where do you...? They go over your heart. Now *nobody* has to feel anything.

"Lizabeth," Joe whimpers, watching her, "once and for all, what's eating you?"

He watches and we watch as Elizabeth, in something like a mechanical trance, begins removing hangers of clothing from her side of the closet, flinging them emphatically but unhurriedly onto the bed.

"Elizabeth?"

At last she pauses and turns to him, a bouclé suit on a hanger in her hand. "In a very short time, I will be arriving at the end of my patience. On behalf of myself and the children, I would like to say it's been our pleasure to live with you until today."

Electrified with surprise and horror, Officer Dogma leaps out of the bed, and finds himself standing stupidly in the middle of the room, flat-footed and pleading.

"Elizabeth! Please, honey, don't go! I mean it. You can't leave me."

There was another pause at this point, longer and more dramatic, as Elizabeth regarded her husband with a cool and clear- eyed stare. Then, after an almost endless moment, she began picking her clothes off the bed, and returning them to the closet.

Sweating with relief, Joe bounded over to her and began, moistly, to kiss her hand.

"Thank you, Lizabeth! Honey, thank you!"

Coldly, however, she pulled her hand away from him, and in a white shaft of moonlight that flooded the room, she regarded him with a remote glacial stare.

ELIZABETH: Please make your exit this evening through the door provided at the front of the house.

JOE (*taken aback*):   Exit? What exit? I thought you'd decided that—

ELIZABETH: And kindly check all drawers, closets, and underground storage areas for any and all personal belongings you may have brought with you into this marriage.

JOE (*shrieking*):   Elizabeth! You mean now you're giving *me* the gate? Just like that? And you won't even tell me why?

Eerily caught by moonlight, Elizabeth turns to him with a seraphic smile, radiant yet oddly impersonal. "Thank you for choosing to marry Elizabeth Dogma. This is the termination of Joe and Elizabeth's marriage. Should you require any divorce information, kindly check with the lawyer's office, conveniently located in the—"

At this moment, I must have been groaning and twitching violently, for suddenly I felt the cool hand of a stewardess, shaking me gently awake.

"Thank God you woke me up," I said, my face bathed in a cold glistening sweat. "I was having the most horrifying dream. It was about women, you see, nice normal women whose bodies have been inexplicably invaded by the souls of automatons.

"Normal sunny personalities obliterated by a terrible impersonal civility. Individuated modes of speech wiped out in favour of a kind of Fortran language that reminded me of nothing so strongly as the sort of vocal pattern you find aboard commercial aircraft, broadcast over the inflight intercom by the voices of..."

As the stewardess stared back at me with a flinty little smile, her grip tightened convulsively on my arm, and I felt my words die in my throat.

The voices of airline stewardesses. That was what I'd started to say, and it was clear that she knew it. Knew it and resented it because, of course, these days they insist on being referred to as flight attendants.

The Invasion of the Airline Stewardesses. Just a crazy dream... or was it?

"For your continued travelling pleasure, a complimentary alcoholic beverage will be served to you at this time," said the flight attendant, still with the glint of her knowing smile. "Please remain seated for your own safety and comfort, with your seat belt securely fastened."

As she hurried away (too quickly?) to get me a sedative glass of wine (and perhaps to alert the rest of the crew that someone on board was on to their plan for world domination?), I reached casually into the pocket located directly in front of my seat for the safety-features card provided for my information while travelling and scanned it quickly to see what it might have to say about the possibility of the type of eerie inflight invasion I was beginning to hypothesize.

Just as I'd suspected, there wasn't a breath of a mention. Damned clever, these flight attendants.

Agnes Macphail
(Elected to the House of Commons in 1921 and held her seat until 1940)

———

Heckler (*during speech by Agnes Macphail*): "Don't you wish you were a man?"

Miss Macphail: "Yes. Don't you?"

———

IF I HAD $1000000

———

Barenaked Ladies

If I had $1000000
If I had $1000000
I'd buy you a house
If I had $1000000
If I had $1000000
I'd buy you furniture for your house
Maybe a nice chesterfield or an ottoman
If I had $1000000
If I had $1000000
I'd buy you a K-car
A nice Reliant automobile
If I had $1000000
I'd buy your love.

Richard J. Needham

They should put the Gideon Bible in the hotel lobby, not in the hotel bedroom; by the time you get to the bedroom, it's too late.

I'd build a tree fort in our yard
If I had $1000000
You could help it wouldn't be that hard
If I had $1000000
Maybe we could put a refrigerator in there
Wouldn't that be fabulous.

If I had $1000000
If I had $1000000
I'd buy you a fur coat
But not a real fur coat, that's cruel.

If I had $1000000
If I had $1000000
I'd buy you an exotic pet
Like a llama or an emu
If I had $1000000
If I had $1000000
I'd buy you John Merrick's remains
All them crazy elephant bones
If I had $1000000
I'd buy your love.

If I had $1000000
We wouldn't have to walk to the store
If I had $1000000
We'd take a limousine 'cause it costs more
If I had $1000000
We wouldn't have to eat Kraft Dinner
But we would. We'd actually make the tree fort from the first chorus out of it. Mmm.

If I had $1000000
If I had $1000000
I'd buy you a green dress
But not a real green dress, that's cruel
If I had $1000000
If I had $1000000
I'd buy you some art
A Picasso or a Garfunkel
If I had $1000000
If I had $1000000
I'd buy you a monkey
Haven't you always wanted a monkey?

Haven't you always wanted a monkey?
If I had $1000000
I'd buy your love.

If I had $1000000
If I had $1000000
If I had $1000000
If I had $1000000
If I had $1000000
I'd be rich.

Stevie Ray Fromstein

So I'm in my hotel room. It's the middle of the afternoon...I'm completely naked...and the maid walks in.
Finally.

BUDDY COLE SKETCH

The Kids in the Hall
(by Scott Thompson)

They say, ooh, that the notion of love at first sight is an impossible idea. Now, I may have been born yesterday, but I still went shopping. It happens. Well, it happened to me. Oh, it was years ago when I was living in Baghdad. On the day in question, it was a sexy, sunny, rocky day, and I was lounging about the pool at the Danish consulate, wearing next to nothing. In fact, at one point all I was wearing was a diplomat's hand. Ooohh, it was a crazy, crazy time for me. I was the top male model for an Egyptian line of jeans, and my face and figure were plastered on billboards all over the Middle East. And still the fighting continued.

Serge, the man, came striding into the pool area like the Colossus of Rome and shot me a look of raw passion that heroes have been shooting at heroes for thousands and thousands of years. I froze, and buried my face in a copy of Omar Kazam's *Kubla Kham*. But it was upside-down, so I feigned dyslexia. He saw right through my onion-skin cheroot and dove into the pool fully clothed. And in one, clean, swift movement, he was there beside me. A pepper miller looking for a salt seller. Oh, yes, Serge was black, which is odd, don't you think, him being Danish and all. But figure: if the French can worship Jerry Lewis and the Turks can invent the croissant, anything's possible in this crazy, crazy world.

I turned to Serge with the spontaneity of champagne in a slipper and said, "I need a lover." And that was it. We were together for six months, which in heterosexual terms is three incarnations with the same mate.

But Serge is dead to me now. They're all dead to me now. He walked out of my life and smack into the front of a bus. All my lovers have been killed by buses. I really must get a place in the country.

Oh well, live and learn. You know, it's hard for a faggot to take risks nowadays, but you've gotta try, for example, you know that

Susan Ryan

I enjoy a good man occasionally. After a meal. Instead of a mint.

feeling you get, when you don't know whether it's going to be a shit or a fart, but you let 'er rip anyways?

I hesitated to use that analogy in front of a heterosexual audience because when we mention anything even remotely anal, they rush out to vacuum their car. It all reminds me of something Molière once said to Guyamo Passant in a café in Vienna: "That's nice. You should write it down."

ME, ON MY HONEYMOON
FROM *THAT'S ME IN THE MIDDLE*

Donald Jack

Finally we went upstairs. I was about to barge into the bedroom; then hesitated, and knocked.

"Who is it?" Katherine said from within.

"It's me," I said.

"Who?"

"Bandy," I said.

"Bandy?"

"Yes," I said. "Don't you remember?"

"Oh," she said in a muffled voice. "You mean Lieutenant Bandy?"

"That's right," I said through the door. What on earth was wrong with the girl?

"What do you want?" she asked.

I didn't quite know how to answer this. I was beginning to feel somewhat foolish, lurking about in the hall talking through a closed door. "Can I come in?" I asked.

There was no answer; so I took a firm grasp of the doorknob and pulled. "It's locked," I said in surprise. "Why have you locked it?" There was no answer. "Katherine?" I said.

Katherine pulled the door inward, and without a word went back to combing her hair at the dressing table. The door hadn't been locked at all. I'd become so used to doors that opened outward, and...Well, the Nissen hut doors opened outward, and so did the doors of the Spartan Hotel.

Our room was frilly with lace, flowery pelmet, ornamental fireplace, patterned antimacassar, and fussy lamp, and had a tiny adjoining room, presumably for the ladies because it contained only a dresser, chair and a large mirror for powdering the nose, and so on; and it was this little room that Katherine went back to. She was wearing a blue silk nightgown that trailed around her ankles and the awful quilted dressing gown I'd seen her in at Burma Park. She didn't say anything, so I shuffled around the bedroom for a while, picking things up and putting them down. Then I gazed out the window. Then I realized the curtains were drawn, so I pulled them back, which enabled me to gaze out the window. But not being able to see anything, it being quite dark outside, I took up my towel and my little toilet bag and went to the door.

"I'm going to the bathroom," I said.

There was no answer, so I went and had a bath, brushed my teeth and cut my toenails, and when I got back Katherine was reading in bed. I wandered about the room for a bit, tidying my clothes and so on. Finally I got into bed.

Katherine went on reading. I sat there for a while, having a little stretch. It was a huge bed, and there was considerable acreage between us. After some time I got up on my hands and knees and crawled across to Katherine and leaned over to look at the book. "What are you reading?" I inquired.

She showed me the cover, then went back to her reading. It was *Quentin Durward*.

"Oh, yes," I said. "Walter Scott."

Five minutes later I said, "Is it any good?"

"It's not bad when you get into it."

A couple of minutes later I said, "I see."

Katherine had been sitting bolt upright, very stiffly. She now lay back on the pillows. This outlined her bosom. It pouted very prettily against the silk nightdress.

"Well," I said, feeling short of breath. "It must be getting late."

"It's only half-past ten," she said. "I forgot to tell you: I always read until dawn. Then I like to go for a long walk."

"Mm," I said.

She turned a page. I took a deep breath, drawing it in as unobtrusively as possible, and put my arm round her shoulders.

"It's been a long day," I remarked conversationally.

There was another of those damned pauses; then she put the book aside and looked at me. She had long since lost any self-consciousness about her slight strabismus; I'd told her so often it made her look all the more desirable. It did now. My face was fiery.

"Yes," she said. "It's been a damned long day." And laughed a bit shrilly.

I started to put my other arm around her. She was apparently wearing nothing beneath the blue silk, and as my fingertips brushed her stomach she twitched and hid her face against me. "Put the light out," she whispered. Her breath tickled my neck, and I started twitching too.

The frilly lamp was on her side of the bed. I didn't want to kneel up and lean over because my pyjamas were noticeably bunched, so I got up and walked around the bed, sideways.

With the light out, the room was pitch dark, and walking back to my side of the bed I smashed my toe against the doorpost.

"What's the matter?"

"I hit my toe."

It was all the more painful because it was the same toe I'd broken when I kicked that rock in France. However, the throbbing soon died down, and I groped my way back, but all that hopping around had sent my compass spinning, and I went in the wrong direction. There was a tremendous clatter as I fell over some fire irons.

"What on earth's the matter now?" Katherine asked in a despairing tone of voice, and switched on the lamp again to find me in the

Bob Edwards

Anxious correspondent inquires: "Is it proper for a young lady of seventeen to go walking after dark with a young gentleman with no chaperone?"

Yes, perfectly proper, if you keep walking.

—*Summer Annual,* 1920

Bob Edwards

When we hear a woman say that all men are alike we wonder how she found out.

—*Eye-Opener*, March 6, 1920

fireplace about twenty feet away. Fortunately the fire wasn't lit, but one of my hands was black with soot and I had to go back to the bathroom to wash it. I met McIntock in the corridor. He stopped and looked at my hand.

"I expect," he said, "you were trying to get away up the chimney. Is that it?"

"Of course not," I said coldly. "I was on my way to bed but walked into the fireplace instead, that's all."

"Aye," McIntock said.

When I got back, the lamp was still on and Katherine was all covered up in bed, pretending to be asleep. I switched off the lamp once more, being careful to take my bearings properly this time, and I managed to navigate back to bed successfully.

There was silence for some time. Katherine didn't stir.

I reached over inch by inch, my heart pounding.

It certainly was a large bed. I couldn't locate her at all. I moved over three or four feet and reached out again, but even though my arm was stretched to the limit I still wasn't making contact. I felt around. I was damned if I could find her.

After a moment I whispered hoarsely, "Where on *earth* are you?"

She didn't answer. I expect the poor girl was suddenly a mass of nerves, and, making allowances for this, I moved over another foot or two and whispered tenderly, "Where the hell are you, Kath?" But again drew a blank. My hand was swishing over the sheets, searching for her. "I can't find you," I complained. Really, this was a bit much. There *was* such a thing as excessive modesty. I moved again, a trifle impatiently, and fell out of bed.

Feeling myself fall, I naturally tried to grasp for some support, and in so doing grabbed the tasseled cloth covering the bedside table, and the next moment there was a shocking din as the table, the tasseled cloth, the frilly lamp, two or three ornaments, and I crashed to the wooden floor. I got a splinter in my behind. The door to the little powder room was flung open and Katherine appeared, outlined against the light.

"I fell out of bed," I explained.

She leaned against the wall for support.

I got up and trod on some glass from the shattered lamp.

When Katherine had pulled herself together, she said, "You'll have to ask McIntock for some first aid for that foot."

I knocked at McIntock's door. He emerged, blinking, to find me smiling ingratiatingly, balanced on one leg in my pyjamas, which now had blood as well as soot on them.

"Sorry to disturb you," I whinnied, "but would you happen to have anything that might be helpful in stopping the flow of blood?"

McIntock looked terribly concerned. "You rotten beast," he said. "Oh, the puir wee girl," and started to rush along the corridor.

"Come back," I said. "It's not Katherine; it's me."

"Great thundering McGubbins," he said. "It's the first time I ever heard of—"

"I trod on some glass," I said.

There was quite a long silence.

"I fell out of bed, you see," I went on, but then dried up, possibly because of his expression.

Lady McIntock came out. "What's up?" she asked.

"Nothing yet," McIntock said. "It seems Bartholomew has fallen out of bed now, and cut his foot on the lamp. I did not dare ask him what the lamp was doing on the floor, of course."

"No," Lady McIntock said. She stared at me balanced on one leg and smiling fatuously, looked as if she was going to say something, but apparently decided against it and fetched the first-aid kit instead, and fixed up my foot there in the hall.

When I got back to the bedroom once again, Katherine had just finished clearing up the mess and was talking to herself. She soon stopped, however, and switched off the light in the adjoining room and we got into bed once more. I gave a grunt and got up again.

"*Now* what's the matter?" she said.

"Oh, it's nothing."

She got up and switched on the powder-room light again. "What is it?" she said, shaking me. "Come on, tell me. Out with it; it's something else now, isn't it? Tell me, tell me!" She sounded just a trifle hysterical and was shaking me so hard my answer was a tremolo.

"I have a splinter," I quavered. A couple of minutes later there was a knock at the door and McIntock and his wife came in with a bottle of iodine for my foot and found me lying face down on the bed, and Katherine holding a large safety pin poised over my right buttock.

The McIntocks stood transfixed for a moment, then slowly began to back out, obviously fearing that they'd interrupted some dreadful perversion culled from the pages of the Marquis de Sade's *Philosophie dans le boudoir*, or *Les Crimes de l'amour*.

"It's all right," Katherine said, almost inaudibly. "It's only a splinter."

"Aye," McIntock said.

"We forgot to put iodine on his foot," Lady McIntock faltered.

They gathered around. By this time I wouldn't have cared if they'd brought in the butler, half a dozen upstairs maids and a poacher or two. I just shut my eyes and tried to think of other things. They took turns trying to pry the splinter out. Lady McIntock won.

Finally we were alone once more, and in the light of the powder room—by this time Katherine didn't dare switch it off—we snuggled up, our two faces jammed together like workmen's braziers. I was rather inept, I'm afraid, for though I knew the technique in theory, in practice it didn't seem to be quite so simple. Still, Katherine appeared to be happy enough at the end of it, and I was reminded of what Queen Victoria was supposed to have said to Albert: "Do you mean to say," she was supposed to have said, imagining, I suppose, that supreme bliss was somehow a royal prerogative, "Do you mean to say that the common people enjoy this just as much?"

I mentioned this to Katherine, but she was not amused.

LOVE POEMS, WITH RHYMES EK AND EP

John Robert Colombo

You're worth more to me than
    the most valuable antique,
As I watch you lying there,
    sound asleep.
Now let me think aloud! Our
    love'll never be bleak
For we've lots of cheek.
We're fashionable and chic,
Having formed our own clique.
There's no need to creep
Before others, or endure the
    critique
Of some foul-mouthed freak.
My love'll keep
Us vibrantly alive. Loneliness'll
    leak
away, unhappiness'll drop off
    some lover's leap.
From Martinique
We'll be the opposite of meek
To Mozambique.
Let's have another peep
At your eye-catching physique!
I love you like a Sheik
And you shriek
Like a sex-starved Sikh.
Cradled in each other's arms we
    slip into sleep,
Our bodies wet and sleek.
There's no need to sneak
Glances, let's loudly speak
Out, and across our bedroom
    streak,
Our bodies stained like teak,
Our love-making assuredly
    unique.
There's no need to weep:
I feel like this seven days a week.

DAUGHTERS OF FEMINISTS

Nancy White

Daughters of feminists
love to wear pink and white
short frilly dresses,
they speak of successes
with boys—
It annoys
their mom.
Daughters of feminists
won't put on jeans
or the precious construction boot
mama found cute,
ugly shoes
they refuse—
how come?
Daughters of feminists
think they'll get married
to some wealthy guy
who'll support them forever,
Daughters of feminists
don't bother voting at all,
Daughters of feminists
beg to wear lipstick
each day from the age of three,
Daughters of feminists
think that a princess
is what they are destined to be.

How do they get so girly?
How come they want a Barbie?
Why does it start so early?
Why, when we bring her up just like a fella,
Who does she idolize? Cinderella!

Daughters of feminists
bruise so easily,
Daughters of feminists hurt,
Daughters of feminists
curtsy and skip,

Daughters of feminists flirt,
They say "Please, mommy,
can I do the dishes?"
And "Let's make a pie for my brother!"
Are they sincere? Are they crazy?
Or are they just
Trying to stick it to mother?

How do they get so girly?
How come they want a Barbie?
Why does it start so early?

GIRLS: "Daughters of feminists just want to play with their
toys!"

Daughters of feminists
love to wear pink and white
short frilly dresses
They speak of successes
with boys.

Susan Ryan

What is a woman without a man? She's a flower without a stamen, an artichoke without a heart, a tree without one of those big, sticky, funny-smelling wads of sap stuck to the side of it.

"I know I'm not supposed to interfere, but how's the dog going to climb through that?"

—UNGER

Stevie Ray Fromstein

Ever notice on a soap commercial, they show people taking a bath, and on a toothpaste commercial, they show people brushing their teeth, but on a tampon commercial, they show people playing tennis?

SIMMERING
FROM *MURDER IN THE DARK*

Margaret Atwood

It started in the backyards. At first the men concentrated on heat and smoke, and on dangerous thrusts with long forks. Their wives gave them aprons in railroad stripes, with slogans on the front—Hot Stuff, The Boss—to spur them on. Then it began to get all mixed up with who should do the dishes, and you can't fall back on paper plates forever, and around that time the wives got tired of making butterscotch brownies and jello salads with grated carrots and baby marshmallows in them and wanted to make money instead, and one thing led to another. The wives said that there were only twenty-four hours in a day; and the men, who in that century were still priding themselves on their rationality, had to agree that this was so.

For a while they worked it out that the men were in charge of the more masculine kinds of food: roasts, chops, steaks, dead chickens and ducks, gizzards, hearts, anything that had obviously been killed, that had visibly bled. The wives did the other things, the glazed parsnips and the prune whip, anything that flowered or fruited or was soft and gooey in the middle. That was all right for about a decade. Everyone praised the men to keep them going, and the wives, sneaking out of the houses in the mornings with their squeaky new briefcases, clutching their bus tickets because the men needed the station wagons to bring home the carcasses, felt they had got away with something.

But time is not static, and the men refused to stay put. They could not be kept isolated in their individual kitchens, kitchens into which the wives were allowed less and less frequently because, the men said, they did not sharpen the knives properly, if at all. The men began to acquire kitchen machines, which they would spend the weekends taking apart and oiling. There were a few accidents at first, a few lost fingers and ends of noses, but the men soon got the hang of it and branched out into other areas: automatic nutmeg graters, electric gadgets for taking the lids off jars. At cocktail parties they would gather in groups at one end of the room, exchanging private recipes and cooking yarns, tales of soufflés daringly saved at the last minute, pears flambées which had gone out of control and had to be fought to a standstill. Some of these stories had risqué phrases in them, such as *chicken breasts*. Indeed, sexual metaphor was changing: bowls and forks became prominent, and *eggbeater*, *pressure cooker* and *turkey baster* became words which only the most daring young women, the kind who thought it was a kick to butter their own toast, would venture to pronounce in mixed company. Men who could not cook very well hung about the edges of these groups, afraid to say much, admiring the older and more experienced ones, wishing they could be like them.

Soon after that, the men resigned from their jobs in large numbers so they could spend more time in the kitchen. The magazines said it was a modern trend. The wives were all driven off to work, whether they wanted to or not: someone had to make the money, and of course they did not want their husbands' masculinity to be threatened. A man's status in the community was now displayed by the length of his carving knives, by how many of them he had and how sharp he kept them, and by whether they were plain or ornamented with gold and precious jewels.

Exclusive clubs and secret societies sprang up. Men meeting for the first time would now exchange special handshakes—the Béchamel twist, the chocolate mousse double grip—to show that they had been initiated. It was pointed out to the women, who by this time did not go into the kitchens at all on pain of being thought unfeminine, that *chef* after all means *chief* and that Mixmasters were common but no one had ever heard of a Mixmistress.

Psychological articles began to appear in magazines on the origin of women's kitchen envy and how it could be cured. Amputation of the tip of the tongue was recommended, and, as you know, became a wide-spread practice in the more advanced nations. If Nature had meant women to cook, it was said, God would have made carving knives round and with holes in them.

This is history. But it is not a history familiar to many people. It exists only in the few archival collections that have not yet been destroyed, and in manuscripts like this one, passed from woman to woman, usually at night, copied out by hand or memorized. It is subversive of me even to write these words. I am doing so, at the risk of my own personal freedom, because now, after so many centuries of stagnation, there are signs that hope and therefore change have once more become possible.

"After 32 years Malcolm,
I've decided that you were just a phase."

—ARNOULD

The women in their pinstripe suits, exiled to the livingrooms where they dutifully sip the glasses of port brought out to them by the men, used to sit uneasily, silently, listening to the loud bursts of male and somehow derisive laughter from behind the closed kitchen doors. But they have begun whispering to each other. When they are with those they trust, they tell of a time long ago, lost in the fogs of legend, hinted at in packets of letters found in attic trunks and in the cryptic frescoes on abandoned temple walls, when women too were allowed to participate in the ritual which now embodies the deepest religious convictions of our society: the transformation of the consecrated flour into the holy bread. At night they dream, long clandestine dreams, confused and obscured by shadows. They dream of plunging their hands into the earth, which is red as blood and soft, which is milky and warm. They dream that the earth gathers itself under their hands, swells, changes its form, flowers into a thousand shapes, for them too, for them once more. They dream of apples; they dream of the creation of the world; they dream of freedom.

THE MOTOR TRADE

Norm Foster

THIS SCENE HAS PHIL AND DAN, TWO PARTNERS IN A USED CAR DEALERSHIP, TALKING ABOUT PHIL'S WIFE, DARLENE

PHIL: Darlene. What, am I supposed to live my life according to her likes and dislikes?

DAN: Well, she is your wife.

PHIL: Uh-huh, well, not exactly there, Danny boy. (*He stuffs another stick of gum in his mouth.*)

DAN: What's that supposed to mean?

PHIL: Nothin'. She just...she left.

DAN: Darlene? She left you?

PHIL: Yeah.

DAN: Go on.

PHIL: I'm serious.

DAN: Get out.

PHIL: She did.

DAN: When did this happen?

PHIL: Couple of nights ago.

DAN: Get out.

PHIL: It's the truth.

DAN: Darlene??

PHIL: Yeah.

DAN: And you didn't tell me?

PHIL: What's to tell? She left. So what?

DAN: So what? She's your wife for godssake.

PHIL: Ahhh.

DAN: Jesus, Phil. I...I don't know what to say. I'm sorry.

PHIL: Oh, don't be sorry. It wasn't right to begin with. I shoulda seen that.

DAN: Well, listen, maybe she'll come back.

PHIL: No...

DAN: Maybe you can work things out.

PHIL: Uh-uh.

DAN: Sure. These things work themselves out sometimes.

PHIL: Dan, she's not coming back, all right? And even if she was, which she won't be, I wouldn't take her back.

DAN: Oh. It's that bad, is it?

PHIL: I'm afraid so.

DAN: Well, where'd she go? Do you know?

PHIL: Oh, yeah, I know all right. She moved in with Turk Schumacher.

DAN: The Dodge dealer?

PHIL: Hm-hmm.

DAN: Oh, no. God, Phil, I'm sorry.

PHIL: A goddamn Dodge dealer.

DAN: Jesus.

PHIL: Hey, go figure women, huh?

DAN: And you didn't even know they were...

PHIL: Had no idea. Not a clue. I shoulda known though. About a month ago she comes home with this Dodge Omni. A shit can, right? Nothing on it. Says she bought it for herself. So, I says, what'd ya do that for? I coulda put you in a loaded Tempo at cost plus the dealer discount. She says she doesn't want me buying her stuff. She wants to be independent. Independent. She's never paid for a thing in her whole life. That's when I shoulda caught on.

DAN: She bought an Omni? You didn't tell me.

Briane Nasimok
Comedian

I met the girl of my dreams. But we didn't exactly hit it off—sexually speaking. She was really into foreplay and I didn't like the other three guys.

PHIL: Hey, it's not something I wanna spread around, okay.

DAN: Right.

PHIL: So, that's it. Finito. Two years down the drain. (*He takes out his comb and starts to comb his hair.*) What a pair though, huh? Her and Shumacher? I'll tell you, Dan, they deserve each other. I've never liked that guy. Well, you know what he's like. Big shot, right? Vain, self-centred, always strutting around like some goddamned rooster. I mean, big deal, so he's only thirty years old and he owns a major dealership. Big freakin' deal, huh? Punk.

(*Phil moves to his desk and throws his gum away again. Then he goes and gets another doughnut.*)

DAN: Before she met you, wasn't she living with...uh...oh, who was it?

PHIL: Harry Farmer.

DAN: Harry Farmer, yeah. The Chev-Olds dealer, right?

PHIL: Right.

DAN: And before that?

PHIL: Paul Janetti.

DAN: Lincoln Mercury.

PHIL: Right.

DAN: Yeah. (*Beat.*) Well, on the positive side, at least she's stickin' with the North American makes. (*He smirks and then laughs a little.*)

Doug Sneyd

"There's little comfort in your observation that we can expect a record low in recalls, Smedley!"

PMS AIRLINES

Royal Canadian Air Farce

(Sound: 737 fly-by cross fade to 737 interior.)

FLIGHT ATTENDANT *(filter):* Good afternoon, passengers. Welcome aboard today's flight. We hope you are enjoying your trip. *(Mood change.)* And if you're not it's your own fault! *(Back to normal.)* If we can assist you in any way please let us know and we'll help you if we feel up to it. Thank you for flying PMS Airlines.

ATTENDANT 2 *(pleasant):* Magazine, sir?

PASSENGER: What do you have?

ATTENDANT 2: *Cosmopolitan, Flare, Ladies' Home Journal, Vogue, Chatelaine...*

PASSENGER: Do you have *Sports Illustrated*?

ATTENDANT 2 *(suddenly surly):* No. You got a problem with that?

PASSENGER: Um, no, no. I couldn't help noticing all your magazines are women-oriented.

ATTENDANT 2 *(loud):* So. That's just the way it is, okay!

PASSENGER: Yes, okay, fine. I'll just take a pillow.

ATTENDANT 2 *(bursts out in tears):* A pillow, oh, a pillow, he wants a pillow...*(Then suddenly very bright and cheerful.)* Would you like a blanket, too?

(Sound: steps on.)

FLIGHT ATTENDANT: Tracy, get a hold of yourself. Get back to the galley this instant. It's time for the meals anyway.

ATTENDANT 2: Yes, alright, whatever you say. *(Going off—under breath.)* Bitch.

FLIGHT ATTENDANT: Sir, on behalf of PMS Airlines, let me offer my sincerest apology. I'm awfully sorry about Tracy. She has this occasional problem.

PASSENGER: It's quite alright. I understand.

FLIGHT ATTENDANT: Thank you, sir. Please allow me to offer you a bottle of our special French wine, with our compliments of course.

PASSENGER: It isn't necessary but thank you very much.

FLIGHT ATTENDANT: Do you prefer red or white?

PASSENGER: Red.

Susan Ryan

Everyone secretes hormones when they have an orgasm. For women, it's the same one as when they're nursing a baby. For men, it's the same one as when they beat a speeding ticket.

Flight Attendant (*suddenly cold as ice*): What's wrong with the white?

Passenger: I'll have the white.

Flight Attendant (*cheerful*): Very good, sir. White it is.

Passenger: Great.

Flight Attendant: As long as I'm here I'll take your dinner order now. You have a choice of fish or chicken.

Passenger: Ah...um...which would you recommend?

Flight Attendant: They're both very good.

Passenger: So it doesn't matter to you which I have?

Flight Attendant: It's your choice, sir. You're the passenger.

Passenger: I'll have the fish.

Flight Attendant: You bastard!

Passenger: I mean the chicken!

Flight Attendant: Too late, you ungrateful potato head. After all the trouble I went to, making you a delicious chicken dinner and you throw it in my face.

Passenger: Chicken is fine, really. I love chicken.

Flight Attendant (*crying, calling off*): Tracy! One fish dinner for Mr. Hot Shot!

Attendant 2: Coming up!

Passenger: Look, chicken would be okay.

(*Sound: steps on wheeling food cart.*)

Attendant 2 (*full exorcist*): Here's your fish, you scum-sucking maggot. Choke on a bone and die!

(*Sound: food tray thrown on passenger.*)

(*Attendant 2 cackles madly.*)

Passenger: Hey, you spilled food all over me!

Attendant 2: It looks good on you. (*Perfectly normal.*) And I'll be around with tea and coffee later.

(*Sound: fast steps on.*)

Pilot: Hey, keep it down here. What's all the commotion? What's wrong?

Flight Attendant (*sobs*): Captain, this trouble maker...he doesn't want the chicken dinner. (*More sobbing.*)

Pilot: Is that what all this commotion is about, a simple dinner order! Francine, get a grip on yourself. You go up and help Tracy fly the airplane. I'll look after this mess. Sir, I apologize for my crew.

PASSENGER: It's alright, really.

PILOT: Are you sure?

PASSENGER: Yes. I just want to get off this plane and forget the whole incident.

PILOT (*defensive*): What is that supposed to mean? Are you knocking the way I'm running this flight? (*Getting worked up.*) I'll have you know I never wanted this pilot's job in the first place. I wanted to be home raising the kids, but no-o-o, I'm stuck in this career of my own. You've got one hell of a nerve, buddy. I ought to pop you one right in the kisser, you wussie.

(*Sound: steps to washroom, door closes.*)

PILOT: Oh now, now he's locked himself in the bathroom.

(*Sound: banging on door.*)

CAST: Come out you coward/Open the door, slime/I'll rip your lips off.

(*Sound: banging ends; plane whoosh.*)

ANNOUNCER: PMS Airlines. It's not just a trip, it's a flight to hell, once a month.

(*Music: play off.*)

STEVIE RAY FROMSTEIN

———

So I'm on the beach, and there's this woman in a bikini, and she says, "Would you mind helping me put a bit of oil on my back? I can't *reach*."
    So I said, "OK."
    So she said, "Maybe my *legs too*?"
    So I said, "Alright."
    So I said, "What's a beautiful girl like *you* doing on the beach all alone?"
    And she said, "No, I'm with my boyfriend. He went to get some Cokes. He's been ignoring me all day. I thought I'd make him jealous.
    (*Beat.*) The sky goes dark.
    And there's this *huge* guy standing there—a tough-looking guy. He had a tattoo on his arm of a happy face with a dagger going through one of the eyes. And he's wearing this Motley Crue button. No shirt, just...
    He says to me, "What the hell you think you're *doing*, buddy?"
    And I said, "Well, right now I'm thinking about all the things I'll never do with my life."

Susan Ryan

———

It's great for your ego to go out with someone younger. Everybody knows why. Because, no matter what, you can always look over at that person and think, "Was I ever *that* much of a dink?"

    There can be problems, though. You can be having dinner in a nice restaurant and all of a sudden he'll start crying, "My potatoes are touching my peas." But, hey, I don't mind moving some vegetables around if it makes a guy that happy.

He says to me, "OK, pal, that's *it*. Come on. Let's *fight*."

So I figure—OK, what the heck. He was already punching me. I might as well get *in* on it.

But I'm not into violence. So finally, we decided to settle our differences by having a race—down the beach. Of course, it coulda looked like he was chasing me.

FROM *MOO*

Sally Clark

ACT ONE, SCENE TWENTY
(HARRY *and* MAUDE GORMLEY. MAUDE *is his second wife.*)

MAUDE: Do you think I should get a nose job?

(*No response from* HARRY.)

MAUDE: Well—do you?

HARRY (*looks up*):   No. I don't.

MAUDE: Why not?

HARRY: Your nose is fine the way it is.

—JOHNSTON

MAUDE: I don't know, Harry. It's all bent over to one side. See.

HARRY: Looks okay to me.

MAUDE: Nah. It's all twisted. I think I should get a nose job.

HARRY: OK. Get a nose job.

MAUDE: But will you love me?

HARRY: Pardon?

MAUDE: I'll look different then. Will you still love me with a nose job?

HARRY: I hadn't thought about it.

MAUDE: Do you really think my nose looks funny?

HARRY: No. I think it looks fine.

MAUDE: Really?

HARRY: Yes.

MAUDE: Not too bent?

HARRY: No.

(Pause.)

MAUDE: I wonder how much a nose job would cost.

(HARRY looks up.)

MAUDE: What if it's expensive? Could you afford it?

HARRY: Probably.

MAUDE: Maybe, I will get one done. I really don't like my nose, Harry.

HARRY: Mmmmmmmmmmhmmmmmmm.

MAUDE: I think it's ugly. It's a blot upon my face. You know. A real blot.

HARRY: Mmmmmmmmmmmmm.

(Pause.)

MAUDE: Have you always thought my nose was ugly?

(HARRY gets up, walks over to MAUDE, picks her up and throws her down the stairs.)

ACT TWO, SCENE ONE
(1960. HARRY and his third wife, PATSY, sitting in front of the television set. He is about sixty years old. She is slightly younger.)

HARRY: You know, I was a heartbreaker in my youth.

PATSY: You?

HARRY: Don't act so surprised. Yes, I was a cad.

PATSY: Gowan.

Richard J. Needham

Most people lie in bed, but an occasional one tells the truth.

HARRY: I was. A real heartbreaker.

PATSY: Aww come off it, Harry, you're a real sweet guy.

HARRY: Now, maybe. But not then. I've been married twice, you know.

PATSY: I'm sure you didn't mean it, dear.

HARRY: Yes. I did. Both times. For a year there, I was a biga-mist. Saw both of them. Did a lot of commuting.

PATSY: You're a kidder, Harry.

HARRY: I threw my second wife down the stairs.

PATSY: Did she upset you?

HARRY: Well, yeah. I guess so. I guess that's why I threw her down the stairs. Can't really remember why. Curious, isn't it? I could always call her up and ask her. She'd remember.

PATSY: You must have had a reason, Harry.

HARRY: I think I was mad at her.

PATSY: There you are.

HARRY: You're a wonderful woman, Patsy.

PATSY: Harry.

(Pause.)

HARRY: I put my first wife in an insane asylum.

PATSY: Why was that, dear?

HARRY: She was crazy. I was mad at her. Something to do at the time.

PATSY: I'm sure you weren't thinking, dear.

HARRY: I knew what I was doing.

PATSY: Harry.

HARRY: You don't believe me, do you? I threw her in, locked the door and threw away the key.

PATSY: Did she get out?

HARRY: Oh yeah.

PATSY: Well, no harm done then, is there?

HARRY: No. No harm done. *(Pause.)* She's mad as a hatter, now, though.

PATSY: Have you seen her recently?

HARRY: No.

PATSY: How do you know, then?

HARRY: She was crazy when I last saw her.

PATSY: When was that?

HARRY: Oh. Let's see now. Twenty years ago.

PATSY: You don't know then, do you? She might not be mad. She might be dead for all you know.

HARRY: That's true. She might be dead.

PATSY: And if she's dead, then it's all over and done with and you've nothing to worry about.

HARRY: That's true, Patsy. That's very true.

(Pause.)

HARRY: What if she's alive?

PATSY: You should send her a Christmas card and let her know you're thinking of her.

HARRY: I don't think so.

PATSY: Huh.

HARRY: I don't think I want to send her a Christmas card.

PATSY: Suit yourself. Everyone likes to get cards, though.

(Pause.)

HARRY: Did anyone ever put a bullet through your brain, Patsy?

PATSY: You're a kidder, Harry.

STEVIE RAY FROMSTEIN

———

To me, there's a difference between being a wimp and wanting to avoid unnecessary physical confrontations. I remember once, we were in a bad part of town, and we saw these eight big guys pushing this old lady around. And my girlfriend says, "*Do* something about it!"

And I said—(*acts as if pushed*)—"*I'll* investigate."

So I go over and I say—I'm not as strong as I look—so I say, "Fellas, is that *any* way to treat an old lady?"

So they said, "It's *one* way."

So I thought, *that's* reasonable.

Well, we *didn't* see it start—Maybe she *said* something.

Then, one of them says to me, "*Why*? You wanna *make* something of it?"

So I said, "Yeah, I want to *make* something of it. I'll make you sorry you were ever born, you greasy punk!"

Well, I didn't use those *exact* words.

I think what I said was, "No sir, I don't."

WOMEN'S NOVELS

Margaret Atwood

FOR LENORE

1. Men's novels are about men. Women's novels are about men too, but from a different point of view. You can have a men's novel with no women in it except possibly the landlady or the horse, but you can't have a women's novel with no men in it. Sometimes men put women in men's novels but they leave out some of the parts: the heads, for instance, or the hands. Women's novels leave out parts of the men as well. Sometimes it's the stretch between the belly button and the knees, sometimes it's the sense of humour. It's hard to have a sense of humour in a cloak, in a high wind, on a moor.

   Women do not usually write novels of the type favoured by men but men are known to write novels of the type favoured by women. Some people find this odd.

2. I like to read novels in which the heroine has a costume rustling discreetly over her breasts, or discreet breasts rustling under her costume; in any case there must be a costume, some breasts, some rustling, and, over all, discretion. Discretion over all, like a fog, a miasma through which the outlines of things appear only vaguely. A glimpse of pink through the gloom, the sound of breathing, satin slithering to the floor, revealing what? Never mind, I say. Never never mind.

3. Men favour heroes who are tough and hard: tough with men, hard with women. Sometimes the hero goes soft on a woman but this is always a mistake. Women do not favour heroines who are tough and hard. Instead they have to be tough and soft. This leads to linguistic difficulties. Last time we looked, monosyllables were male, still dominant but sinking fast, wrapped in the octopoid arms of labial polysyllables, whispering to them with arachnoid grace: *darling, darling*.

4. Men's novels are about how to get power. Killing and so on, or winning and so on. So are women's novels, though the method is different. In men's novels, getting the woman or women goes along with getting the power. It's a perk, not a means. In women's novels you get the power by getting the man. The man is the power. But sex won't do, he has to love you. What do you think all that kneeling's about, down among the crinolines, on the Persian carpet? Or at least say it. When all else is lacking, verbalization can be enough. *Love.* There, you can stand up now, it didn't kill you. Did it?

5. I no longer want to read about anything sad. Anything violent, anything disturbing, anything like that. No funerals at the end, though there can be some in the middle. If there must be deaths, let there be resurrections, or at least a Heaven so we know where we are. Depression and squalor are for those under twenty-five, they can take it, they even like it, they still have enough time left. But real life is bad for you, hold it in your hand long enough and you'll get pimples and become feeble-minded. You'll go blind.

   I want happiness, guaranteed, joy all round, covers with nurses on them or brides, intelligent girls but not too intelligent, with regular teeth and pluck and both breasts the same size and no excess facial hair, someone you can depend on to know where the bandages are and to turn the hero, that potential rake and killer, into a well-groomed country gentleman with clean fingernails and the right vocabulary. *Always*, he has to say. *Forever*. I no longer want to read books that don't end with the word *forever*. I want to be stroked between the eyes, one way only.

6. Some people think a woman's novel is anything without politics in it. Some think it's anything about relationships. Some think it's anything with a lot of operations in it, medical ones I mean. Some think it's anything that doesn't give you a broad panoramic view of our exciting times. Me, well, I just want something you can leave on the coffee table and not be too worried if the kids get into it. You think that's not a real consideration? You're wrong.

7. *She had the startled eyes of a wild bird*. This is the kind of sentence I go mad for. I would like to be able to write such sentences, without embarrassment. I would like to be able to read them without embarrassment. If I could only do these two simple things, I feel, I would be able to pass my allotted time on this earth like a pearl wrapped in velvet.

   She had the startled eyes of a wild bird. Ah, but which one? A screech owl, perhaps, or a cuckoo? It does make a difference. We do not need more literalists of the imagination. They cannot read *a body like a gazelle's* without thinking of intenstinal parasites, zoos and smells.

   She had a feral gaze like that of an untamed animal, I read. Reluctantly I put down the book, thumb still inserted at the exciting moment. He's about to crush her in his arms, pressing his hot, devouring, hard, demanding mouth to hers as her breasts squish out the top of her dress, but I can't concentrate. Metaphor leads me by the nose, into the maze, and suddenly all Eden lies before me. Porcupines, weasels, warthogs and skunks, their feral gazes malicious or bland or stolid or piggy and sly. Agony, to see the romantic frisson quivering just out of reach, a dark-winged butterfly stuck to an over-ripe peach, and not to be able to swallow, or wallow. *Which one*? I murmur to the unresponding air. *Which one*?

THERE'S NOTHING GOOD ON TV, ANYWAY

SPORTS IN CANADA

BOBBY CLOBBER, PUBLIC RELATER

Dave Broadfoot

(Music: sports show theme.)

BIG JIM *(voice-over):*   Hi, sports fans. Big Jim Harrison here. It's that time again. Time to hear words of wisdom from the world of sports. So let's bring out my special guest, a man for one season...Hockey Super Star, Big Bobby Clobber!

(Music: Brief play on.)

BIG JIM: Big Bobby!

BOBBY: Big Jim!

BIG JIM: Good to have you back.

BOBBY: My back's fine, Big Jim, now, and I'm glad you're here, too.

BIG JIM: I understand you're working as a P. R. for the team this season.

BOBBY: It's not that bad of a job. It's more like public relations. Like I'm a spokesperson. That's like a spokesman without any sex.

BIG JIM: So tell us what you do.

BOBBY: This morning. About 7:30? I got out of bed? Then...I had a big breakfast?

BIG JIM: And then...

BOBBY: I got back in bed?

BIG JIM: I meant, what do you do in public relations?

BOBBY: I get myself invited to lunch.

BIG JIM: Oh. So you're on the rubber chicken circuit.

BOBBY: OK. On the question of circuits...no one talked to me about that yet. So I can't really say the one way or the other way on that for sure. As far as the rubber goes, when I got this job, that word never came up. Or about being chicken. So, you know, I have to be honest. I don't understand the question.

BIG JIM: What do you do at these lunches?

BOBBY: I...eat. Then I talk about the team. I tell how the team has a low moral right now.

BIG JIM: You mean "morale."

BOBBY: Hey, come on, Big Jim. Don't you ever watch "Jeopardy"? Morale is a kind of fancy mushroom.

BIG JIM: What else do you talk about?

BOBBY: About how you can't just only judge a team by what it does during a game. You've got to see it practice. Like us. We pair off...into groups of three. Then we line up...in a circle. Our philosophy is "The only way to start at the bottom is to improve."

BIG JIM: So you're trying to give the team a new image?

BOBBY (*moved*): Thanks, Big Jim. I always tell the lunch people...even when you've *got* a team...sometimes you can't win. And other times you're going to lose. But you can never lose unless you try.

BIG JIM: So...you're really enjoying P. R. No retirement yet for Big Bobby, huh?

BOBBY: No way. I can't. Not now.

BIG JIM: Why is that?

BOBBY: I loaned every nickel I had to a guy who used to be our goalie. He said he needed the money for some plastic surgery on his face. I figured it was kind of my duty as a human being to help another human being at a time when he needed my help. We're all human beings, eh?

BIG JIM: Well, that was a nice thing to do. I'm sure he'll repay you eventually.

BOBBY: No way, Big Jim. He's disappeared. And after the plastic surgery I have no idea what the son of a bitch looks like.

BIG JIM: Well, Bobby, we're almost out of time. How about a word of wisdom for young athletes out there who may be living in hopes of a career in professional hockey?

Gord Paynter*

I love sports...I still downhill ski. I go out with my friends, they tell me what to do. "Gord, go right." "Gord, go left." "Gord, go right."

Works out pretty well. Although I don't trust my friends quite as much as I used to. Not since they put me on that ski jump. Some of you may have seen me?—I do the opening for "Wide World of Sports." I'm very proud of myself. I just wish they'd got it on the first take. It was kind of like, "Do you want to haul the blind guy up there again? Well, *push* him if he won't go!"

*Gord is blind.

BOBBY: OK, kids...as far as living goes...if there's something in your life that you don't know and want it to become, you just got to figure it out what it is and you got to go ahead when it happens to you, or, for you, to become it...OK? Don't.

BIG JIM: Thank you very much, Big Bobby Clobber.

(*Music: play off.*)

SHAKESPEAREAN BASEBALL GAME

Wayne and Shuster

(*A heraldic device background over which to super titles. It is crossed baseball bats and a catcher's mask.*)

(*Orchestra: fanfare.*)

(*Zoom in Super:* THE ROYAL WAYNE AND SHUSTER FESTIVAL PLAYERS)

ANNOUNCER (*voice-over*): The Royal Wayne and Shuster Festival Players present...

(*Lose Super. Zoom in:* A COMEDY OF HITS, RUNS AND ERRORS)

ANNOUNCER: A comedy of hits, runs and errors.

(*Dissolve to: graphic of baseball stadium or crowd on tape. Super:* BOSWORTH FIELD, A BASEBALL STADIUM NEAR STRATFORD)

ANNOUNCER (*voice-over*): Enter, two Umpires.

(*Dissolve to dugout set empty. Two umpires enter from either side. Orchestra: fanfare.*)

FIRST: Hail, Bernardo...

SECOND: I give you greetings, Antonio.
Thou hast the line-ups?

FIRST: Aye...The batting orders duly
Signed by managers both.

SECOND: 'Tis well...what o'clock is it?

FIRST: 'Tis at the stroke of two.

(*Music: short modal fanfare.*)

SECOND: Hark...The players come. To our appointed places
Shall we go. You at first and I behind the plate.

FIRST: 'Tis done. (*He turns and second takes his arm.*)

SECOND: This game depends on how you make your call.
Farewell until you hear me cry Play Ball.

(They exit. Music: big fanfare to herald entrance of baseball team. They enter Stratford style, with a flourish.)

FRANK: My excellent good friends, may fortune smile upon
   our enterprise today. As manager of this most valiant club,
   I swear by all that's holy in our game,
   I shall not rest until the pennant over Stratford flies.

CAST: *(Cheer.)*

RICHARD: Most noble manager...

FRANK: Who calls?

RICHARD: 'Tis I...Richard.

FRANK: Speak, oh faithful Richard.

RICHARD: I pray you tell us how doth the starting line-up go?

FRANK *(takes out card)*:   'Tis as it was before. With Harry,
   Joe and Pete out in the field. Rusty?

RUSTY: Sire?

FRANK: Thou the shortstop spot will play.
   And you three guarding your accustomed bags.
   Sam, the first; Bill, the Second; and Richard, the Third.

(To pitcher, rubs up ball.)

   And as for you, most noble Sandy,
   Hie thee to the bull-pen.
   So that if our pitcher from his box is knocked,
   you shall go upon the mound and take his place.

(Flips him ball.)

SANDY: I go. *(He picks up jacket and exits.)*

FRANK *(follows him)*:   For this relief much thanks.

PEEWEE: Most noble manager...a word.

FRANK: Speak, oh Peewee.

PEEWEE: Where is the Captain of our Team? The mighty
   Rocky.
   The man whom all the sports reporters call...
   The noblest catcher of them all.

FRANK *(sadly)*:   Alas, the mighty Rocky sits and mopes in
   yon locker-room. And well he might,
   for in these last ten games he has not hit the ball.
   Not even once. Yes, hitless has he gone,
   and twenty times has been called out on strikes.

(Orchestra: entrance music. Sad modal.)

PEEWEE: But soft, he comes.

(Cut to JOHNNY'S entrance. Cut back to FRANK.)

Frank Peppiatt

———

I'd give my right arm to be a Big League pitcher.

———

THE ANSWER IS: Goldie-locks and the Three Bears.
THE QUESTION: Name a lousy Chicago backfield.

FRANK: To think he led the league in RBIs...
And now he reads the record book and cries.

(Orchestra: soliloquy background.)

JOHNNY *(enters reading record book)*:

Oh, what a rogue and bush-league slob am I...
Is it not monstrous that this player here,
But in a fiction, in a dream of passion,
Should gaze upon the record book and find
That he has ten games hitless gone...
Oh, cursed fate...
That I who led the league
Should now bat 208.
A hit...A hit...My kingdom for a hit.
Once more to hear that welcome crack of bat upon the ball...
And then to run from first to second then to third.
And then to dig for home.
To slide...slide... slide...
Aye, there's the rub.
There's a divinity that shapes our ends.

FRANK *(moves to him)*:   Most noble Rocky.

JOHNNY: Who speaks?

FRANK *(bends down)*:   'Tis I, the mentor of your team.

JOHNNY: Ah, sweet, my manager. Gaze not upon my face.
This is the poison of deep grief
and springs from a batting slump.

FRANK *(puts hands on his shoulders)*:   Take heart, Gentle Rocky
For today your batting slump will end.

JOHNNY: What say you?

FRANK: I have devised a plan wherein you will bat five for
five.

JOHNNY: A hit for every time I go to bat?

FRANK: 'Tis so.

JOHNNY: Angels and ministers of grace, defend us.
(Crosses right, to players.) He has gone bananas.

FRANK: Here is the instrument of your success...Bat boy,
hither.

(Enter bat boy with bat on velvet cushion.)

JOHNNY: 'Tis but a bat.

FRANK: Not but a bat.

JOHNNY: Not but a bat?

FRANK: But a special bat. A Louisville slugger that once
To Babe Ruth did belong.

JOHNNY: Thou puttest me on.

FRANK: I put thee not on. A slugger with which
The mighty Bambino sixty home runs did hit.

(Orchestra: low background as Johnny kneels.)

JOHNNY: Is this a slugger...which I see before me?
The handle towards my hand.
Come let me clutch thee.
And with this mighty staff of Birnam Wood
shall I win the day.

FIRST UMPIRE *(off stage)*: Play ball!

FRANK: The game begins!

(Orchestra: fanfare.)

CAST: *(Cheer. Go for gloves.)*

JOHNNY: Pitchers, catchers, shortstops, lend me your ears.
The game begins and we must win—

FRANK: And win we shall. All hail Stratford.

CAST: All hail Stratford. *(They all kneel.)*

FRANK: A manager's blessing upon you all...
And as for your Captain, Noble Rocky, give me your hand.

JOHNNY: 'Tis gladly given.

FRANK: Play well, valiant Captain. And remember,
this game is being televis-ed.

JOHNNY: Televis-ed?

FRANK: And the TV will record each passing play.

(Orchestra: mod background up and fade.)

JOHNNY: TV or not TV, that is not the question.
We shall play with might and main *(Cheer.)*
Where is my battery mate? The pitcher, the mighty Burford.
(He enters.) Art thou prepared to take thy place
upon the mound?

BURFORD *(thick Southern accent)*: Marry Sire, I am.
I shall do everything thou dost desire.
I shall throw a goodly mixture of curves, sliders
and changes of pace that will cause them
to saw the air mightily with their bats.
And on the scoreboard
there will be a giant goose egg for all to see.
Farewell, y'all.

Frank Peppiatt
(A favourite line, delivered by Jackie Gleason on a special filmed in Florida, 1973.)

———

None of my diets have been working, so my doctor told me to run five miles a day for a year, and that would do it. Well, I religiously ran five miles every morning and at the end of the year, I hadn't lost any weight and I was seventeen hundred miles from home!

JOHNNY: He is indeed a southpaw.
His Paw is from the South.

FRANK: And now, sweet Rocky—lead your players to the fray!

CAST: *(Cheer.)*

JOHNNY: To our appointed places shall we go.
Before this evening sun is set,
we'll win the day for Stratford—and Gillette!

(Music: flourish into lapse of time music. Montage of baseball shots and crowds — batters hitting, sliding into base, pitching, etc. Sound: crowd up and down. Dissolve to scoreboard: ninth inning, 1 : 0.)

RUSTY: How goes the game?

FRANK: Not well...'Tis the bottom of the ninth
with one away,
and they do lead us by the score
of One to Nothing. *(Crosses right.)*
Who's next to bat?

MACDUFF: 'Tis I...Macduff. Ready am I to do thy bidding, Sire.

FRANK: Then take thou thy bat...
and hie thee to the plate.

MACDUFF: I go. *(He exits.)*

P.A.: Now batting, Macduff.

(Sound: crowd up.)

JOHNNY *(enters):* How goes it, cousin?

FRANK: Our chances dim with every pitch.
'Tis one away...
Macduff is at the plate.

JOHNNY: Lay on Macduff. And watch out for that breaking stuff.

(Sound: crack of bat and cheer. Cut to crowd cheering on tape. Back to FRANK.)

FRANK *(walks left as he follows ball):* A hit...a very palpable hit.

UMPIRE *(off):* FOUL BALL!!!

BACK BENCH

–HARROP

CROWD: Ohhhhhhhhh!

FRANK: Foul ball...He called it foul?
A plague upon him. That ball was fair.

JOHNNY: Fair, it was indeed. You, sirrah...
(Walks forward to umpire.) That ball was fair.

SECOND: That ball was foul.

JOHNNY: So fair a foul I have not seen.
Accursed knave with heart
as black as the coat you wear upon your back.
Get thee a pair of glasses.
Get thee to an optometrist.

SECOND: *(Snarls long gibberish at him.)*

JOHNNY: I would the gods had made thee more poetical.

SECOND: *(Snarls again. He exits.)*

JOHNNY: Thou art a robber and a crook.
Thy name should be in Jim Bouton's book.

FRANK: Calm thyself.

JOHNNY: And foiddermore...

FRANK: Calm thyself, sweet Rocky.
(Yells.) Come on—Macduff—
Take thou a cut at it.

SECOND *(voice-over):* Strike three!

(Sound: crowd groans.)

JOHNNY: That was the unkindest cut of all.

(MACDUFF enters and sadly heads for dugout.)

FRANK: Now is the summer of our discontent.
That was our second out.
One more time at bat do we have to win the game.
(Crosses left.) Who's next?

JOHNNY: 'Tis I.

FRANK: 'Tis you.

JOHNNY: Marry, 'tis.

FRANK: Then go, my friend, with aid divine
And hit that Pepsi-Cola sign.

(Bat boy brings in bat and baseball helmet. JOHNNY goes to plate. Split screen. Cut to FRANK and RUSTY.)

RUSTY: See how the valiant Rocky stands at the plate,
like some mighty colossus,
the bat resting gently on his shoulder.

Q. What do you get when you cross a maple leaf with a groundhog?

A. Six more weeks of crummy hockey.

FRANK: But soft...Here is the windup, here is the pitch.

(Sound: beanball on head.)

CROWD: *(Groans.)*

FRANK: No...(*Turns away.*) I cannot look...
The sight doth sear my eyes.

RUSTY: The ball did strike his head. The pitcher bean-ed him.

FRANK: He comes this way...I cannot look!

(Orchestra: business. Cut to JOHNNY singing.)

JOHNNY: Take thou me to the ball game,
Take thou me to the park.
Buy me some peanuts and crackerjack,
Wash it all down with a flagon of sack.

FRANK: Oh, what a noble mind is here o'erthrown.

JOHNNY *(picks up catcher's mask)*: Ahh...Alas, Poor Durocher,
I knew him...A man of infinite lip.

(Sees FRANK. Picks up bats.)

Ah, greetings to you, sweet nymph.
I would have brought you violets but they withered. *(Hands him bats.)*

FRANK *(turns to camera)*: Oh horror. Not only hitless, but witless.

JOHNNY: Two outs damned spot—
Life's but a walking shadow,
a poor player that hits and bunts his weary hour
upon the field, and then is heard no more.
It is a tale told by an umpire,
full of sound and fury, signifying one-nothing...

(JOHNNY passes out.)

(Orchestra: undertone background.)

FRANK *(kneels)*: Now cracks a noble head.
Goodnight, sweet catcher.
Flights of shortstops sing thee to thy rest.
(He rises sadly.) Let four bonus players bear Rocky,
like a soldier, to the dugout. *(They lift him.)*

(Orchestra: snare drum.)

FRANK: No more will Stratford watch him play ball.
I'm trading the bum to Montreal.

(Super: exeunt with a flourish of bat boys.)

(Orchestra: Up Dead March to finish.)

(Silhouette lighting.)

Super: THE END

GREAT ONE GOES

Susan Musgrave

The poster says, "We have a prophetess in our midst. She will be reading her poetry August 9 at 8:00."

In Toronto one year I read on Black Monday after the stock market crash, in Sudbury after INCO laid off two thousand workers, and now I've arrived in Edmonton where the headlines scream GRETZKY TRADED. If I were a true prophetess I wouldn't be reading again on the eve of another disaster.

The imposter, with six-year-old daughter in tow, climbs a flight of stairs to the Off-the-Wall Gallery. The walls are covered with etchings of mutilated organs: my daughter wants to know what they mean. I'm about to tell her that all art should be, not mean, when the artist introduces himself. I avert my eyes from his "Ovarian Cyst" while he explains how his vision complements my poetry.

Early in my career I felt duty-bound to read my most depressing stuff—poems of despair and tortured love, of failed suicide and unrequited lust. I had a dedicated following. In Winnipeg one winter, for instance, I read to a handful of homeless derelicts who had come to the library to get warm. They even applauded after every poem—to warm their hands. One, with newspapers wrapped around his feet in place of shoes, came up to thank me after the reading was over. My poetry, he said, had been an inspiration—to end it all that night.

At this point my perspective changed. I didn't want a successful poetry reading to be one where people felt like slitting their throats after listening to me, so I switched to stand-up comedy. I'm not sure that anyone noticed.

The Off-the-Wall Gallery is packed; it was built to seat fifty. I'm used to giving poetry readings in this kind of space. I'll be expected, afterwards, to help stack the chairs.

The director of the gallery comes forward to introduce me. After being touted, once again, as a prophetess, I begin my reading.

In Canada, I tell my expectant audience, hockey is the poetry of the masses. To press my point, I ask how many hockey fans there are in the crowd. When no hands are raised, I tell them the reason for there being only fifty people here tonight is that the other fifty thousand have stayed home, mourning the loss of the Great One.

What if there should come a time, I prophesy, when poets, like hockey players, are treated as depreciating assets and traded by publishers for hard cash to foreign countries: "Canada lost its finest poet Tuesday," the papers might report, "when Margaret Atwood was dealt to Los Angeles in the most stunning poetry deal in history. She packed her word processor and the best years of her life and headed south...to what? To millions of Los Angelenos who don't give a damn, to a town that doesn't know a poetry book from a surfboard. ..."

Gord Paynter

I'm from Brantford, Ontario, hometown of hockey star Wayne Gretzky. People back there love Gretzky. They still talk about the six million goals he scored while playing minor hockey there. Big deal. I was the goalie.

Did you hear about the horrible mistake that the construction men made when they built Maple Leaf Gardens?

All the seats were built *facing* the ice.

The expectant faces have become incensed. Once again I am being taken deadly seriously.

"In Toronto," I continue, undeterred, "before the deal was announced, outraged poetry fans jammed all incoming phones to her publishers. One NDP MP argued against free trade in poets. He urged the federal government to stop the sale of Margaret Atwood, saying she is a national symbol, like the beaver."

Having thoroughly convinced my audience, I launch into my first poem, "Two Minutes for Hooking." I wrote it ten years ago, but it seems downright prophetic now. "You are leaving..." it begins. When I finish the poem it is so quiet you can hear hearts breaking.

We take our symbols seriously. After the reading I am overwhelmed by fans. I autograph books, I shake hands. For fifteen minutes I'm famous, until I catch my daughter, who's always been my most reliable critic, looking skeptical in a corner.

I push through the crowd. "Well, how did I rate?" I ask when she isn't forthcoming.

"Did you see the size of my yawn, Mum?" she replies. Peter Pocklington says Gretzky has an ego the size of Manhattan; my ego shrinks to the size of the "Ovarian Cyst" on the wall of the Off-the-Wall Gallery.

When the audience has gone my daughter shows me how to put away the chairs. She makes it clear I'm a mother first of all. I may be a great one, but I'm still a depreciating asset.

Wheetabix

SECOND CITY
(by John Candy and Peter Aykroyd)

Guy: Hello.

Cecilia: Oh, hello. You must be, uh...

Guy: Guy.

Cecilia: Guy Lafleur! Hello, I'm Cecilia Walters.

Guy: Hello, Cecilia.

Cecilia: Walter Thompson will be out in a minute.

Guy: Big place, eh?

J. Walter: Hello, I'm J. Walter Thompson, your director. You're Guy Lafleur, is that right? Uh huh, uh huh, can you speak English?

Guy: I can talk.

J. Walter: Good. Cecilia, good to see you. The crew set? Where the hell's Sittler?

Guy: I don't know. He has a different dressing room.

(Sittler enters.)

J. WALTER: This is Guy Lafleur. Oh, yeah—you know each other.

GUY: Oh, that's for sure.

J. WALTER: I see. Well, I guess you know what we're here for. Look, we sent you your scripts about a week ago. Is there any chance at all you know your parts?

GUY: I know it.

J. WALTER: You do?

DARRYL: I know mine, sure.

J. WALTER: You do? Well, that's just golden. Why don't we try it now, maybe we'll just get lucky right off the top; we'll get one the first take. Alright, let's try it now. The tables are here, the bowls, the Wheetabix. OK, you're all set? Good. WHEETABIX, Take One and—Action!

GUY: Hello, I'm Guy Lafleur.

DARRYL: I'm Darryl Sittler.

GUY: And I use a Darryl Sittler hockey stick.

DARRYL: I use a Darryl Sittler hockey stick.

J. WALTER: CUT!

CECILIA: That's a *Guy Lafleur* hockey stick.

DARRYL: Yeah, I know. I wouldn't use that stick if you paid me.

CECILIA: But we *are* paying you.

DARRYL: Sure, I'll do it. What the hell—No one will believe me.

J. WALTER: Alright, that's the only problem? OK, try it again. No problems, right?

DARRYL: Right, Guy.

GUY: I got it, yeah.

J. WALTER: Alright? Good. WHEETABIX, Take Two—and Action!

GUY: Hello, I'm Guy Lafleur.

DARRYL: I'm Darryl Sittler.

GUY: And I use a Darryl Sittler hockey stick.

DARRYL: I use a Guy Lafleur hockey stick. Hey Guy—how about some Wheetabix?

GUY: OK.

DARRYL: Alright.

GUY: Hey, that's got a good malt flavour eh, Darryl?

DARRYL: Smells good. Oh, fuck, I can't eat these things. They're too hard on my gums...

J. WALTER: What's the problem?

DARRYL: I lost my plate in St. Louis.

J. WALTER: Can we get him some teeth?

CECILIA: Too late for teeth.

J. WALTER: Too late for teeth. Well, look: maybe you could just mime eating it or do something else with it.

GUY: Why don't you mush it up with the milk and then push it through? (*Mocking him.*) Hey, Darryl forgot his plate! Hey, Darryl!

DARRYL: I think someone stole it.

J. WALTER: Well, that's fine. OK, you can just mime eating it or something. OK, no problems? Good. WHEETABIX, Take Three—and Action!

GUY: Hello, I'm Guy Lafleur.

DARRYL: I'm Darryl Sittler.

GUY: And I use a Darryl Sittler hockey stick.

DARRYL: I use a Guy Lafleur hockey stick. Hey, Guy, how about some Wheetabix?

GUY: OK.

DARRYL: Alright.

GUY: Hey, that's got a good malt flavour, eh, Darryl?

DARRYL: Sure does. Smells good too. Let's see what it's got in it. It's got...*pour de sonne*. Oh, shit. This is in *French*!

GUY (*angry*):   This is a bilingual country.

DARRYL: It *isn't* a bilingual country. It's *one* country and it's got *one* song: God Save the Fucking Queen. Go back where you came from!

GUY: Lots of packages have only English and I have to read them.

J. WALTER: I think the simplest way is to read the language of your choice. Alright? There is English on the package. Alright?...Alright, Guy??

GUY: Yah, yah, OK.

J. WALTER: Alright, WHEETABIX, Take Four—and Action!

GUY: Hello, I'm Guy Lafleur.

DARRYL: I'm Darryl Sittler.

GUY: And I use a Darryl Sittler hockey stick.

DARRYL: I use a Guy Lafleur hockey stick. Hey, Guy! How about some Wheetabix?

GUY: OK.

DARRYL: Alright.

GUY: Hey, that's got a good malt flavour, eh, Darryl?

DARRYL (*malicious*): Want some Pepsi-Cola to go with it?

J. WALTER: CUT!!

(*The two men start to fight with each other.*)

J. WALTER: Alright, stop it. *Stop it*! *You* take five minutes in your dressing room to cool off—and *you* take five minutes.

GUY: Five minutes!!

DARRYL: Hey, something's burning here. (*Nasty.*) I smell *pea soup*!

(*More hockey-like fistfighting as we go to black.*)

STANLEY CUP SEDER

Shel Krakofsky

Our seder is longer
though the story's the same
we'll get it all in now,
there is no big game.
Once we skated through it
the Answers could wait,
the seder was rushed,
"...the game's on at eight!"

Bubie and Zaida told us
to eat slower, read more,
but we'd leave our Haggadas
to find out the score
and watch on TV
our regular seder guests,

Glossary

---

seder: the meal and home service celebrating the Exodus from Egypt.

Bubie and Zaida: (Yiddish) Grandmother and Grandfather.

Haggadas: the booklets used to follow the Passover service.

Elijah: Great Jewish prophet who is believed to visit Jewish homes during the Passover seders; a cup of wine is set out for him.

maror: "bitter herbs," or horseradish, set out on Passover table to remind participants of the bitterness of Egyptian slavery.

Afikoman: Dessert; in the case of Passover, unleavened bread.

Howe Hull Mahovlich
the Richards at their best.

We knew who escaped
the Egyptian plagues and sins
but with the Leafs and Canadiens,
who'd first get four wins?
So the door was kept closed
Elijah barred from his cup
Zaida could only resume
after Lord Stanley's Cup.

Four cups of wine
this seder's full length
expansion, a longer schedule
have cut NHL strength
and our passion for hockey.
Baseball's now the game,
the Blue Jays and Expos
their seders not the same.

Puck finals after Pesach
are certainly no treat,
now baseball overlaps hockey—
like mixing milk with meat.
With Gordie Howe missing
bitter maror we eat,
and without Bubie and Zaida
it's even more incomplete.

We eat the afikoman
and make a wish for later:
Next year in Jerusalem,
another Stanley Cup seder.

GLOVE THEATRE

The Frantics

ANNOUNCER: The Frantics proudly present, Glove Theatre.

(*Graphic:* GLOVE THEATRE)

(*Puppet theatre stage. Bedroom scene. The characters are all hands wearing gloves. A Montreal hockey glove and a woman's glove enter on hands.*)

HOCKEY (*French accent*):   Are you sure your husband won't be home?

WIFE: Don't worry. He's playing golf. Come to me darling!

(*The hands strip off each other's gloves. The wife puts the hockey glove on the stage out of the way so it doesn't block the action.*)

HOCKEY: Oh darling…

WIFE: Be careful.

HOCKEY: Oh right.

(*Ducks down under and immediately pops back up wearing a rubber glove.*)

(*Sound effects: door opens and closes.*)

HUBBY (*off*):   Honey, I'm home early.

WIFE: It's my husband! Quick, hide!

(*The rubber glove—hockey player—runs into the closet. The wife pops down and then up again wearing an oven mitt. The hubby enters in a golf glove.*)

HUBBY: Hi honey. What are you doing?

WIFE: I was just…baking. Why are you home early?

HUBBY: Game was rained out. Say, when did you take up baking?

(*Hubby does a double-take and sees the hockey glove lying there.*)

HUBBY: And whose is this? Stand back, woman!

(*Wife spreads herself over the closet door to keep hubby out.*)

HUBBY: Whoever he is…

(*Hubby goes down and pops up in boxing glove.*)

…I'll kill him!

WIFE: Honey, don't hit him!

HUBBY: Come on out!

(*Cupboard door opens. Out comes naked hand. It is downcast.*)

You jerk you! You…you…you're Guy Aurvoir of the Montreal Canadiens? My wife's been havin' it off with Guy Aurvoir?

GUY: I'm sorry dere, mister.

Frank Peppiatt

THE ANSWER IS:
The Long Count.

THE QUESTION:
What will they call Monte Cristo after two weeks on the rack?

HUBBY: You're the greatest left-hander alive.

WIFE: I'll say.

HUBBY: How many times did you score this year?

GUY: Just this once, I swear it.

HUBBY: Oh come on, you got Pobodkin and Rivers out there with you.

(Two more hockey gloves appear.)

BOTH: Oh, so you know about us too.

HUBBY: Wow! Wait till I tell the guys at work about all of the great hockey players that came to my house.

WIFE: You're not mad?

HUBBY: How can I be? I love hockey!

WIFE: How do you feel about baseball?

(Five baseball gloves pop up, filling the room. They laugh the way only baseball gloves can.)

THE BIG GAME EXPLAINED
FROM *URBAN SCRAWL*

Erika Ritter

Contrary to the impression sportscasters like to give, not everybody in this country looks forward to the Grey Cup game.

There are, in fact, enormous gangs of you out there to whom the Cup, the teams who vie for it, and indeed the hallowed sport of football itself (hereinafter referred to as The Game), mean nothing at all.

Fortunately, I am not one of them. I adore the Grey Cup, and exist for that November weekend on which it is competed for. That's because I have the distinct advantage of being knowledgeable about The Game in general, and about the Grey Cup game (hereinafter referred to as The Big Game) in particular.

Furthermore, it's my determined belief that any of you who understand The Game will become interested in it, and any of you who take the trouble to familiarize yourselves with the history and psychology of The Big Game cannot fail to turn into devoted fans, faster than you can say Frank Tripuka.

So, let's begin our crash course on The Game and The Big Game with a quick look back to Where It All Began.

Where it all began, naturally enough, was in the States. And that's pretty much where it has stayed. The best players of The Game are still Americans, and the less talented among them still regularly move up to Canada to help us out with our version of The Game, which we've managed to keep distinctly Canadian by adding a man (Canadians never see any harm in hiring on extra personnel), reducing the number of downs (Canadians never see any harm in making things harder) and altering the size of the field (for the same reason that we have a two-dollar bill; in this country, it's the *illusion* of autonomy that counts).

Way back when, however, when a team from McGill University went down to play The First Game against Harvard, Canadians had no reason to suspect that we were not going to be equal participants in the creation of The Game.

As far as I know, no clear records of that first scrimmage are extant, but I bet I can make a few shrewd assumptions as to how the day went.

First of all, there's no question in my mind that Harvard had the better-looking cheerleaders, not to mention a classier half-time show. No doubt the Harvard players were also paid much better, and could augment their incomes through lucrative product endorsements. While the poor McGill players found themselves with nothing more tempting than requests from the Heart Fund to do free commercials, and the opportunity to appear on talk shows in Chicoutimi.

As if all that weren't humiliating enough, I can just imagine what it was like out there on the field for the Canadians, in a game where the rules were presumably being made up as things went along.

I'll bet you anything that tackling was introduced by the Americans, and probably in the most unceremonious way. While the McGill team was still discussing how to decide to form a committee to investigate various methods of player interception, the boisterous Yanks probably just jumped them, thereby forcing a point of view upon their gentle northern neighbours.

As for the ball itself, doubtless McGill brought a live pig with them, which was slaughtered, tanned, stitched, and stuffed by American labour, then sold back to the Canadians at the end of the game at an exorbitant mark-up.

But in spite of its inauspicious beginning, The Game has taken feverish hold in this country, and nowhere is this more evident than in an examination of The Big Game, and of the cup for which it is named.

The Grey Cup (more properly referred to in these metric times as the Grey Quarter-Litre) is quintessentially Canadian, as a close analysis of its name reveals. First, the significance of the fact that it is a cup. The Americans—a more lavish people generally—measure their football in bowls. And they take care that it's always a bowl of *something*—roses, oranges, cotton; even 'gators will do in a pinch.

What have we got? A cup full of grey. A colour evocative only of dirty snowbanks, slightly soiled flannel jackets marked down at The Bay, and mid-winter Canadian skin tones. Ugh.

But despite the uninspiring nature of the trophy, The Big Game is an important cultural event, and there's absolutely no reason you should let yourself be left out, simply because some of the traditions attendant upon it make no sense to you.

Howie Mandel

I started aerobics. I like doing aerobics now. I bought one of those Jane Fonda tapes, and boy, that's hard. I don't know if you've tried it. I bought *On Golden Pond.*

I should've got one of the earlier ones—like *Barbarella.*

Howie Mandel

I'm living in California now, and I want to be like everyone else. So what I'm doing is, everybody there wants to get into shape, and the shape I've chosen is a triangle. So I was getting up every morning and I was jogging for like half an hour, and then I said to myself, "If I take the car, I could save *so* much *time*."

To better your understanding, I've prepared a Quick Checklist of some of the most common questions asked about The Big Game.

QUESTION ONE: If The Game is a popular pastime all across this great land of ours, how come no teams from the Maritimes ever compete in The Big Game?

ANSWER: For the same reason there are no Maritime hockey or baseball franchises. The names Nova Scotia, New Brunswick, and Prince Edward Island are simply too long to be printed neatly across the back of an uniform.

QUESTION TWO: How come you didn't say anything about Newfoundland?

ANSWER: All right, if you insist. How many Newfound-landers does it take to make up a football team?

QUESTION THREE: I don't know. How many?

ANSWER: Twelve. Ten to hold them down, and two to apply the make-up.

QUESTION FOUR: How on earth did you come up with a joke as terrible as that?

ANSWER: Oh shut up. Anyway, you're supposed to be asking me questions about football.

QUESTION FIVE: Why is it that The Big Game's location is continually shifted from East to West and back again?

ANSWER: Because that's how a sense of tension is provided. Every year we get to wonder if it's going to rain during The Big Game (Vancouver), or will it snow (Toronto)?

QUESTION SIX: But doesn't Vancouver now have a domed stadium?

ANSWER: Hey, you're brighter than you've been letting on. You're right, Vancouver does have a dome, so now we have to focus our tension on whether it's going to rain or snow on The Big Parade preceding The Big Game. Of course, if Toronto ever gets its domed stadium [*With the coming of SkyDome in 1989, Toronto did.*] , the distinction between the two cities will keel over on the astroturf faster than you can say Sam Echeverry. The only distinguishing feature then will be that in Toronto people say, "Have a nice day, eh?" while in Vancouver they say, "Hey, have a nice day."

QUESTION SEVEN: Why is it that—

ANSWER: I'm sorry, that's all the time we have for questions. Time to move on to a Short Glossary to explain some of the more puzzling terms associated with The Big Game.

Short Glossary of Big Game Terms

TIGHT END–The way the players look in those funny pants during The Big Game.

DEFENSIVE END—The explanations the players offer for why they have to wear those funny pants during The Big Game.

QUARTERBACK SNEAK—When one of the TV viewers of The Big Game surreptitiously removes twenty-five cents from the pile of money everyone has chipped in for pizza.

HANDKERCHIEF ON THE PLAY—Phenomenon of lachrymose wives who wanted to watch Shakespeare on PBS, but their husbands insisted on seeing The Big Game instead.

SACKING THE QUARTERBACK—When the person who surreptitiously removed twenty-five cents from the pizza-money pile surreptitiously slips the coin into a bag while everyone else is caught up in watching The Big Game.

Now that your most pressing questions have been answered, and the more puzzling terminology has been elucidated, you're ready to join the rabid thousands to whom The Big Game embodies a quality of meaningfulness otherwise absent from their lives.

Just make sure nobody suckers you into playing a game of *electronic* football during half-time. Electronic football (in whose evolutionary history Canadians played no part whatsoever) is a whole other story, which you must remind me to tell you about some time.

In fact, if you're very good, quicker than you can say Cookie Gilchrist, my guide to electronic football (hereinafter referred to as The Little Game) will become available in a bookstore near you.

–UNGER

I Can
Get It For
You Retail!

CONSUMERISM AND THE CONSUMER SOCIETY

INVASION OF THE YUPPIE CLONES!
AN '80S HORROR STORY

Murray Soupcoff

*Warning! The Following Story Contains Lifestyle Scenes that May Be
Frightening to Those Without Sufficient Discretionary Income!*

The night was cold, misty and damp, as I trudged along one of our
neighbourhood streets, our trusted cocker spaniel in tow. It was time
for his usual late-night constitutional. Suddenly, about two hundred
yards ahead, I noticed it—a strange unfamiliar yellowish glow, breaking through the mist.

The spaniel yelped in fright, and then began to bark anxiously.
Behind ominous beams of yellow light, I could make out the outline
of a huge aerodynamic vehicle whose metallic paint seemed to glow
in the street lamps' aura. I shuddered involuntarily, my hands trembling with fear.

I realized I was in the presence of an alien force the likes of which
I had never before encountered. Trembling, I pushed forward, our
spaniel reluctantly following behind, barking at his loudest.

What extraterrestrial aliens had we chanced upon in this late-night
encounter? Did they mean us any harm? Though inwardly frightened,
I was determined to find the answer.

As we drew closer, the mist seemed to part, revealing an awesome sight. There it stood in all its magnificent grandeur, its LED
displays blinking an uncertain welcome.

The beams of light, I soon realized, emanated from its ornate
fender-mounted fog lamps. Nothing, however, could have prepared
me for the mystical sense of awe I felt in its presence. There before
me stood the neighbourhood's first BMW, complete with silver-grey
metallic paint, sunroof, tinted glass, blacked-out trim, brushed
aluminum wheels and stylized front-air dam.

I squinted through the mist, trying to determine the presence of the late-night interlopers attached to the idling vehicle. Suddenly, my eye caught the glint of a brand new Rolex watch. There they were, standing proudly in front of a freshly implanted SOLD sign.

I tried to shield my eyes from the glint of so many gold accessories sported by the alien strangers. They were a handsome pair, dressed in finely cut imported fashions, even their fashionably coiffed hair styles signalling assured affluence. They appeared relatively friendly.

I drew closer, my heart still pounding. Little could I know that this was just the beginning. Little could I realize the significance of this seemingly benign meeting. How could I know that an invasion had begun—an invasion more terrifying and unnerving than watching a full hour of "The Tommy Hunter Show": the invasion of our innocent, unspoiled neighbourhood by...the Yuppie Clones!

Close Encounters

I approached nearer. Despite their strange garb, they seemed not that different from other neighbourhood residents. Suddenly, the male member of the duo spoke: "Good evening. A bit chilly tonight, isn't it?"

I recoiled in surprise. Here were these strange aliens, sporting gold chains around every available limb, and owners of such a magnificent vehicle, and they spoke the same language as me. What a pleasant surprise. Or so I first thought.

The female of the species then spoke, using a strange vernacular I could barely decipher: "What a lovely neighbourhood. Would you know the location of the nearest après sweat boutique? What about a greengrocer with an adequate selection of fennel, celeriac or radicchio? Not to mention somewhere handy to pick up some shallots, ground sesame seeds or coriander? Don't you just adore cooking *la vrai chose*!?"

"Uh, yes, it is a chilly evening," I answered lamely. "Well, I must be on my way. I think there's going to be another teen suicide on 'Degrassi Junior High' tonight, and I don't want to miss it."

Quickly I made my escape, anxiously turning the corner to the safety of the familiar beat-up Chevettes, Tercels and Civics lining our own thoroughfare.

Bring on the Clones

After this close encounter of an affluent kind, I attempted to take a different late-night dog-walking route. However, as the weeks and months passed, I began to see growing evidence of a frightening phenomenon that caused me increasing concern. Slowly but surreptitiously, the extra-neighbourestrial aliens were colonizing our neighbourhood, and in the most extraordinary manner.

The original alien home buyers had somehow brought with them the secret ability to clone duplicates of themselves. As more and more SOLD signs proliferated in our neighbourhood, home after home became populated by strangers bearing an uncanny resemblance to the original alien encroachers.

Those new residents all drove similar model, fuel-injected automobiles (all bearing those enigmatic initials, BMW). They sported the

Richard J. Needham

After visiting your friendly neighbourhood supermarket, you wonder what the hostile ones must be like.

same blow-dried hair styles, the same designer jogging suits, and the same fashionable footwear. They all served cumin carrot salads and cream cheese brownies for Sunday brunch, frequented the same pasta bars, thought *The Big Chill* was profound, admired Jane Fonda's thighs (not a trace of cellulite!) and agreed that if only politicians were as knowledgable and caring as David Suzuki, the world would be a better place. ("If only they'd let an informed individual like David Suzuki sit down with Gorbachev, we'd have a disarmament agreement in no time!")

The more I looked, the more I realized the breadth and efficiency of this secret cloning process. How else could one explain the amazing similarities of the new residents, all of them apparently incapable of displaying any trace of individuality, or any deviance from what seemed to be a standardized norm.

The similarities *were* incredible. They all referred to television as the boob tube, though they did take time to watch "Street Legal" ("They're almost like family") and "The Journal" ("It's so superior to American television, but I wish Barbara Frum would do something with her hair!").

Amazingly, in the 1984 election campaign, every one of them noted what a decent and compassionate individual Ed Broadbent was, and how he stood for "the right things," and then secretly voted for Brian Mulroney ("Can you imagine how much taxes would go up under a socialist government!?"). They were all proud of having black friends, commented on how eloquent Jesse Jackson was (though they were never quite sure what exactly he was saying) and inevitably belonged to an exclusive tennis or squash club with no black members. They all publicly praised cabinet minister Flora Macdonald as a role model that any mother would want her daughter to look up to, and privately questioned why Flora never married and had children.

Yes, it was obvious that there was an extraordinary cloning process under way, all part of what appeared to be an organized effort to subvert our neighbourhood. Just how extraordinary, I didn't initially realize.

There Goes the Neighbourhood

I should have realized just how insidious the process was when I stopped in at our corner milk store, a few months later, for a loaf of white bread. The store was gone! The proprietors, Mr. and Mrs. Chan, were gone! The white bread was gone too! All of them had disappeared, perhaps whisked away during the night by unknown forces.

The Chan's Groceteria: Wine & Beer sign was replaced by an elegant, pink plastic canopy with the words, McGoo's Food Emporium, illuminated in very large white letters. Gone was the soft drink cooler, the cartons of cigarettes, the Ruffles potato chips, the Hostess Twinkies, and of course the Wonder Bread. In their place were discreetly stained pine shelves filled with strange cheeses (derived primarily from goats and other esoteric creatures), freshly ground coffee beans imported from every mountainous region in the Western hemisphere (none of it instant either), nuts and dried fruit, croissants, cheese, bread, fresh salads and pasta and racks and racks of every spice and vinegar known to humankind.

"Can I help you, sir?" My god, it was another one of them, same hair style, same Gucci loafers, same smarmy smile! They had absconded with the Chans, and replaced the Chans with another one of their robot-like clones.

"Hi, I'm Kenny Kinsley. I'm helping my wife today. She just opened this shop. Actually, I'm an accountant; but I'm being naughty and took the day off to help out (little chuckle)."

God, he was personable. But he couldn't fool me. I didn't even want to imagine what they had done with the poor Chans.

"You know, we bought this store from the Chans. Had to pay a bundle for it too. And now they're down South soaking up the sun in their new condo in Clearwater, while we're working our butts off up here!"

They were a crafty lot, but I knew how to put him to the test.

"What's your favourite movie of all time?" I asked subtly.

"Well, *The Big Chill* of course, but—"

"Aaaaaarggghhhh!" I screamed in fright. They were everywhere! And forgetting to even tell him that *no one* buys whole wheat bread (it tastes funny), I raced out of the store to safety. There was simply no escaping them. They were everywhere.

Creeping Gentrification

Indeed, they were now everywhere. Even our own street was being transformed by the interlopers. Off came the porches, on went the pseudo-Victorian facades, brass lamps, ornaments and door knockers. There seemed to be nary a home that didn't have a BMW parked in front of it. Each morning, at 8:00 a.m., it was as if a collective alarm sounded, as rows on rows of suitably coiffed gentlemen and ladies, complete with leather attaché cases, simultaneously exited their front doors, chatted amiably for forty-five seconds with their neighbours (about their tennis game and the high cost of brie) and then went off to their office towers to fiddle with their PCs and discuss whether there is life after Lotus 1-2-3.

How had they done it? I could not understand. Here the aliens were slowly taking over a neighbourhood, reproducing themselves at a rate sufficient to alarm even Xerox, and yet there had not been one ounce of organized opposition. The portrait of the Queen in the local bank had been taken down, replaced by an autographed photograph of Loblaws President Dave Nichols, proudly brandishing a jar of President's Choice Dijon Mustard. Our garbage collectors now insisted on being addressed as sanitation workers, and now only took cappuccino breaks. Yet, not a sign of resistance.

I knew I had to do something.

Organizing the Resistance

There were now too many of them to permit visible resistance. However, there still could be clandestine opposition; and with this in mind, I invited two potential co-conspirators to my home for a late-night meeting.

If ever there were two individuals that I knew to be sympathetic to the cause, it was Rick Smythe and his wife Mary Beth. Rick and Mary Beth had never had a dinner party, had never joined Amnesty

JiCi Lauzon

Have you noticed that they never display size thirteen shoes in the window? The only time I ever saw size thirteen shoes in the window was in the wax museum. First, you choose the style in the window that is in a seven or an eight. Then, you go back inside and ask the salesperson if he has the same style in size thirteen. And he looks at you as if you're crazy, and says, "In thirteen? I don't have any in stock. But I could maybe have some made for you, and have them sent to you."

When there is a pair, he brings them to you, and it's always a disappointment. On the seven, there are ten holes for the laces; with size thirteen, there are twenty-two holes. The laces to go with the shoes come in a roll—fifty feet of laces. It's useful. For example, when the shoes are worn out, there are enough laces to knit a poncho. And with the soles, you could build a patio.

International and even bought leisure suits at Sears. Culture was a non-existent concept in their home. To the best of their knowledge, *The Jewel in the Crown* was 100 proof premium Canadian whiskey and Yitzhak Perlman was the Prime Minister of Israel.

"Rick and Mary Beth," I began. "Do you see what's happening to our neighbourhood? *They're* taking over! We've got to do something. The situation is getting desperate."

"They? Who's they?" asked Rick incredulously.

"Who's they?" I gasped. "*Them*! The ones with $100 fold-away aviator sunglasses! The ones with the leather pants, the customized aluminum tennis rackets, the Filipino nannies, the aerobic classes, the tanning salons, the Nathan Pritikin diets! *Them*!"

"Oh, them," answered Mary Beth nonchalantly. "Why didn't you say so in the first place?"

"Them? What's wrong with them?" asked Rick politely.

"What's wrong? I'll tell you what's wrong. They're everywhere! Our people are disappearing in the night! One day they're with us, the next day they're gone!"

"Well, of course," answered Mary Beth. "Do you realize how much money those strangers are offering for our homes? Rick and I figure if we can hold out another six months, we'll clear two hundred thousand dollars! Just think, six months from now, Rick and I can be in our new RV, on our way to Graceland to visit Elvis's resting place."

"But don't you understand?" I countered. "It's a plot to drive us out, so they can take over! They want to make the whole world over in their image, make everyone look, think, speak and even vote the same way! We have to take a stand for individuality! We have to resist!"

"Uh, sure," agreed Rick unconvincingly. "But it's getting late and Mary Beth has a jazzercize class first thing tomorrow morning. Why don't we talk about it another time, maybe in seven months or so."

My god, they had got to Rick and Mary Beth too! We were doomed!

Epilogue

I am sitting here writing this piece in my private room in our regional Mental Health Centre. Now don't get the wrong impression. They treat me very well here, and there are no locked doors, and we have groups every day.

Dr. Finley tells me all this worry about "them" is just a paranoid projection. It's all part of my too vivid fantasy life. He says that if I can control these destructive projections, then I can go home very soon.

I know he's right, and I'm trying to change. The little blue pills I take seem to help, and all those fears seem quite hazy now and part of the distant past.

It's just that something about Dr. Finley bothers me. I don't know whether it's the gold chain he wears on his wrist, or the Gucci loafers, or when he tells me to get in touch with my feelings, but something bothers me. I wish I could remember why.

He is a very nice doctor. He's a very caring person too, worried about the environment, just like David Suzuki. He told me so himself. In fact, he said that if only they'd let an informed individual like David Suzuki sit down with Gorbachev, over a pasta salad and a glass of the best beaujolais nouveau, we'd have a disarmament agreement in no time.

Well, I must close this little story. I'm sorry if I upset you unduly with my original ravings. It's all quite clear now that they were the result of an overactive imagination.

I must go now. We're all going to watch a movie on the video tonight. Dr. Finley says it's a dramatic tour de force. Something called *The Big Chill*.

—KING

Lenin Statues Liquidator World

———

Double Exposure
(Linda Cullen and Bob Robertson)

A pre-break-up-of-the-Soviet Union sketch

(Music: something Russian with Balalaikas.)

Sergei: Hallo! I'm Sergei Knocitov, owner of the Lenin Statues Liquidator World.

Ludmilla: Hallo. I'm Ludmilla Knocitov. Have we got a great deal for you!

Sergei: Lenin Statues Liquidator World warehouses are piled high with thousands of statues of Lenin. Everything must go!!

Gord Paynter

My neighbour has a very interesting breed of dog. He's got something called a Besanji. They're African dogs and kind of unusual because they don't bark. Nothing. Which is great. You get a burglar and the thing's doing mime. "Two words. First word—sounds like gun butt." They put the Beware of Dog sign around its neck, you flip it over, it says Woof-Woof. Because the dog couldn't bark to get in, they taught the dog to ring the doorbell. Two weeks later, it was selling Amway.

LUDMILLA: So, if you are looking for a good deal on a statue of Lenin, see us today!

(Sound effects: large crane noise, then crash.)

SERGEI: Every hour, the trucks drive in, unloading statues of Lenin. Look at this one here...sixty-two feet high, weighs forty-seven tons. Clean the pigeon droppings off the head, it will make great lawn ornament.

LUDMILLA: And we are letting it go for only ten thousand rubles. And remember, nothing down. Do not pay for six months. If there is still Soviet Union then, kindly pay up.

SERGEI: But, Ludmilla, we don't just have one size. Look here...

(Sound effects: he rolls out heavy trolley.)

SERGEI: Lots of small Lenin statues. Perfect for your bookshelf. Use them as door stoppers. Throw them when the cats fight.

LUDMILLA: Lenin Statues Liquidator World will not be undersold! Come to the place that sells only Lenin Statues. You want Stalin Statues? Go to Stalin Statues Liquidator World, not here!

SERGEI: No, Ludmilla. Stalin Statues Liquidator World do not exist anymore.

LUDMILLA: What happened?

SERGEI: They were liquidated! Ha ha ha.

LUDMILLA: Ha ha ha.

SERGEI: So, remember: if you are looking for a statue of Lenin for your home, office, or cottage, come to Lenin Statues Liquidator World.

LUDMILLA: I'm Ludmilla Knocitov...Owner.

SERGEI: No, Ludmilla. I am owner.

LUDMILLA: I am owner!

SERGEI: No! No! I am owner!!

LUDMILLA: Who cleans off all pigeon droppings?

SERGEI: You do...

LUDMILLA: Who cleans off all anti-Communist slogans?

SERGEI: You do...

LUDMILLA: Then I am owner. So, keep quiet Sergei, or you will suddenly become ill.

ANNOUNCER: Lenin Statues Liquidator World, with stores in Kiev, St. Petersburg, and opening soon in the new "Lenin's Tomb Mall and Mini-Golf Land," Red Square.

(Music up and out.)

AD NAUSEA

Jim Cormier

Memo to: Theodore J. Bassett, VP, Marketing, The Canine Cuisine Corp.
From: William T. Plugman, VP, Beelzebub Advertising
Re: Woofer's Global Product Placements

Dear Ted:
As per our previous discussions with Paramount, we are pleased to confirm a placement deal for your flagship brand, Woofer's Cookies ("The Dog's Breakfast That Tastes Good All Day").

By paying to have your upmarket canine treat appear in Mr. Robert De Niro's latest film, you will build critical brand-consciousness with discriminating cineastes worldwide.

By the terms we've struck, Mr. De Niro's character will feed a morning pick-me-up to his dog, Fuffles. Holding up the Woofer's package, in full frontal view for 3.7 seconds, Mr. De Niro will say, "Does Fuffles want a little snacky?"—a slight amendment on your originally scripted "Does Fuffles want a little snacky-wacky?" (Mr. De Niro's agent explained that the longer version doesn't organically align with the character's narrative trajectory, and to resolve the dramatic contradictions he would require another $150,000 in personal-development fees.)

To update you on other exciting highlights of our global campaign:

1. The endorsements department at *The Norton Anthology of Poetry* has agreed to place Woofer's jingles in reprints of John Keats's steamy classic, "Ode to a Nightingale." Our poetry consultants advise that Keats is a Jim Morrison-type personality of the nineteenth century with a durable brand presence in the eighteen- to twenty-two-year-old female college demographic. Our deal will replace two lines of his widely enjoyed ode ("O, for a draught of vintage! that hath been/Cool'd a long age in the deep-delved earth") with the updated "Oh for a bowl of Woofer's Cookies! that hath been/Heated up toasty in the microwave!" It's good, second-stanza positioning, and for another 10 percent *The Norton* may throw in boldface.

2. We have made ground with the Kunsthistorisches Museum in Vienna to place one tin of Woofer's in the right foreground of the sixteenth-century Flemish masterwork *Peasant Wedding*, by Pieter Breughel the Elder. Our art people advise that this Breughel character is an unpolished Robert Bateman who speaks to vacationers from heartland America. Apparently, we can paint a legible likeness of Woofer's packaging straight onto the canvas, under the snout of a hungry terrier, without compromising the original Woofer's corporate logo.

Briane Nasimok

The one thing I like to read most on the toilet is the *National Enquirer*—it inspires me. And the articles are so insightful.

They had an exposé on Morris the Cat—this isn't the first one you know—it's like the twelfth or something—but there was this story on the original Morris and the controversy surrounding his death.

You see, the original Morris *didn't* die of natural causes like they said—the *Enquirer* found out the truth. He didn't choke on a hairball—he OD'ed on nip. Seems he was having an affair with Miss Mew, and Sylvester took her away—so Morris did himself in. They know that it's true because Morris had the same vet as Elvis.

Stevie Ray Fromstein

There's lots of crime on television. I've noticed the latest thing on TV is showing cops breaking into those crack-houses—and sometimes they do it *live*.

I mean—that's *amazing* television! Police sneaking around the bushes, about to *burst* into a house—

What I was wondering is—what if the people inside are watching the program?

"Hey! Looks a lot like *our* place!"

"Hey, Larry—get the door, will you? I don't wanna *miss* this!"

"Keep it down! They're goin' in!"

(Holds his arm up behind his back.)

"Hey—that's *me*!!"

3. We are talking with the Metropolitan Opera Company to script a Woofer's promotion into Wagner's *Die Meistersinger von Nürnberg*. It might seem odd to market canine cookies through an operatic parable of art set in sixteenth-century Nuremburg. But here's the clincher: we believe we can swing a joint promotion with Madonna, who's negotiating to star in *Die Meistersinger* as part of her "Collar Me Blue in '92" World Subordination Tour. Considering the leash motifs running through her upcoming road show, there are natural synergies here for all parties.

Well, Ted, that's it for now. I'll update you soon on our talks with Salman Rushdie and the building management at the Sistine Chapel. Until then, as we like to say around here, where there's a Woof there's a way (ha ha).

Sincerest regards,

Bill

FROM *NAPALM THE MAGNIFICENT*
A PLAY ABOUT TRUTH, SEX AND BAD ATTITUDE

David S. Craig

NAPALM: I read newspapers, you know. I've got opinions. I may be short but I'm not stupid. I run a news-stand at Union Station here in T.O. Papers, bundles, mountains of news, and I read it all. I read it so I know what's going on. And everyday there's something new going on so I read that. And I read and I listen and I watch until I can't have a single fucking thought of my own.

I'm not the only one. Did you see the new opinion poll? They asked Canadians, "Which of these political leaders would you vote for in the next federal election?" The most popular leader was d) none of the above. The second most popular leader was e) no opinion.

Everyone's talking but no one's thinking. Clyde Wells. Did you hear why he's willing to let Quebec drop out of Confederation? He thinks it'll be faster to fly from St. John's to Ottawa.

What we need is another little war to perk us up. C'mon. Aren't you looking forward to another little war? I am. And next time I'm going to be right in there. Well, not me personally, I just want to watch it on TV. Hey, don't get me wrong; I'd enlist but they won't have me. Flat feet.

I just wanna see it live through a camera on the nose of the bombers as the flak comes streaking up from the ground, and then cut to a shot looking down the bomb bay doors watching those smart bombs go off like mushrooms and then, suddenly, cut to a long dogfight in action with one of our CF 18s (Canadian content) and watch as the pilot dives and turns locking on to the enemy, thumb down, white trail and BLAM!, fire and smoke in a clear blue sky while I sit in my Laz-E-Boy eating Fritos and drinking Coke Classic.

I want to be there when an enemy pilot locks on to one of our guys. Warning light flashing, pilot screaming into the radio, diving and twisting, fear and sweat, until suddenly—shhhhh—the screen turns white, and cut to commercial.

You deserve to see that, don't'cha think? I mean who pays for these planes, anyway? *You do.* So my idea is this. You want to reduce the deficit, right? So why don't you sell off the military? Make it a private company. Hell, if we're fighting for free enterprise, why can't free enterprise pay for it? And when you do, you should make me chairman of the board. I could make millions selling television rights alone. Millions? Hell no. Billions. I mean if you knew you could watch a war live on TV, would you be reading a book on humour? Hell no. You'd be watching TV. The whole world would be watching TV. It'd be bigger than the Academy Awards. Corporations would line up to advertise. Just think of it: "Ladies and gentlemen, this bombing run was brought to you by Exxon." Or what about Pepsi on the side of the cruise missiles, The Bomb of a New Generation, or Greenpeace in big block letters on the 100-percent biodegradable body bags. Oh yes, friends, the war of the future will have a camera on every plane, on every tank, on every cruise. And *I'll* be running that war. Because Sadam is a prick, and George is a prick, but I'm the biggest prick of all.

JiCi Lauzon

I bought myself a pre-arranged funeral. My family was really happy about that! Well, it's a beautiful casket. I have my tombstone. I have my place reserved in the cemetery. So you see, I know *exactly* where I am going. It was a great deal! The kind of deal that goes "Don't pay a penny until the first of October!" That kind of a deal. That means that I could die tomorrow, allow myself to be buried next week and then, not make any payments until the month of October. And then, it's satisfaction guaranteed, or your money back.

Evidently, this implies reincarnation.

FROM *THE PROMISED LAND*

Martin Waxman

The Birth of a Mall
BY *MARTIN MALL*

And there was heaven and there was earth.

And the Lord said, "Not bad for My first try."

And there was day and there was night. And there was winter and there was summer.

And in the winter the days were freezing cold. And in the summer the days were hot and humid.

And there were deodorants.

And there was air conditioning. And there was heat. And there were big woolly sweaters.

And there were power mowers and televisions and hair dryers and electric can openers.

And there was formica.

Yea, there were all these condiments to be bought and sold and a plethora of places to buy and sell them, but still the people were edgy.

And they complained to each other on a regular basis.

"Why should we have to drive all over town just to go shopping?"

"Why should we have to worry about validated parking?"

"Why do all the stores close before we get home from work?"

Why...why...why...

Until the day they set up a grievance committee and made an appointment to see the Lord.

This is the gist of the proposal they submitted unto Him: "Technology is no Eden. We want everything under one roof!"

...FLOATING DOLLAR.

—MALLETTE

"Can't you leave Me alone?" said the Lord. "You're never satisfied." And He started muttering to Himself, "Everything under one roof. They want everything under...one...roof...Everything under one roof. That's it. That's the answer. It's so simple, I can't believe it."

And he said to the delegation, "Look, you may have come up with something decent for a change. Let Me sleep on it. I'll get back to you tomorrow."

That very evening, the Lord summoned up the finest Architects, Draftspeople, Builders, Engineers, Designers and Optimists (in short, His peer group). And he ran the proposal up the flagpole for them.

And lo and behold, though nary a one had served a moment in the military, the Lord's words so inspired them that they saluted in unison and remained at attention until the Lord was forced to say, "at ease."

And the proposal became an idea. And the idea became a concept. And the concept of malls was born.

And the Lord said, "I've got to give credit where credit is due."

And so there was Visa and Mastercharge and American Express.

And the people rejoiced.

In the days that followed, the seeds of many malls began to spout and blossom in every corner of the land.

There was Cloverdale and Westdale and Southdale and Southwestdale.

And Southwestdale begat Parkdale. Which begat Parkdale Gardens. Which begat the Lincoln Overview Development Corporation. Which begat five scores of malls from coast to coast...

Which begat Garden Park.

And Garden Park was a full five and twenty years old. And it had led a successful and profitable life.

On the eve of its Grand Reopening and Anniversary Celebrations, let us raise our glasses in a toast to Garden Park: "May your cash never cease to flow..."

HALLELUJAH!

THE NEW CORPORATE TESTAMENT

Ed Hailwood

INSPIRING BIBLE STORIES, EACH WITH A MORAL FOR THE MODERN EXECUTIVE, TRANSCRIBED FROM ANCIENT SCROLLS.

"GO, AND DO THOU LIKEWISE."—LEE IACOCCA

Adam and Eve Fail to Resolve Their Differences

Now the LORD God, having created man, said, It is not good that man should be alone in the workplace. I will make an helpmeet for him, to get his coffee, and add a feminine touch.

And the LORD caused a deep sleep to fall upon Adam, and took one of his ribs, and with it made a woman, and brought her unto the man. And the woman looked upon the man as he slept, saying, It figures. There he is, dead unto the world, and paid roughly half as much again for work of equal value, or slightly less, if you ask me.

And Adam, upon awakening, said, I will call you a dame, for there is nothing like you. In fact, you are quite beautiful without your clothing, and do you come here often?

But the woman said, Put a sock in it, Charlie, that is harassment, and let us get down to brass tacks. Dost thou know a good tailor? And so forth, so that the man did yearn for the beasts of the field, over which he had dominion, but not the woman, apparently.

Now the serpent was more subtil than the general run of beasts, having been to law school, at nights. And he said unto the woman, How do you like them apples? Thou art paid far less than the man, who oppresses thee, and what about sisterhood?

And the woman said, There are no sisters, insofar as I can see, and I do not have a thing to wear to court, so as to seek redress.

And the serpent answered, Hark now unto the Charter, Section 15 [2], of which, in this pastoral backwater, you may not be aware.

For in the day ye stake thy claim thereto, then shall your eyes be opened, and ye shall be equal, and no more hassles, take my word for it.

And so the woman did mount a challenge, and her eyes were opened, but not immediately, for it took many days to be resolved. And in the meantime, she did not bring the man his coffee, and objected mightily to his taste in furnishings, and networked with the serpent, on an hourly billing, so that she was sensitized. And both she and the man became aware that they were naked, and so both were tailored, indistinguishably.

And the LORD God dropped by for a warranty check, and they downed tools, and hid beneath a filing cabinet because they were afraid, having monkeyed with the prototype.

And the LORD said, Beguiled, wert thou? I shall curse the serpent for this, upon his belly shalt he go, and forced to take legal aid cases, at a loss.

Unto the woman he said, Thou shalt fight hammer and tongs with thy co-worker, and he shall leer at thee, and no paid maternity leaves, either.

And unto Adam he said, Because thou hast colluded in this, thou art doomed to struggle with postfeminism, whatever that may be, and thou shalt sweat for thy bread, which will fall bitter side down, ho, ho.

So he locked the man and the woman in their workplace, and set at its gateway Human Rights Commissioners, armed with broad swords that swept to and fro with each passing breeze, fanning the flames of perpetual litigation.

Moral: Settle matters quietly amongst yourselves. The law is an asp.

Joseph and His Inappropriate Wardrobe

Now Israel (the Old Man) loved Joseph more than all his co-workers, because he had a proven track record, and he made for him a suit of sombre hue, and conservative cut, that Joseph wore all the day, and his shirts were purest white, and buttoned down.

And when his co-workers saw that Israel loved Joseph more than all of them put together, they hated him, and conspired against him, and advanced the kilometrage on his automobile, which was leased, so he surpassed his limitation.

But Joseph conceived a strategy, and told it to his co-workers, and they hated him the more for this.

For he said unto them, Hark, I pray thee, to this strategy, that cometh to me as in a dream, thanks to an extension course that you should take, too.

For behold! we were closing orders in the field. And lo! my order book was filled to bursting, and also legible, I might add. And behold! your order books were all unmarked, and the leaves withered away, save only your expense accounts, which were padded past belief, and you had better shape up next quarter.

And his co-workers said to him, Shalt thou indeed outpace us in the field?

And he replied, Be assured of this, and I will gain a bonus for the third year running.

So did Joseph's co-workers go into the field, there to tend their clients by night and day. And by chance, they met in the wilderness, and compared their notes, and said, When Joseph doth appear, we will lie in wait for him, and slay him, and cast him into a PCB disposal site, and that will fix his wagon.

But one of their number, Reuben by name, a pragmatist, said, Let us not do anything hasty, for he is our co-worker, and hath powerful friends.

So it came to pass that Joseph appeared among them, at a motel, and they fell upon him, and stript him of his sombre cloth, and clad him in a coat of many colours, of polyester made, and of a grievous weave, not to mention two-toned elevator shoes, and a tie on which might land a 747. And so were they revenged.

And they said to one another, Behold! Joseph cannot cut the mustard wearing such a suit, we would not be caught dead in a ditch clad thuswise, and when the Old Man sees him, it will be curtains, which is what yon cloth resembles.

And they took a photograph of the incident, and sent it unto the Old Man, who sayeth, Hath Joseph come to this? An evil taste hath taken him, and there goeth the dress code I have set.

And the Old Man adjusted his garments, and put sackcloth upon his loins, for he had lost a top producer, saying, This might fly in Egypt, but not in my tribe.

And he refused to be comforted, and gave Joseph's place unto a straitlaced junior, who would toe the line.

Moral: Wider lapels are coming back, but slowly. Never dress for excess.

Job's Attitudinal Problem

There was a man in the corporation of Oz, whose name was Job, and he was perfect and upright, one that feared God, and eschewed evil, and his loyalty was not in question.

And there came to him great merit for this, and stock options, and other perks. His substance also was a corner office with a view, and a seat at the high table, and a personal computer, upon which his children did their sums.

And Job arose early in the morning, and went unto the squash court, and thought pious thoughts, for he was very content. Thus did Job continually, to the point of boredom.

Now there was a day when experts came to present themselves unto the LORD, and a shrink came also among them, who said, Let us test thy servant, for thou hast made it too soft for him. But stretch forth thy foot, and trip him up, and he will fall down, and curse thee, and go unto the competition.

Richard J. Needham

There is one thing to be said for inflation. It enables you to live in a more expensive neighbourhood without moving out of your home.

And the LORD said, Behold! all that Job hath is in thy power, and ye may subject him to a battery of tests, but assault not his person, lest word get around.

So the shrink did probe at Job, and counselled him and showed him inkblots, and made him to associate words, and inquired as to his sex life, and drinking habits, and his very motivations, writing it down, in triplicate.

Then Job arose, and rent his mantle, saying, Naked came I into this firm, and naked shall I depart, if necessary. The LORD giveth, and the LORD hath set this bimbo upon me, for reasons that, quite frankly, remain obscure. Whereupon he drank a single Perrier, and sang the company song, so to raise his spirits.

And in all this, Job sinned not, despite the shrink, who waxed wroth, for his tests did not avail.

And again there was a day when experts came unto the LORD, who chided the shrink, saying, Thou hast not got to Job, more fool thee, and thy tests are humbug, and there goeth thy retainer.

And the shrink replied, saying, Thou hath not seen nothing yet, for Job will revile thee, if thou uppest the ante, for a degree of stress is a healthful thing, and spurreth output, but tamper not with Job's sanity, this week.

So the shrink went forth, and smote Job with a neurosis, induced by constant observation, so he did itch, and twitch, and jump at small sounds, and his effectiveness was not enhanced, and he did snap at his wife and children when he returned unto his home, late for dinner.

Then said Job's wife, Thou art not the man I married, and she departed unto another place, with the BMW.

Now when Job's cronies heard of this, they rallied about him, bearing strong potions, and sat down with him, and strove to boost his morale. But they succeeded not in this, for behold! their words were much as follow: Lusteth thou for thy mother, or mayhap for comely youths? There is a skeleton in thy closet, else why doth the shrink pry therein? Perhaps thou art a crazy person, and the LORD knoweth something we do not. And this went on, for several days and nights, whilst Job protested, far too much, for he was on the defensive.

But the LORD spake to Job from out a heavy overcast, saying, Dost thou question my decisions? Who hath built this firm up from nothing, anyway? Consider thou thyself indispensable, or what? And dost thou expect a job for life, no pun intended?

And Job answered the LORD, and said, Thou wert correct to unleash the shrink upon me, and I will mend my ways, for I abhor myself, and will confess my sins if thou wilt give me a memo enumerating them, for I am broken in spirit. And the LORD sayeth, That is what I like to hear. We must have lunch sometime.

So Job returned unto the fold, being somewhat dazed, but took early retirement, and was seen no more.

Moral : If you're perfect that's no (a) excuse, (b) guarantee, (c) great hell. Check one.

God Frustrates the New Technology

And it came to pass, as business folk embraced the postindustrial age, that they felt need of wondrous devices, to enhance their daily tasks, and speed communication.

And they said, Let us have intelligent machines, and place our faith in them. And from silicon were they made, thanks to a wizardry understood by few, save only certain high priests, who instructed the business folk how to plug their acquisitions in, with varying results.

And they said, Let us venerate the machines, for they are a salvation unto us, and devise us a language, so they may speak, one to another. And the high priests said, We shall get back to thee on that.

And the LORD looked down, and saw these things, saying, Behold, the business folk are one, and nothing will be restrained from them. So they will access all the firmament, and here cometh a three-day week, which was not my original intent. So I will thwart their schemes, causing
a slippage of their disks, and treasured documents will disappear unto the void, and other glitches too horrible to mention. I have not had one this good since locusts.

So the LORD went down and fragmented the technology. And lo! there came a great array of wondrous machines, each with bells and whistles of its own, so each did outmode its predecessors, and did not interface, driving the lesser priests, or comptrollers, to distraction, and emitted rays that circumcised the operators thereof, and made the business folk to attend workshops in a distant land, to keep abreast of developments.

Therefore was the name of this place called COBOL, because the LORD did here confound the language of the machines, and they were incompatible, until reinvented by peoples from the East, which is surprising, since they wrote backward, but there you are.

Moral: Deus ex machina, loosely translated, means that God moves in mysterious ways. D-d-d-d-data's all, folks.

–RAESIDE

RRDSP

Double Exposure

(Music: something commercial-sounding.)

BOB: Here's news of recent federal legislation that should be of interest to all Canadians.

LINDA: Now, you can put away hundreds or thousands of daylight hours for your retirement years, simply by contributing to Registered Retirement Daylight Savings Plan.

BOB: And none of those daylight hours are taxable, if you leave them in your plan till retirement. Imagine all those extra daylight hours to use, as you wish, after age sixty-five. Yes, you could go through your twilight years without even seeing any twilight.

LINDA: With the right plan, your retirement years could bring you as much as twenty-four hours of daylight every day. Your hydro bills will be way down, and you can throw away expensive bedroom furniture.

BOB: Registered Retirement Daylight Savings Plans go into effect this weekend.

LINDA: So, don't let retirement scare the daylights out of you. Get an RRDSP now, and make your last years sunny and bright.

BOB: Call your nearest weather office now, for details. The Registered Retirement Daylight Savings Plan!

LINDA: And say "Goodnight" to goodnight!

(Music up and out.)

—MACKINNON

So Canada failed to celebrate your birthday again this year Sir John...

In our country the people get a holiday on <u>our</u> birthdays and go to stores to shop for birthday bargains.

Och weel, if **Canada** had a holiday for **me**, our people would just go to stores and shop for birthday bargains in <u>your</u> country too.

—PETERSON

A Disney Minute

Radio Free Vestibule

(Music: a lush rendition of the classic "When you wish upon a star," as from the opening and close of the Walt Disney TV show. The music continues under the entire sketch.)

ANNOUNCER: It's time for a Disney Minute! Today—a visit from Mickey Mouse!

MICKEY *(high, squeaky voice, à la Mickey)*:   Hello, kids! How'ya doin'? I'm fine! Bye-bye!

ANNOUNCER *(with passion, drive and threat)*:   Mickey Mouse is a registered trademark of the Disney Corporation. Any unauthorized reproduction of his likeness in any medium is strictly prohibited. These regulations apply both to private and public use, as well as to any other use which the Disney Corporation deems unacceptable in regard to their rules and regulations concerning the infringement of copyright law. Moreover, any use of the name "Mickey Mouse," and/or the names "Mick," "Michael," "Mike" or "Morey," and/or the words "Mouse," "House," "Louse" and "Blouse" will be considered an infringement of applicable copyright laws. Similarly, any person whose ears are seen to be overly round and large, i.e., exceeding an ear-to-body ratio of one to three shall be subject to litigation and possible criminal prosecution. Also, any person whose voice registers a frequency above fifteen kiloherz is forbidden to speak unless authorized to do so under a licensing agreement with the Disney Corporation. Furthermore, the Disney Corporation forbids

the wearing of white gloves, red shorts with large buttons—
and don't even think about big shoes. Lastly, any mouse
caught owning a pet dog shall be subject to severe penalties
as provided for under the copyright laws of the United States
and Canada. *(Pause; deeper voice.)* This has been a Disney
Minute!

Mickey *(high, squeaky, warm):*   Bye-bye!!

(Music: up and out.)

FROM *Cum Buy the Farm*

Don Harron

The Bertha Yer Aggrybizness

The wun thing peeples cant seam to do thout nowadaze is munny.
As yung tads reered durin our Deep Depressyun, we had no choist.
But we had a cow, a hawg, a chick er too and we got along fare enuff.
Not like in the sitties ware they hadda line up fer bred er soop, and
this is happnin agin today.

But a famly farm wuz a self-contane liddle eunick that maid all
of us in it self-defishunt. Nowadaze farmin is called Aggravibizness
and yuh gotta be a speshulist to be part of it. God noes we gotta hav
speshulists like docters or even bankers and liars, but we never had
better meddlekill care took of us than by our old Jeepy, hoo noo all of
us and our fokes frum berth, and spent haff his time sayin: "Don't
ever do that dam fool thing agin." In our day that wuz preventiv
meddlesin.

The speshulists in yer Aggrybizness is pritty well all frum
universaltys. They is all trained to mine ther own partickler bizness
and run around like won-ide munsters without bothrin to look over
yer academickle fents at the uther fella's facultys. Oldtimer farmers
like me is consider by these peeple to be unskill workers cuz I don't
fit into enny of ther neet cattygorys. Yer Aggry perfessers figger they're
in charge of farmin like liars is in sold charge of laws, and fillosofers
is in charge of marales and ethnics, wile they both leeve God to yer
theeorylowjins.

Thanks to our aggerculcher speshulists, farms are now divide up
into two kinds: them as takes hevvy ekqipmint and them as don't.
That's why farms has got so big, cuz you need a lotta akers fer to
justinfy poorchasing wun of them air-condishun combines with a
glasscab feechurin yer a.m. and yer p.m. raddio with a steereo-foney
Victorola attach.

Git bigger or git out, that's farmin today. Morn more small farms
is gettin abandon into weed patches, wile the big ones is gittin ploud
past ther fentsposts rite to the hi-way. I think this all start up in yer
fiftys wen gaslean replace otes as the mane prime moover. So we sole

off our horses and fed our otes to the cows cuz everybuddy in Northamerka wuz gittin into the backyard barby-queue, and the high steaks wuz in beef cattel. Weet becum a bit of a drag on the markit back then too, so we fed it to our beefs.

To farm big yuh has to borry munny and that's wen bankers, not yer aggryonomist, becums the speshulist in charge of us. If you heer sumbuddy describe as a farm experk, you kin bet yer gumboot he's not makin his livin as a farmer. Mebby a common-tater or bawd-caster, spoutin frases like "Aggrypower ginrates aggrydollers thru aggryexports." And they luvs to boast that thanks to yer hy-tex in Ammurrica oney three purrsent is feeding the uther ninety-seven with morn enuff leffover to meat the markit demands of the resta the wirld. Well, that tiney minerority is so good at ther jobs in yer You Ass, Canda and yer Yerpeen Common Mark-up that the wirld is drownin in mountins of weet, milk, and aigs, wile them poor Thurd Wirlders cant afford to buy a thing frum us. They say the problim is distrybushun, but mebby its retrybushun for all them bank lones.

I giv up my horses thirty yeer ago, and my Herferts five yeer ago, and went hevvy into weet. I dun good fer three of them yeers, but now it's the vicey of yer versy, and I'm sellin weet to my breeder nabers at bargin prices, cuz the oney beef I got is agin the guvmint.

Now if I'd staid in both biznesses I mite a cum out even, but I don't noe that I'm ever likely to git even agin. It's a littel like that tonick Valeda makes me take evry winter, Beef Iron and Wine; bilds you up as it tares you down, so that wat you lose on yer rustybouts you ganes on yer swingers. Bak in yer fortys we use to hav round our parts wat they called yer Beef Ring. It wuz kind of a co-hop of a few farmer nabers that kep us out of the butchershop, sints we took terns assastinatin one huge heffer or bullox every munth and passed the parts around prive-it.

Farmers allwaze mange to co-opulate in tuff times. Nobody in yer thurtys seem to own a combine or even a thrasher. We all gang up together and rent one in consert, and then we'd all gang-thrash eech other. Yer farmer has bin a genrullist hoo noo a liddle bit about everybuddy eltses speshulty, but our mane speshulty wuz takin care of the land. This is not wat farmin is about today. Yer speshulist farmer has tern into a exploiter hoo likes to git into the land and git out fast—a wambam- thankye mam. But a reel farmer noes he kin deepend on the land oney if the land kin deepend on him. We are not jist extrackters; we are nurcherers.

Modren aggrybizness trys to tern farmers into facktry werkers hoo happen to liv in the country, but not nessessarly close to ware they works. Jist punch in and out, and leeve the controlls to a absentease landlard hoo cood be a big malty-nashnul corpulation. The thurd wirld has not yet folla soot, most farms on this planit is three to four akers and they still diversifys ther crops. But in Canda yer small farm is sloely goin the way of yer buffloe. Sept that them beggers is thrivin with reservayshins, mostly in nashnulized parks. If Sassakat-chewon wuz put to grass, them farmers wood make more munny cleenin up on yer bison. They cud fatten them up with all that weet. Lets hope

Gord Paynter

If I go grocery shopping, I make it a point to rip the label off every single tin I buy. I figure, if I don't know what I'm getting, why the hell should the cashier?

they don't speshullyize like them wite hunters dun a hunderd yeer ago, takin out the tung and leevin the uther two tun of carcase fer to rot on the planes. They're doin the same now huntin poler bares with a helluvacopper and oney takin the rug part home.

Environly-Mentalism is in the papers every day now. Our first inhibitants wuz practissin all that before we land on them. In fack it was ther relijun. The Injuns didden think of yer invyronmint as seprit, but as spearit. And they was all part of it, no more ner less than anythin else on yer Muther's Erth, and they all had a persnal relayshunship with that big Muther. Accorn to yer Redman relijun, Her and Them is in a constant whirl of goin thru the changes. All of us, plants and aminals, passes thru eech other and out the tother side. We is part of whatever sirrounds us, so that nobuddy ever feels aloan, long as ther fulla erth spearits. We cant jist liv by and for arselfs and eggnore our Muthers Naycher, fer she is a too-way street. Yule notiss that sitties is gittin to hav morn more 1 way streets.

But we solvd our natif problim by pennin them up and teechin them to fowl ther own nest. And we suds-siddyize this squaller like a crop we don't wanta grow no more. Peeple fergit that Injuns wuz our first farmers. Yer Eeryquoits wuz groan corn in the middel of Trontuh twelve hundert yeer ago, and even then they had a better plitickle sistern than we got now. Now they're backd into corners fite-in fer ther rites to look after therselfs in the old waze before pro-grass overtuck them.

So our first famlys has bin kick into the corner of histry. But ther is a bunch follyin the saim kinda beleefs, putting yer eckollogy over yer teckology. I'm tockin bout yer Aimish, yer Hutaright, and I dunno

-ARNOULD

how menny Mennanite. They is the best peeple at restrainin therselfs
I ever see. You probly seen them as you wiz by them in yer car. Both
of youse is goin to markit: yer in a helva hurry to stock up before the
hoarders gits ther, but these fokes is jist a clip-cloppin along in a horse
with a buggy

behind. You'd think they wuz all goin to a funerall the pace they is
goin and the close they is ware-in. Or cherch, mebby. Funny enuff,
they ain't got no cherch. They hold servisses regler, but it's in ther
homes or even ther barns. And ther's no minster lordin it over them
by degrees. Their preecher is chose by lottry, if they ever use sich a
word. And nobody gits paid fer doin any of that. Them tellyvishun
vangelists must think these peeples is stark stare-in nuts.

But these peeple got the saim altitude to Naycher as our Ab-origi-
nals. You gotta giv back to Muther Erth wat you took. Modren
aggerculcherists hoo is outstandin in ther feelds say leeve it to the
experks to figger out, speshully if they is in the hire of a kemikle
cumpny. Wile ther all erjin farmers to git morn more expansive, these
Aimishable peeple gits morn more restrainin. And modrens sorta
snickers at them as sum old-time relick, like a scarecrow. But the point
of tillin yer erth is helth. Not jist fer yerself and yer land, but yer hole
commoonity, yer land and yer planit. And yer Mennanite bunch has
dun this by restricktin therselfs in every way, frum masheens, frum
wore (they are all patsy-fists) and, as much as they kin, frum
guvmint—federast, pervinshul and moony-pissiple.

Everybuddy elts thinks these peeple is kwaint, pitcheresk, weerd,
exstream, backerd, probly slubversiv, and certny over-relijuss. But any
farmer hoo noes his salt, noes that they're the best at ther job of any
of us. With small farms fallin on all sides, these so-call relijuss
fannyticks kin take them over and expand, but not into a meggy-
bizness. They is self-contaners, pervidin ther own wellfair, secyourity
and sociabull insurience, by ignorin guvmints with ther undivide
attenshun and stickin to ther own famly and common-unity.

Wat's ther secreet? They don't compeats with one anuther! They
don't use all ther no-how fer to pray on eech uther, and they don't
cast-off ther old peeples or bandon ther childern. Summa ther childern
is leevin the farms, but that's cuz this bunch is so blaim furtle that
sum of the yung has to make ther way in the towns, cummin back on
weak ends fer all that home-cookin that makes yer lips shmeck together. Fer them that staze, everybuddy is bizzy and everybuddy has
a use. And wat we mite call demeenin drudjery they calls Good Helth-
keepin fer the sake of awl.

They wood say that the werd perduckshun is a dillusion of yer
mail eego, witch thinks it duz things all by itself, and is out to brake
all reckerds. But reaperduckshun needs yer femail part too, and this
act happens not once, like in a stripmine, but agin and agin, seizin
after seizin. I got a distaff on my staff and I'd abin bankrupchured
long ago if she hadden bin round fer to keep our books and me outa
the porehouse.

I'll tell you ther uther secreets. Wile the rest of us farmers is sayin
"let us spray," they're out rowtatin ther crops every yeer frum rye to

Harland Williams
———
I bought one of those milk-
shakes in a carton the other
day. It said "Shake twenty-two
times." I shook it twenty-three.
Blew my hand off.

weet to corn to clover and First and Second Timothy. That givs them bugs no chants to settle down and raze a famly over the winter, and also lets yer goodlady bug do her work fer free. These Mennanite noe that erthworms duz more good than trackters in yer long runs, fer them little burrowers brakes up yer soil, and makes it eezier to work. Them trackters compacks the ground like a horse don't. And horses gives you less erozeshun not to menshun instant-on the spot-deliverd fertlyizer.

Mebby we shud all take lessins frum these Cristchun farmers. We all got eclectic lites but sumhow I think we're more in the dark. Speekin of witch we pert neer cum close to freezin in the dark a duzzen or so yeers ago wen the Arbs had us over a barl, but we restraned ourselfs and becum oily conservayshunists so that now them sheek peeple is up to ther barenooses in glutz of oil. Mind you, the same short-edge cood happin agin if we don't take a kew frum our best farmers, yer Aimish, woo ar a lotless Aimlesh then the rest of us.

TRAPPER

The Frantics

(Door light fade up. The trader is onstage behind a table. A trapper hops in on one leg.)

RENÉ: I'm a trapper!

TRADER: Yes?

RENÉ: I'm here to trade some furs.

TRADER: What do you got?

(René pulls out a little ratty squirrel tail. Trader holds onto it and just stares.)

RENÉ: Here you go. *(Reading from list.)* Now I'd like four pounds of flour, three pounds of dried beef jerky, two pounds sugar, one pound salt, sour dough bread, a couple of knives, eight rounds of gun shot, three pouches of gun powder, salted cod, birchbark canoe repair kit, insect repellant, fishing rod, fishing line, deck of Bicycle playing cards, coonskin cap size six and seven eighths, snow shoes, back pack, paddle, leghold traps—the kind that don't hurt, case of wine, and a set of lawn darts.

TRADER: Mister, this is a squirrel's tail.

RENÉ: No, that's a mink tail.

TRADER: This mink—was it a cute, perky bucktoothed li'l feller or a long, wiry vicious-looking cuss?

RENÉ: It was, yeah, like the first one.

TRADER: That's a squirrel.

René: Not worth as much as a mink?

Trader: Not quite.

René: Oh well then forget about the lawn darts. I'll just have to rough it.

Trader: You don't get it mister. Squirrel tail ain't worth diddly! I can't trade you nuthin' for it.

René: But you don't know what I went through to get that pelt. Don't I get anything for effort?

Trader: Sorry.

René: Now listen here you...you...Hudson Bay trading company scum! You know nothing of the conditions which I, as a rugged fur trapper, have had to endure! The endless cold nights! The cries of wolves and moose and ducks that scare the shit out of you! Weeks at a time spent following your own footprints. The low-hanging branches that poke you in the eye. Setting down leghold traps only to step in them yourself, then chewing off your own leg.

(The trader looks at the missing leg.)

So here I stand after traversing the most northern reaches of this unchartered, desolate land, pelt in hand, and you dare tell me that this is worthless.

Trader: Yup.

René: Oh...Can't I get anything for it?

Trader: No.

René: A pickle?

Trader: No.

René: A mint?

Trader: No.

(This goes on for a bit until...)

René: Can I have that bit of thread on the floor?

Trader: Sure.

(René snatches up the thread, hands the trader the tail, and skips out.)

René: I'm a trapper! I'm a trapper! I'll see you in two months.

Trader *(to audience)***:**   Two months later.

(René comes in, both legs gone, shuffling on the floor. He stops and pulls out a dead cat.)

René: I got a mink!

(Blackout.)

Howie Mandel

I ordered a chicken and an egg, 'cause I just wanted to see what would come first.

FROM *ST. FARB'S DAY*

Morley Torgov

Barney's at lunchtime is the New York stock exchange at the height of the crash, D-Day at Normandy, the entire Middle East crisis, all contained within a narrow corridor about forty feet in length and just wide enough to swing a chopped egg on a kaiser. There is a sense here that Western civilization has already declined and is on the verge of falling and that only the speedy delivery of short-order food may stem for a time—perhaps an hour or two, a day at most—the extinction of the human species. The phones ring incessantly with take-out orders and Barney answers them, often all three at a time, with unconcealed impatience, a man biting the hands that he feeds. Steaming plates of food are passed over patrons' heads and behind their backs andbetween their noses and the newspapers they are trying to read while they sit either on stools at the long counter or in the cramped booths that line one wall of the place. Muttering mutinously, Barney's waiters and short-order cooks (every one of whom has the face of somebody who has done time in maximum security) move surefootedly from counter to grill to freezer to sink to fryer doing everything with vengeful expertise, asking nothing of the customer save that he or she order, eat and get out so the next customer can order, eat and get out.

"I *hate* this place," says Kelly Greenglass. He and Farb occupy a booth at the rear of the restaurant. "You can just feel the cholesterol in the air." Greenglass's shoulders shiver with disgust.

Farb holds out the palm of his hand in the aisle, testing the air. "I don't feel a thing," he says, "except acute hunger. Know what I love about this joint? Order a green salad, they throw you out—right on your exercise-loving ass. It's against the law here to drink coffee without 18 percent cream and double sugar." Farb grins. He knows this is getting to Kelly.

Young Greenglass watches a waiter deliver an order of salami and fried eggs with a side of french fries and toast to the man in the next booth. "I asked for toast well buttered," the man says to the waiter, his hands pleading for a little justice and compassion. Like a robot, the waiter removes the toast and heads for the butter pot.

"These people are killing themselves," says Greenglass.

"My dad's eighty-nine. Ate lunch here every day for years right up to a couple of years ago when he had his stroke. Eighty-nine!"

"He never would've had that stroke if he'd watched his diet," Greenglass asserts, righteous as a glass of skim milk.

"Pish tosh, Greenglass. Give the man here your order."

Regarding the dirty-aproned waiter as if the poor fellow has just been convicted of rape, Greenglass says curtly, "Two poached eggs, dry whole-wheat toast, large orange juice."

"We don't poach 'em at lunch. Only breakfast. Fried or scrambled?"

Farb enjoys watching his young partner commit nutritional suicide. "Okay," says Greenglass to the waiter, "scrambled, but with margarine. I don't use butter."

The waiter couldn't care less. "Anything you say, chief," he says to Greenglass and looks to Farb.

"The usual for me, Charlie," says Farb. The usual, for Farb, is a chopped liver appetizer with coleslaw, sliced tomatoes, two thick slices of dark rye, tea and lemon.

"I don't know why I let you drag me to this place," Greenglass pouts after the waiter yells their order halfway down the corridor to one of the short-order cooks behind the counter. "I could've been at the club having a good game of squash instead of sitting here filling myself with calories."

"Honest to God, Kel," says Farb, a thin edge of sarcasm in his voice, "I wouldn't have asked you to make the ultimate sacrifice except something important has come up and I need your input." Farb begins to relate the morning's happenings, going into such meticulous detail that the only thing missing is the actual punctuation. Greenglass, who was a law clerk in Farb's office and readily accepted Farb's invitation to join the firm after graduation, never ceases to be amazed at the older lawyer's awareness of mood, nuance, snippets of dialogue. To Farb, a woman glancing ever so fleetingly at her fingernails, a man brushing his hand quickly across the knot of his necktie...such barely perceptible acts often warrant as much of his attention as the stacks of documents and affidavits and letters that swell his case files into rows of highrises atop his desk.

Farb pauses in the narrative while the waiter sets down their food, observing with some inner satisfaction that Kelly Greenglass's scrambled eggs are afloat in a sea of melted butter. This fact Kelly—who is now absorbed in Farb's story—chooses to overlook. "Go on, go on," Kelly urges.

"Well," says Farb, after he has finished both the narrative and the chopped liver, "the question now is how the hell do we play the next act? Seems to me, no matter what tack we take, it's a no-win situation for the firm of Farb & Greenglass. As I see it at the moment, like it or not we're on the hook to *both* sides. On the one hand, I think I'm obligated to inform Kopman and Slatkin (a) that Shahani, alias Black and White Investments, is a client of ours, and (b) that Shahani's partners in the deal are the very people who are purporting to act as Kopman and Slatkin's agents, and since there's no disclosure of this latter fact in the papers, that's a triple A no-no. On the other hand, if I pass all this information on to Kopman and Slatkin, then surely I'm acting to the detriment of another client, namely Patrick Shahani. On top of which, I've already planted clearly in the ladies' minds that Black and White Investments must be a speculator, so already the old girls are out for blood. Once they find out exactly how this guy Hagan and his fellow genius, Rebecca Schwab-Henderson, are involved, even blood won't be enough."

Without realizing what he is doing, Kelly reaches across the table, filches a crust of Farb's double rye, and begins to munch on it thoughtfully. "Haven't you already solved the problem?" he asks. "After all, you've told Shahani our firm can't act for him in this deal and sent him away. He'll get himself another law firm and that'll be that, won't it?"

"Not quite, Kel. Trouble is, I should've sent him packing the minute he opened those papers and I spotted that he is Black and White Investments. I shouldn't 've let him open his mouth beyond that point. Before I knew what the hell was happening, he'd spilled most of his guts. You know Pat—he's like a big sheepdog; not an ounce of guile in the man."

Greenglass, having polished off the crust, absentmindedly reaches for a second piece left over on Farb's plate.

"You still hungry, kid?" Farb can't help it; whenever his younger partner shows signs of hunger, a cold, a headache, or any kind of indisposition, Farb becomes older-brotherly and takes to calling Kelly "kid." So far, in the decade or so they've been together in the practice of law, Kelly Greenglass has raised no objections to being called "kid" on occasion, especially since Farb is at least sensitive enough not to use the term when clients are present.

Chewing slowly on a piece of crust, Kelly says, "A big sheepdog Shahani may be. But as for his not having an ounce of guile, I'm not too sure. Patrick's got his own bag of tricks, you know. He didn't get his millions by being Mr. Nice Guy all the time. I mean, look at the way he plays with his own kids. About the only thing Rose and Pat Jr. haven't got around to doing yet is turning themselves into burnt offerings just to please the old guy. Talk about a professional manipulator!"

"C'mon, Kelly, lots of people, especially parents, are clever at that sort of stuff. It doesn't mean they're crooks and conspirators."...

Greenglass nods in the direction of Farb's plate; there is one lonely slice of tomato remaining. Farb slides the plate across the beige Arborite tabletop. "There's a bit of coleslaw left," Farb says. He slides a side dish across the table as well, and watches Greenglass finish off the leftovers. The word "devour" comes to Farb's mind—Greenglass has obviously been starving himself to death. How else can the young lawyer fit into Italian-made suits cut for men who have no waistline, no hips, no buttocks, no thighs, and, presumably, possess removable genitals which they leave in a drawer at home during the day? "Tell you something, kid," Farb says. "Has it ever occurred to you that maybe you're starving to death?"

"Given a choice," says Greenglass, "I'd prefer to die thin."

"Why? So it'll be easier on your pallbearers? C'mon, for Chrissakes, give in a little, kid. I'm gonna order you dessert. They got great rice pudding here—"

"With raisins?"

"Just like your dear ol' mom used to make." Farb catches the waiter's eye. "One rice pudding with whipped cream, Charles."

"Why one?" Kelly asks. "What about you?"

"Hate the stuff," Farb replies.

Kelly accepts the rice pudding without protest but carefully removes the whipped cream topping, as if transforming sin into virtue by a single stroke of his spoon. Catching this, Farb smiles. "Y'know, kid, you got it all wrong. When you die and go to that great fitness institute in the sky," he says to Kelly, "they examine your *soul* up there, not the contents of your stomach. You worry too much."

"Let's stick to legal ethics, Farb," says Greenglass, gulping a heaping spoonful of rice pudding. "Religion, I'll get tomorrow morning at my nephew's bar mitzvah."

ADVENTURES IN THE NIB TRADE

Douglas Fetherling

A person can read a lot into the fact that sales of fountain pens have more than doubled in recent years, both in Britain and the U.S., where industry-wide figures are kept, and probably also in Canada, where apparently none are. In 1988, for example, Americans bought 12 million of the objects at a cost of $82 million in their money, as what at first seemed like a mere fad became a longer-term condition, one that already looks to be as permanent as such trends in public taste usually are. Various reasons are being advanced for this phenomenon.

One of the commonest explanations is that the fountain pen is a sign of token resistance to the accelerating pace of greed in Western society, a mild attempt to pretty up the surface of daily life without altering the substance. There's certainly no denying that the heft of the fountain pen, or perhaps the way the ink flow seems to adjust itself to the speed of one's thoughts, restores a little bit of dignity, a note of elegance, to the act of writing. But surely the fountain pen is a protest not against materialism (wait until you read how much some of these things cost, below) but against the ballpoint, which is to say against the headlong rush towards awful efficiency. Fountain pens are conservative all right, but they're definitely not Thatcheristic, Mulroneylike or Reaganesque.

Reagan preferred felt-tip pens (it figures) until the Parker Pen Co. persuaded him to use one of its famous products when he signed the intermediate nuclear weapons treaty with Mikhail Gorbachev in 1987. We don't know what he's used since or what George Bush prefers (hard to figure out the stylus preferences of a Yaley who moved to Texas) and we have no idea what Mr. Gorbachev's tastes are in these matters. Anyway, the Parker firm enjoys a thick slice of the market, with pens costing as little as $30 and as much as $3,500, though many specialty concerns routinely charge even more for theirs. For example, Cartier, the New York jewelers which hadn't dealt in fountain pens for years, got back into the market in 1981, a beautifully timed reappearance. There's no question whatever, though, that it is the Parker people who have done so much to bring about the revival or at least to egg it on. Their PR has come out as smoothly as blue-black ink from the gold-wing nib of, say, a hand-engraved Mont Blanc

Meisterstuck (you don't want to know the price except that it's in guineas, not pounds.)

The fountain pen, with its self-sustaining ink bag, made the hand-dipped pen obsolescent in 1884. The date seems perfect if you think about it; fountain-pen technology must of course be contemporary with the elevator, the typewriter and the telephone, rather than with, say, the motor car, the wireless and the wristwatch of the succeeding generation. The first colossal figure of the industry was George Parker, the founder of the Jamesville, Wisconsin, company that bears his name. The earliest of his famous promotional coups was seeing that one of his products was used to sign the treaty that ended the Spanish-American War of 1898. The treaty was signed in Paris. It had long seemed appropriate that treaties should be executed there. But from that day forward, diplomatic etiquette seemed to require that the deed be done with fountain pens specifically. The idea lasted slightly longer than the demand that the signatories wear striped trousers and claw-hammer coats.

The story is told of George Parker beating his way back and forth across China, looking for a particular resin—"mandarin yellow," it's called in the parlance of the nib trade—to use on what became his Big Yellow line. A restored Big Yellow can run to about $1,500 now. Parker's best known design, however, was the Parker Duofold. It became ubiquitous, the four-door sedan of writing implements. A replica of a first-generation Duofold from the 1920s might be had for $350 these days; but the series has been resuscitated, and you may buy a current original for between $125 and $300.

Like Steve Jobs of Apple Computers feeling that he had to top the Macintosh with the NeXT, Parker was at some pains to go beyond his initial success. So it was that in the 1930s he introduced the Parker 51 (today, perhaps $175 from one of the rare pen dealers found here and there in London, the world pen capital). It was with a Parker 51 that General Douglas MacArthur accepted the Japanese surrender ending the Second World War. This fact was significant, indeed ominous, for the fountain pen was one of those things that would never be the same in the new post-war world. In 1939 Lazlo Biro had invented the ballpoint or *biro* as it is known in other than North American English. When the world economy went back to a peacetime footing, his was one of the cheap products seized on with greatest force and celerity.

In certain circles, the fountain pen had always seemed bankerly and corrupt. ("Some people rob you with a sixgun/And some use a fountain pen"—Woody Guthrie.) But now the object became even more of a symbol as it became less of a utensil. It came to symbolize the wretched prewar world with its powerful old men, prepared, like Stalin, to do anything in pursuit of power—when they were not, like Neville Chamberlain, prepared to do as little as possible. Try this quiz. The f——— pen was to Mackenzie King as the b——point was to John F. Kennedy. The ballpoint was the new thing for the new era. James Bond's fountain pen was not used for writing but for blinding and immobilizing the agents of SMERSH and SPECTRE. Nevertheless it was the ballpoint that fought the Cold War.

Ballpoints come in batches, each unit indistinguishable from all the others. They go click-click-click like guns, cameras and other implements of destruction. They can be chained to counter-tops in banks and post offices. They are *de rigueur* in the breast pocket of a short-sleeve shirt that's 50-percent polyester, thus limiting their attraction even more to people who promised Mother on her deathbed that they would never wear blends. The blind beggars you still see on street corners in cities like Marseilles refuse to have any truck with ballpoints and continue to fill their tin cups with pencils exclusively.

Ballpoints often come with advertising messages along the shaft but nothing too clever, nothing the boys down in Creative would ever sully themselves with dreaming up at lunch, but only some sentiment such as E-Z Tax Service, Napanee—"We deliver." In fact, one is constantly ending up with pens whose apparent provenance is a bit of an embarrassment. No, really, I've never been to the Can-Am Erotic Wax Museum in Niagara Falls ("We're never clothed"). The CIA issues ballpoint pens from particular places to its agents in the field, along with matchbooks, candy wrappers and other such "pocket litter."

Virtually all credit card purchases involve the use of ballpoint pens since fountain pens don't disturb the serenity of carbon paper. This circumstance merely emphasizes what was so apparent already: ballpoints are the instruments of credit, fountain pens are instruments of capital. Ballpoints, by tradition, are agents of paranoid bureaucracy, fountain pens expressions of *noblesse oblige*.

**"I'm sorry, I haven't laughed
like this for months."**

–UNGER

Like all small appliances, ballpoints promise to enrich our lives but merely make our sorrow cost effective. They keep the record of dehumanization they cause or at least of that which they contribute to. People inherit good fountain pens, as well as shaving mugs with brushes in them, but no one has ever inherited Bic pens or Bic razors, not even in prisons where Bic products are used as currency, not even in the shyest of the newly emerging countries of the Third World.

As for fountain pens by contrast, I hope we have established that they are the natural enemies of ballpoints.

Let us go forward in the hope they are also a cure.

Thank you for your attendance here this evening.

BAG BABIES

Allan Stratton

(The condo of DICK and JANE JONES. It's in a trendy complex overlooking a park. Decor is minimal, perhaps including marbled floors, glass furniture, mirrors, tile: opulence. In the living room, prominently displayed, is an easel with large promotional flip cards designed for a business presentation. The card on top, in bold lettering, reads "HAVING WITH HEART." DICK and JANE are welcoming RICK and ELAINE into their home. They are all dressed in something Italian.)

ELAINE: Our apologies, please, it's barely eight.
We really intended to be fashionably late
But traffic was good—God, your condo's so sleek!
So Spartan! Postmodern! Dramatic! Unique!
The most radical reno I've been in all week!

RICK *(embarrassed, extends hand)*: By the way, I'm Rick.

ELAINE *(also extending hand)*: Whoops, I'm Elaine.

DICK: Good to meet you at last. We're Dick and Jane.

JANE: Now, if you'd like to give me your mink,
Make yourselves comfy.

DICK: Care for a drink?

ELAINE: Thanks, we'll pass.

RICK: I want a whiskey.

ELAINE: You're driving, dear. It's very risky.

RICK: Okay. I'll settle for a spritzer.
Gimme a little Schlitz and a mixer.

DICK: I hope this isn't cause for tension.

RICK: Nothing that we'd care to mention.

ELAINE: Just a minor marital spat.

JANE: Oh good I'm glad it's only that.
  Keeps marriages from going flat.
  But take a seat, let's have a chat.

(DICK *gets* RICK *a spritzer as the rest move to the living room.*)

ELAINE: I love your stuff! I mean, your clothes!
  To speak of them defies all prose.
  That brooch, that pendant and that ring!
  Handcarved in jade?

JANE (*nodding*): Yes. From Beijing.
  They're very smart with linen suits,
  Pleated, over leather boots.

ELAINE: I have my boots hand tooled in Stutts (*beat*) Gard.

DICK: You buy German?

ELAINE: Lined in ermine.

JANE: How discreet!

RICK: They really make her look a treat.

JANE: I buy mine on trips to Rome
  From a little shop a Zurich gnome
  Referred to us.

DICK: It's called "Il Dome"

JANE: But I prefer to call it home.

  (*sighs*) Italy.

ELAINE (*same tone*): Italy.

RICK: Sure beats Paris!

JANE: French fashions are fashioned as if to embarrass.

ELAINE: They're designs designed for some dowager heiress.

JANE: And that "*je ne sais quoi,*" my God it's passé—

ELAINE: Unless you're bulimic, anorexic or grey.

JANE: It's "*La Crap*" for "*Les Nouveaux*" what more can one
  say?

ELAINE: Oh for Rome, Milano—

JANE: Even Brindisi.
  Italy makes one's shopping so easy!

ELAINE: Thank God. I used to suffer "shopping stress."
  I'd take to bed, in great distress,
  And gobble pills.

JANE: Let's all give thanks
  That God created booze and tranks.

DICK: But small talk aside, let's get clear
  Precisely why you ventured here.

No need to be shy. We know you're nervous
Or you wouldn't have enquired about our service.

RICK (*to* ELAINE)**:**   Tell them. I'm too ashamed to speak.

ELAINE (*blurts out*)**:**   We live quiet lives of desperate chic.

JANE: Poor dears, that's tragic.

ELAINE: Yes, and bleak;
Lives writ by some cathartic Greek!

RICK: I mean, soon as we'd made it, scaled the peak,
We tumbled down, went up the creek.

DICK: The wheel of fortune?

ELAINE: God, we're weak.

RICK: We realized in shame, to wit:
That both our lives are full of shit.
We may be bright, successful, rich...
But I'm a bastard!

ELAINE: I'm a bitch!

RICK: Our generation once blazed like a comet,
But now we're adults we make the world vomit.
Wherever you look, we're under attack,
Called acquisitive pigs by the media pack.

ELAINE: They've raised the most ferocious rumpus:
Said we've lost our moral compass.

RICK: Okay. We're adult. We can take what they hurl—
But it hurts when their crap hits our little girl.

ELAINE: She's smart, she's cute, she's the best kid alive.

RICK: She has it all. And she's only five.
She can swim, play tennis, ride a pony,
Work a Video-Cam.

ELAINE: She has a Sony.

RICK: She's seen symphonies, operas, David Bowie.

ELAINE: By the way, her name is Chloe.

RICK: Her life was perfect until last May—
I remember it like it was yesterday—
Our angel ran home covered in mud
From a fight at her daycare.

ELAINE: Kids called her a crud.

RICK: With tears in her eyes and pigtails askew,
She sobbed, "Why does everyone hate me and you?
Kids say you're a greedy old bag of worms,
And I'm a rich kid with cooties and booger germs."

ELAINE: We both fell apart.

Rick: Our dreams had derailed
For our babe's perfect childhood.

Elaine: God, where had we failed?
What made her this target for playground aversion?

Rick: Her ballet classes?

Elaine: Her French immersion?

Rick: Confused and angry, I started to drink.

Elaine: I went over the brink.
I took to bed, unable to eat.

Rick: Her shrink called it a psychosomatic retreat.

Elaine: All year, depressed, we had weeping wailies,
Until last week while reading the dailies
We caught an article in the Lifestyle section
That got Rick so aroused he got an erection.
Didn't you hon? *(To* DICK *and* JANE.*)* The first one all year.

Rick: You promised you wouldn't mention that here.

Elaine: The headline said:
"Running on Empty? Make a New Start.
For Renewed Self-Esteem Call 'Having With Heart.'"
So we read ahead.

Rick: All about how you promised, no ifs ands or buts,
To give meaningful life to material sluts.

Elaine: Please help us! What's wrong!

Rick: Are we really depraved?

Elaine: Tell us what, in God's name, must we do to be saved?

*(*DICK *and* JANE *flip to a gold card reading* PLACEMENT.*)*

Dick: All life is buy and sell, a fact well-known to Baby
Boomers.
And what we have to sell is us.

Elaine: We're fodder for consumers?

Jane: Even a Grinch in a pinch will flinch
From attacking a certified hero.
Put a halo in place and your odds of disgrace
Are reduced to practically zero.

Rick: So what's the deal?

Jane: We'll market you both as two of the faces
Seen to be seen in all the right places.

Rick: Like where?

Jane *(very smooth)***:** Glad you asked. Dick?

DICK: Thank you, Jane.
For a Teflon reputation you simply can't afford
Not to be on an arts or social service board.
So, for a fee, we'll place you, through our contacts and channels
On many such high-minded boards and panels.

JANE: Soon the activist types who loathe and revile you
Will do handsprings and backflips to charm and beguile you.

ELAINE: Even radical clones who scream no one can trust us—
That we're just greedy pigs out to screw social justice?

DICK: You'll be their closest friends.

JANE: The little principle that'll make you invincible
Is known as means and ends:
Board connections enhance whatever chance
Those radicals have to get their grants.

DICK: Except when dealing with the terminally stupid
Self-interest plays the role of Cupid.

JANE: But to be realistic, no matter the cause,
It won't gain you any acclaim and applause
Without a little well-heeled promotion
To stir up interest and public commotion.

DICK: So kids, get ready for—

DICK AND JANE: The Platinum Plan!

(They flip to a platinum card. It reads PROMO.)

JANE: According to all of our statistics
Folks believe what they're told by the media mystics.
Our response?

DICK: To make you a hit with opinion makers
Our electronic swamis, gurus, fakes and fakirs.

JANE: And once you get real hotsy-totsy,
To set you up with the paparazzi.

RICK: That's a great spiel, but hey get real,
How will you bring the press to heel?

DICK: If you've access to info you're one of the forces
That newspeople call their "inside sources."

JANE: And Dick and I, we certainly do.

DICK: Because of the nature of our milieu,
We know who's hot, who's not and who's got what.

JANE: Presto! For tips and scoops we get action
An arrangement of mutual satisfaction:
We're helping them help us help them with our work.

Dick: It's called a "Social Circle Jerk!" *(Gasp from the others.)*
I don't mean to imply our connection's erotic
Just that our needs are "symbiotic."

Rick: Hot stuff! To be quoted in all of the papers!

Elaine: But what'll we say? You're giving me vapours!
They can be vicious! Mad dogs in a pack!
I'm having a-panic-a-panic attack!!!

Jane: Hold on, Elaine! There's no need to fuss!
For a small added fee leave the thinking to us.

Dick: You'll love it. We call this plan "Platinum Plus!"

Rick and Elaine: "Platinum Plus?"

(Dick and Jane flip to a platinum card reading POP PUFFS.)

Jane: We'll write you a series of appropriate platitudes
Designed to show you've correct social attitudes.
Old sentiments jazzed up to sound new minted.

Dick: With a leaven of hype to make sure they get printed.

Rick: You'll put words in our mouth?

Elaine: It doesn't sound right.

Jane: My God, Elaine, you're far too uptight.
All public leaders whose speeches are toasted
You'll find, on inspection, have had their lines ghosted.

Dick: With our words, you'll shine as you play to the galleries
Winning respect and far higher salaries.

Rick: Hold on. Did I hear you amiss?
You mean we can even make money on this?

Dick: And how.

Dick and Jane: "The Gold Plan Placement Bonus!"

Jane: Through a number of ethical quirks
Mere placement on boards provides lucrative perks.
Like gold-chip networks.

Dick: These increase your chances
Of landing substantial career shift advances.

Jane: And how about—

Dick and Jane: "The Platinum Plan Placement Promo Bonus!"

Jane: In which we take note of this ethical oddity:
Civic heroes are bought as a market commodity.

Dick: Multi-national thugs who pollute our society
Like to make a big show of their corporate piety.
They need "Good Guys" on staff. Human components
In a P.R. ploy to outflank their opponents.

RICK: If we get praised for our work for the masses
The big buck boys will be kissing our asses?

DICK (nods): Instead of corporate shuffles
Which might otherwise have chopped you
You'll be fending off big business types
Attempting to co-opt you.

RICK AND ELAINE: Wow!!!

JANE: We know what you think: it's too good to be true.
But you kids deserve it. I mean, it's *you*!

A TRULY SERIOUS WINE SNOB'S
GUIDE TO RARE WINES

Jurgen Gothe

The recent rash of renewed interest in wines and oenous subjects generated in this country by wine-and-food publications, unscrupulous wine writers like the author, and brash marketeers ready to foist sparkling bilberry wines from Bechauanaland and other exotics upon us, has made for a spate of articles and broadcasts, telling all and sundry what to drink, and how. This has left the Serious Wine Snob without anything on which to lavish serious snobbery. This matter must be remedied.

Cab drivers now readily engage us in conversation, captiveheld as we are in traffic jams and late for planes, on the subtleties of the Bordeaux harvest last year, on the case of nouveau they have lying in the trunk, on the many methods of cork removal, on the forty-gallon pail of wine entirely made from eggplant they've got bubbling under the stairs and how it tastes just like real grapes.

Restaurants that heretofore served perfectly acceptable steak and chips with a Labatt's nice and cold on the side have gone ahead with renovations and sommeliers. It's to the point where in most pizzerias you can't get anything to drink that doesn't come with a cork. In my favourite deli they have the wine chilling right next to the stainless steel bowl of chopped liver. And that's only the red. The white is strung out across the top of the bagel counter in endless variety: medium Riesling, medium Chablis, medium Meursault and my favourite, Ontario Montrachet (medium).

This may all be very nice for ordinary people, but it is easy to see that there is now a void that wants filling, a void created when those selfsame Ordinary People began to discover all the good prestige wines in the world and—worse!—began to actually drink them, and then told their friends.

It has become tremendously difficult to be a proper wine snob, what with coffeeshop waiters curling their lips when you send back the Dinner Red (medium sweet) because there happens to be some sort of large thing floating in the jug standing on your table between the chili and the garlic bread.

It's all well and good to talk about your Châteaux, your Lafites and Yquems and Petrus and the like. Everyone is doing that these days. But who do you know, I mean really well, who can claim to have sipped the fabled Château Nougat, the rare almond-flavoured table wine of the Ozarks? And while your neighbour may go out and buy the same colour Mercedes as the one that's sitting in your drive-way, can he claim to have tasted the silken treasure of Clos de Loch Glenmorangie, one of Scotland's most magnificent green wines, aged in a sheep's stomach still within the sheep, and then burned to a crisp over a peat fire?

And who is there among us who truly knows the delights of just one sip of Mardirosian Plinth-Bage, Israel's proudest cremant, with its sprinkling of poppyseed over the inside of the bottle, making it impossible to ascertain the true color of the wine, although it is re-puted to be a touch on the blue side?

You see?

In the interests of re-establishing ground for the true, dedicated wine snob, I provide here a guide to some of the world's rarest wines. These are decidedly lesser known, eminently snobbable wines, and the information is presented here for the first time anywhere, doubt-less with repercussions to come.

Now that everyone has a pocket edition of Hugh Johnson's in the glove compartment, it is in the interest of all true wine snobs to seek out some of the wines described here. Around the world, numerous wine treasures repose undiscovered, some of them so rare as to never be exported; others are always exported...because their producers know something we don't.

Seek them, find them, and as contemporary wine parlance has it, get to first base with them!

ALBANIA: An emerging wine nation flexes its disused viniferous muscles and makes us wonder!

One of the most interesting little-known wines comes from this tiny country, shrouded in mystery (both the country and the wine: the country discourages tourism, the wine discourages drinking—the neck of the bottle is encased in cement immediately after bottling). The country is a former friend of China and a more recent football great when the national team took a chunk of the Celtics, all of which makes for an interesting wine culture. Vineyards there are still called com-munist plots; the southern valleys are well suited to corn, wheat, and tobacco, as well as grapes, and there is often some confusion as to which goes into the wine.

The native grape is called rohshoke and is not found elsewhere. A hardy, early-ripening grape, it is thought to have been a successful transplant from China, which no longer wanted anything to do with it. It produces one of the most depressing wines known to man or beast. A drab grey is imparted to the wine by the grape skins. These

Howie Mandel

Before I came here tonight, I was at a restaurant. And I ate dinner there, right? 'Cause the guy at the front door said, "No volleyball." That's what he said.

Anyway, we ate there, and it was one of those revolving restaurants, and it was revolv-ing at, like, eighty miles an hour. There were no tables and chairs; they were just stuck to the wall. Food was going by...I spilled some water on me and it dried right away. It was fun—but leaving was a bitch.

are actually tiny, woollen coverlets designed to protect individual grapes from frost and which someone forgot to remove prior to the crush.

The seaport town of Durres on the Adriatic is a major Albanian wine region. Just south of Durres, or actually below it, is the famous Likerimat region. The great wine here is the All-Peoples' Riesling Breakfast Wine; it is said, with geographic accuracy, to be produced "under Durres." Also important is the onomatopoetically named town of Puke; the wine produced here is a robust vin du pays generically known as drivel, a Gheg word meaning "to walk with the aid of grapefruit." Its price is steep: four goats or, for tourists, surrender of any wide-wale corduroy slacks to the customs officers.

This is obviously a nation to watch, because as wine prices continue to climb, the discriminating buyer will soon be looking for alternative sources of wine energy. Albania's greatest wine is a hock called Schloss Hoxha; chilling renders it inert long enough to take the cork out. It must then be placed in the garden, and if by sundown it has not yet exploded it could be said to be drinkable. As an accompaniment to Chinese food it is quite good, as an antiseptic perhaps even better. The important thing to remember is to be careful in the handling.

JAPAN: The rising sun rising to the challenge of a smaller, more compact wine with better mileage!

This industrial nation is making significant strides in the production of fine wines, and although vineyards aren't plentiful in Japan, there are already two on the northern island of Hokkaido (both owned by Sony) and several more renting space on Mount Fuji. Great advances in computer technology have led the Japanese to produce some stunning wines from materials other than grapes.

Also, the Japanese nomenclature reflects a colourful independence: Ryokan Tarbel is one of the best of the new Japanese transistor wines—light, fruity, quixotic, frivolous and bouncy, it may well be the only wine in the world that can successfully accompany sashimi.

Another unique Japanese wine derives as a logical extension of the traditional rice-wine brewing technique, resulting in Sake Eiswein. Rice is quick-frozen and then subjected to bombardment by high-speed neutrinos, resulting in a tough, viscous wine that can hold water for up to six days.

Finally, no discussion of the new Japanese wines would be complete without mention of Machigai. This wine, produced from certain rarely benign acids, is frequently drunk after the improper preparation of fugu.

CANADA: The land of the maple leaf is in there too!

Yes, we need take no secondary position to anyone when it comes to producing a fine rare wine, because the Blue Wine of Prince Edward Island (Baby Spud) has been eagerly received by appreciators of wine around town and as far west as Summerside.

It is potassium from the potato-field fallow mixed with the characteristic red soil of the island that produces this distinctive blue wine. An unexpectedly delightful feature is the tendency of the wine, due to its high potassium and magnesium content, to burn under water.

Describing its taste in typical Canadian fashion, wine writer Dan Blank wrote in a recent issue of *Vintages of the Laurentian Shield*, a weekly newsletter: "Sort of, oh, I don't know...a bit like...well, it's got a kind of definite...howyoucallit...um, something. But big, oh goodness, yes, big, a big wine. Take the truck when you get that taste happening."

Canadian chronicler of the spoken word John Robert Colombo has taken note of this and is reported to have begun work on *Canadian Quotations About Wine, Volume 1: A to A-Minus*, due next spring from Hurtig of Edmonton.

With all those wines ready for the finding, the serious wine snob need never again be wheedled into ordering yet another tired La Tache or Margaux or Pommery et Greno.

Now you can look the waiter straight in the eye and say: "Bring us six or eight bottles of that Château Malamute '07. Now there's one of the best sparkling wines Alaska ever produced."

And who do you know has even *heard* of that, let alone knocked back a six-pack?

THE BORDER SHOPPING SONG

Moxy Früvous

We were thinking of our shrinking Früvous budget
And we could sit and curse and angrily begrudge it
Or we could spend the weekend in Fort Erie having fun
And while we're at it make a speedy Border run!

Yes we'll be stocking up on sinful little pleasures
And then we'll speed through the express lane with our
   treasures
This border shopping is a lot more fun than one might think,
   in fact
Until last week I didn't smoke or drink!

Drinks are duty free, smokes are duty free
This is gonna be, quite a shopping spree
Toys and gasoline, nylon neoprene
Toilet paper and soap

(To the tune of New York, New York.*)*

Start packing the car
I'm leaving today
I'm gonna buy a ton of it
 In old New York!
Canadian goods
They're yesterday's news
These days I'm buying stars and stripes
Check out these shoes!

I want to buy it in a city that sells it cheap
And find I've gone for a drive
Saved me a heap!

(Our tune here.)

There's a bold new future high on the horizon
And a VCR I've kind of had my eyes on
But does this border shopping have a darker side?
And are we being taken for a ride?

Say what's all the fuss?
Free Trade's gotta grow
But it's a fear of fiscal consequence for Canada
And that our companies will move to Mexico!

But we've got no choice
More taxes each year
But if we're spending all our money in the U.S.A.
Then our social programs may just disappear

(To the tune of The Sabre Dance.*)*

There's lots of merchandise it's super-duper what a price
And Carvel ice-cream will entice,
It's shopping that you simply can't ignore
Buy more!

Spent Sunday in your Honda, fighting crowds in Tonawanda
More exhausting than Jane Fonda
And you've only got ten minutes more

You rush to Onandaga race across to Cheektowaga
Feeling like your shopping saga's Worthy of a spot on
    Channel Four
News Four

Then driving home you wonder if your pillage and your
    plunder
Hasn't been a massive blunder

(*To the tune of* New York, New York.)

Alright let's be frank
We lose at the bank
Free Trade is shutting business down
So Moxy propose—
We trade the G.S.T.
For Jan and Wayne Gretzky
And keep our cash in this country!

OHIP, Medicare, welfare we can share
University, U.I. subsidy
Trough.

THE MAN WHO KNEW TOO MUCH

Charles Gordon

Two years ago D. decided to live without information. Although friends still question his decision, he is convinced that he made the right one. D. (not his real initial) decided to do without information during the week of the two-headed cabbage. You remember it. An amateur gardener grew a two-headed cabbage and took it, as proud gardeners do, to the local newspaper office. A picture was taken, a story was published and the normal information process began. The wire services picked up the two-headed cabbage story and added comments from whichever public officials happened to be in a talkative mood that day. The minister of agriculture was not available, but the minister of science and technology was. He said that the government was unlikely to take a position on two-headed cabbages one way or another.

On network television, the farmer was linked by satellite with a farmer from the Soviet Union and with the Washington correspondent for a British newspaper, who didn't say anything about cabbages but spoke authoritatively anyway. As for network radio, the proud gardener was out when the radio telephoned, but his wife gave an interview.

"How does your husband feel about this?" the radio asked, and when she said that her husband was out, the radio asked her how she felt, then. She said that she felt fine and only wished that her husband was around to answer all these questions. She said her husband was out being interviewed by a magazine, which she didn't name, for a cover story tentatively entitled "Those crazy vegetables."

Network radio also telephoned an Irish pub and got the reactions of everyone there.

D. began to feel the stirrings that would lead him to give up information. His local newspaper prepared a series on strange vegetables in the immediate area and quoted local professors on what might be responsible for two-headed cabbages not being grown around there. The professors refused to be drawn into predicting when the area might have its first two-headed cabbage. "That would depend on a lot of things," one professor said.

Local television interviewed educational experts about whether discussion in the schools about two-headed cabbages would upset students unnecessarily or whether students in the upper grades could handle it. The question of drugs in the schools, as it related to two-headed cabbages, was raised. The local morning show interviewed psychiatrists who said that there was no need to be alarmed. "Are you *sure*?" the morning-show host asked. A psychiatrist said that you could never be 100-percent sure about anything. D. turned off his radio.

When he told people that he had stopped listening to radio morning shows, stopped watching television public-affairs programs, stopped reading newspapers and magazines, his friends were appalled. "How will you keep up?" they asked him. D. said there was nothing to keep up with, just a lot of information about nothing. "You don't understand," D.'s friends said. "This is an information society. Pretty soon 75 percent of all jobs will be in the information field."

D. said that he thought that he liked it better when everybody was drawing wood and hewing water, or however that went. "Well then," said D.'s friends, delivering the clincher, "if you don't read the newspaper, how will you know what's on TV?" D. said that he would figure that out by turning on the TV. And when his friends said that he would never, using that method, be able to plan ahead to watch the public-affairs shows, D. just nodded.

Life without information went fairly well. D. found that he had to be careful at the supermarket check-out counter to keep from reading headlines about Martian diets and the newest diseases of soap-opera stars. But he was able to smile when his friends told him about the latest developments in the information field. "They've got access-to-information laws now," D.'s friends said. "The government has to cough up all kinds of terrific stuff. Yesterday the newspapers got the complete dental records of a former minister of finance. There was a great fuss. Television interviewed a couple of former dentists, and radio had a live interview with some people in an Irish pub." D. said that was nice and went back to his house, where he lived in more or less the same way he had before he gave up information. Talking to people, he found that in giving up information he had joined a group that was larger than he had thought. Many people had given up information, some of them decades ago. There were people who did not know that the Beatles had broken up. There were people who did not know about astroturf, videotape, Grace Jones, nouvelle cuisine and the cuisine before that. They seemed to be getting on all right.

There were people who did not know that disco was dead or even that disco had been born. There were people who wore wide ties and did not know about the several rises and falls of roller skating. The move away from pastels and back to earth colours had escaped the attention of many; many others had missed the earlier move to pastels. These people, when they wanted to paint their walls, just bought whatever colour paint they liked, apparently. D.'s self-imposed abstinence from information caused him to miss several close calls for the government of the day and the leaders of the other parties. Frequently it appeared that the government was about to fragment into internal dissension. Meanwhile, the other parties were consumed with bickering that threatened to explode and dissolve the entire fabric of party unity. Or so it was explained.

It was only by the sheerest of luck that the parties and their leaders survived. D. was unaware of that, as he was unaware of the aerobic calf-roping fad. That was the one where young urban dwellers had lots of fun visiting calf-roping parlours, falling onto the specially imported sawdust and trying to tie up computerized calves before the bar closed.

People said that the best thing about aerobic calf-roping was the marvellous look of the calf-roping outfits everybody was wearing, but D. didn't know about that. Unenlightened and outwardly happy, he went off to his place of work five days a week, leaving his radio on at home, where the sound of information might frighten off potential burglars.

—CLEMENTS

FROM *LETTERS FROM WINGFIELD FARM*

Dan Needles

A ONE-MAN SHOW/TRILOGY OF PLAYS ABOUT A CITY MAN WHO
DECIDES TO BUY A FARM AND TRIES TO MAKE IT A SUCCESS.

July 25

I was trying out the team again in a fairly simple exercise with a stone boat this morning. Since it has no tongue to break and no moving parts of any kind, I thought it would offer good training at low risk to life and property. But within ten minutes we had worked up to a level of excitement worthy of the Calgary Stampede. So I put both horses on report and went up to Freddy's to pick out an older, more experienced animal, before it went to Owen Sound for glue production.

Freddy and I leaned against the corral fence and I watched the herd mill by as Freddy listed the track record, pedigree, and hoof size of any individual he thought might appeal to me. They were a pretty nondescript lot, but Freddy's patter buffed them up a bit.

"Well now, Walt, you see the big chestnut mare there? The one with one ear, yeah. You see the way she holds her head? What a stride! Don't pay any attention to that bit of mange over the withers, Walt. That'd clear up with the sun on it in no time. And you see that two-year-old? He'd make a dandy hunter...with a little work. You could have him registered, if you want."

In Freddy's eyes, any horse who can stagger onto a truck unassisted can be registered. A big colt lumbered by.

"That fella's mother was a thoroughbred...and his father was half quarter-horse."

Great, I thought, That would make him seven-sixteenths dog food.

"Sure, he's ugly," said Freddy, with his auctioneer's gift for perceiving silent skepticism. "Most yearlings are. But strong, you know. His mother won a couple of races at Woodbine. I've half a mind to take that young fella and race him myself. There's a lot of money in him, if you bring him along right."

Despite the brilliant future ahead for this colt, his price was the same as the rest: a hundred bucks.

"You're lookin' for somethin' heavier, are you? To draw, like? Well, come on inside and I'll show you old King."

Freddy opened the barn door and we stepped into the gloom of the stable. It was cold and damp and the air was heavy with the smell of horse, harness and hoof paint. Half-way down a row of hefty Holstein cows, a huge black work horse towered fully three feet above the rest of the animals. Only the shoulders and hindquarters were available for viewing. The head was out of sight somewhere at the bottom of the oat box. It looked like a great big, black grand piano on edge.

As Freddy listed the options on this animal I began to wonder if he came with a head. I reached out to touch him on the flank and an enormous head rose up from the oat box and turned to look at me. For a moment, I felt as if I was looking into the eyes of some ancient priest of Shangri-La. In those luminous brown pools I caught a glimpse of yesterday, before the milk wagon, before the prairie schooner...even before King Arthur's court. This was a very old horse.

"Hullo, King," I said.

The head returned to the oat box.

"I guess this fella would be old enough to vote, Walt," said Freddy, edging up beside the horse to undo his halter.

"But strong. As long as these fellas keep their teeth, they never quit. You fit him up with a set of dentures and he'll last you another twenty years. Hyep!"

Freddy leaned over the oat box and spoke very distinctly into King's left ear as if he were speaking into an apartment intercom.

"Back up, King. Back up."

I understand that the pilot of an airliner has to wait seven seconds after applying the throttle before the engines respond. It was the same with King. The head rose up from the oat box, a blast from the nostrils filled the stall with a fine spray, one enormous hoof rose and came down almost tentatively on the cement walkway. Joints cracked, bulk shifted and King was under way.

There is something very impressive about a really big horse. I remember when I was a kid going down to the Royal Winter Fair in Toronto and watching the big Belgians and Clydesdales line up for their events. I remember most of all their huge soft noses, big kind eyes and hooves the size of dinner plates that came down on the concrete with a clank you could feel through the soles of your boots twenty feet away. I can't say I ever dreamed of owning one; they seemed so impossibly big and far away. But I did dream of having one as a friend some day, to go and visit.

Once he was out in the sunshine, I could see that King was a far cry from those sleek bob-tailed Belgians and Percherons with their nickel-plated harnesses. But the eyes and the nose and the dinner plates...they were all there, all right.

"A hundred bucks, Walt," said Freddy.

Same as the rest. And so I led old King down the Seventh Concession, his great chipped hooves scraping along and his nose barely three inches off the ground, blowing up little hurricanes of dust every few steps. I opened the gate to the pasture, unsnapped the lead rope and gave King a slap on the rump as he plodded by me into his new home. The look he gave his new pasture-mates, Feedbin and Mortgage, was one of unspeakable weariness, as if he had seen so many pastures and so many pasture-mates that all sense of novelty was hopelessly lost for him.

I've never seen Don laugh so hard. I didn't expect Don to see what I see in King. But then I didn't expect him to tell me that I could have saved a hundred bucks by throwing a horsehair rug over a rail fence and emptying the wood-stove ash bucket over it. The reaction

Bob Edwards

"How about that horse you sold me last week," said a man to Johnny Hamilton last Saturday in the Alberta Hotel dining room. "It's as blind as a badger. I thought you said it had no faults."

"So I did," replied Johnny, gazing at the bill of fare. "But blindness is not a fault. It's a misfortune—I'll take some corned beef and cabbage, please."

—*Wetaskiwin Free Lance*, February 20, 1899

elsewhere in the neighbourhood has been much the same. King's age has been estimated at somewhere between eighteen and fifty-five and his pedigree judged to involve Percheron, Clydesdale, Belgian, musk-ox or woolly mammoth...take your pick. But I don't care. I've always wanted a quiet horse with some character, and I've certainly got that.

I can see them all down in the pasture now; my herd—Feedbin, Mortgage and old King. King has a couple of birds perched on his back, just like a dead elm stump. He hasn't moved in over an hour. He just stands there, staring sadly at the ground, as if some great tragedy were unfolding in the ant kingdom below.

This place gets to look more and more like a farm every day.

FROM *LOVE AND ANGER*

George F. Walker

(SARAH *is sitting behind Maxwell's desk. Feet up. Reading Gail's story. Crying gently. Humming an African song. A knock on the outer door. Sound of it opening. Muffled voices.* HARRIS *and* CONNER *come in. Overcoats, silk scarves. Look at* SARAH. *At each other.*)

HARRIS: Excuse me?...Excuse me?

SARAH: Be with you in a minute. Just want to finish reading this beautiful paragraph...Beautiful and sad. This girl's a genius. Someone should tell her. ..I'll do it.

(SARAH *looks up.*)

HARRIS: We're looking for Peter Maxwell.

SARAH: Not here.

CONNER: Yeah, we can see that. Is he coming back?

SARAH: Sure.

CONNER: When.

SARAH: Don't know.

HARRIS: Are you a friend of his?

(*She looks at them for a moment.*)

SARAH: Are you?

CONNER (*to* HARRIS): Fuck him. Let's go.

HARRIS: I think it's worth one final effort all things considered. Don't you?

CONNER: Yeah. I guess.

HARRIS (*to* SARAH): Do you mind if we wait?

SARAH: Sure. Sit on that couch.

Harris: Thanks. We know it's late. But we saw the lights on. I heard he works late. Sometimes even sleeps here.

(They take off their coats. They both have on black and white formal wear. SARAH bolts out of her chair.)

Sarah: Holy shit! You look like a couple of vampires!...You can't walk around with those things on. Don't you realize the images those things conjure up?

Harris: We've just come from a function.

Sarah: You look like you've come from a dinner at the Reichstag. Some family affair of the Third Reich. You look like Goering. You look like Speer.

Conner *(to HARRIS)*: What is all this Nazi crap around here? Are these people living in the goddamn past...I mean, it's starting to really annoy me.

Sarah: Take them off. Take them off!...Come on. They're scaring me. I'm gonna wet my pants or something. Jesus. At least loosen the ties. Undo a button or two. You look like machines. Nazi vampire machines. I'm getting scared. Look guys I really mean it...Loosen your ties!!

(HARRIS does.)

Harris *(to CONNER in a whisper)*: Loosen your tie.

Conner: What for?

Harris: She's scared. Look at her.

Conner: That's her problem. It's a tie. It's just a tie.

Harris: So just loosen it. What's the big deal? It scares her.

Conner: Why?

Harris: I don't know. Ask her.

Conner: Ah. The hell with it. *(He loosens his tie.)*

Harris *(to SARAH)*: Better?

Sarah: A little...So you were at a function. That's nice. I used to function...Now I just dream. *(She starts to read again.)*

Conner: What's she talking about?

Harris: I don't know.

Conner: Who is she?

Harris: I don't know.

Conner: Ask her.

Harris: You ask her.

CONNER *(to* SARAH*):*   Hey you! What are you doing here? Are you a client?

(SARAH looks up. Slowly.)

SARAH: Client? What made you ask that? Why didn't you ask if I was a lawyer? Does it look like I couldn't be a lawyer...for some reason?

HARRIS: Are you a lawyer?

SARAH: Yes.

HARRIS: You work with Mr. Maxwell?

SARAH: I'm his new partner. My name is Sarah Downey.

(She stands, walks to them. Puts out her hand. HARRIS and CONNER look at each other. Shake with her in turn.)

HARRIS: Sean Harris.

CONNER: John...Conner.

SARAH: Perhaps I can help you. Are you looking for a lawyer?

CONNER: We're looking for Maxwell.

SARAH: You have... some reason you don't want to do business with me...You don't do business with black people?

HARRIS: I beg your pardon?

[Anthologizer's note: SARAH is a white woman who thinks she is black.]

SARAH: Oh excuse me. I should have been more subtle. But sometimes the yoke slips you know. The beast escapes. Stand up straight. Tells it like it is. *(She gives them a Nazi salute.)*

CONNER: Let's get outta here.

HARRIS: OK.

SARAH: OK?...OK OK. I've had my laugh. You guys are too much. Lighten up! I'm sorry for stringing you along. I don't know. Maybe it's the way you're dressed. It just brought out the mischief in me. You gotta believe me. I'm sorry. Now what can I do for you...Come on. I'm Peter's partner. Do you want to see my degree?

(And now SARAH is a lawyer. A pretty good one.)

CONNER AND HARRIS: Yes.

SARAH: What is it? The way I'm dressed? I was cleaning up the office. We can't afford a janitor for God's sake. Come on what's the problem? You have some problem with Peter, I take it...Something I can probably help you with.

Conner: I want him off my back. You think you can arrange that?

Sarah: You're going to have to fill me in here. Peter isn't exactly the most professional of individuals these days. It's his illness, you know. The communication around this office isn't what it should be. He's harassing you. Is that what you're implying?

Conner: Yeah he's—

Harris: I think it's better if we wait for Mr. Maxwell.

Sarah: Okay. But I'm telling you you won't get anywhere with him. He's not behaving rationally.

Conner: You've noticed that, eh.

Sarah: Well, it's hard not to. Come on. Seriously. You can level with me. I was just kidding before. It's late. It's been a hard day. I spent most of it covering up for Peter's lack of judgement.

(CONNER *takes* HARRIS *aside.*)

Conner: Obviously she's got lot in common with the guy. Obviously she knows the guy. She's got a bead on him. Maybe we can work this out with her. *(To* SARAH.*)* I'm offering the hand of peace. That's basically what I'm doing. You know me, don't you? You recognize me, I know you do.

Harris: Maybe she doesn't.

Conner: Everybody in this city recognizes me. She lives in this city, doesn't she?

Harris: Maybe she doesn't.

Sarah *(to* HARRIS*):* Whatya mean by that?

Harris: Nothing. Maybe you're from out of town...You know from some other place.

Sarah: I used to be from some other place. I'm from here now. I mean I'm trying my best. Come on, give me a chance. I recognize him. He's famous.

Conner: I wouldn't say famous. I get around though. I make my contributions.

Harris: Mr. Conner is the publisher of *The World Today*.

Conner: She knows that.

Sarah: Yeah I know that...That's the paper with all the colour. Lots of blue and red. I like that paper.

Conner: You do?

SARAH: I like it a lot. I read it. I like the way all the articles are surrounded by colour. Borders, I mean. Colourful borders. And the writers, they're interesting. They're mad. They all write like they're really ticked off. I like their angry attitude. I can relate to it.

CONNER: Do you subscribe?

SARAH: To what?

CONNER: To what? The paper.

SARAH: No. I like it though. I read it on subways. I pick it off the floor. I read it carefully. Then I put it back on the floor before I get off.

They Didn't Mean To Be Funny, Honest

Unintentional Humour

FROM *Outrageously Yours*

Bruce West

This is a paperback from the mid-1980s, in which a Mr. West decided to write anyone and everyone in the world, offering his services, challenging consumerism, maligning politicos, etc., etc., often enclosing a (very nominal) cheque.

T-Bone   .25
With Meat $4.00

—A *"Daily Special"* seen across the Canadian West

Public Service Commission
P.O. Box 2703
Whitehorse
Yukon Y1A 2C6

December 4, 1984

Dear Sir,

Regarding the advertised vacancy for Territorial Court Judge, you need search no further!

My vast legal expertise has been acquired over a considerable number of years, and to the eternal frustration of my opponents thus far I have a spotless record. How many of us can boast that nowadays?

You may be assured that all who appear before me for sentencing will be well advised to prepare themselves for a long detention, with minimal facilities to ease the passage of time. Yes Sir, I intend to crack down on trouble makers, and crack down hard!

I note the salary for this position is a nominal $74,345.00 per annum. I would also have to insist on an aircraft for my personal transportation, and of course a motor carriage commensurate with the status of the appointment.

I am not without means, and I am on first name terms with the Prime Minister. [in earlier letters, Bruce West had written to, and received a letter from, Pierre Trudeau.]

I look forward to receiving confirmation of my appointment, and to expedite same I enclose five dollars to make sure my name goes straight to the top of the pile.

Yours faithfully,

Bruce West

Yukon Public Service Commission

December 11, 1984

Dear Mr. West:

I am in receipt of your letter of application dated December 4, 1984, for the position of Territorial Court Judge.

Please be advised that "an aircraft for (my) personal transportation" and "a motor carriage" are not provided with this position.

I am returning your cheque for five dollars...any attempt to bribe a public official is an offence under the Criminal Code.

Yours sincerely,

Susan L. Priest,
Personnel Officer.

encl.

The Coca-Cola Company
310 North Avenue N.W.
Atlanta
Georgia 30313
U.S.A.

October 2, 1984
For the attention of Roberto C. Goizueta, Chairman

Dear Mr. Goizueta,

In accord with the majority of responsible physicians in North America, my colleagues and I are extremely concerned regarding the alleged toxic properties contained by your dubious products.

You will no doubt be aware of the soon to be published Government Report on "soft drinks," with particular reference to the alarmingly coincident deterioration of digestive function now recognized to be a direct consequence of regular consumption of beverages of your ilk.

My own people have been conducting private research into the harmful effects suffered by innumerable children and young adults, drawn to innocent addiction by glamorous advertisements such as the example currently showing on television, featuring the quintessentially popular song-and-dance mannequin, Jesse Jackson.

I submit sir, that the irresponsible employment of pop stars to foist your wares upon the young and impressionable is a moral and commercial travesty of monumental proportion.

Aside from one's professional commitment to this investigation into the detrimental content of your products, which have always been widely reputed to have corrosive properties, one's personal view to this end is compounded by the recent inexplicable disappearance of a caged hamster belonging to a neighbour's children, subsequent to their playfully "rewarding" the unfortunate rodent with a saucer of Coke.

You may be assured that my staff will be collaborating our evidence with the findings of the Authorities, and that our consequent public disclosures will ensure swift curtailment of your blatant commercial excesses.

Yours sincerely,

Bruce West

THE U.S. WANTS OUR WATER—FLUSH TWICE

—A message above a toilet in Nova Scotia, seen during energy crisis of 1972

COCA-COLA USA

October 24, 1984

Dear Mr. West:

Our Chairman of the Board, Mr. Roberto C. Goizueta, has asked me to personally thank you for your letter. We are glad to have this opportunity to respond.

Coca-Cola and all our other soft drinks are wholesome beverages manufactured in compliance with the Federal Food Laws, the laws of all the states and the laws of more than 155 countries throughout the world where the product is marketed. The long history of use of soft drinks without adverse health effects further demonstrates the safety of our products.

We make no nutritional claims for Coca-Cola or our other carbonated soft drinks. In our view, every item in a person's diet need not be nutritional in the sense that it is "good for you" nutritionally. All of our soft drinks are marketed as beverages to be consumed for pleasure and enjoyment. We believe there has always been, and always will be, plenty of room in a balanced diet for consumption of pleasant soft drinks.

In response to your reference to our commercials using Jesse Jackson, I assume you are referring to the commercials of PepsiCo. with singer Michael Jackson. We are not affiliated with these advertisements in any way.

As you may know, the aim of our advertisements through the years has been to depict our products as being refreshing beverages enjoyed with good times, and to portray how they advance any given situation.

Please know, Mr. West, that The Coca-Cola Company engages in a continuing program of research and development in cooperation with our advertising agencies. Different types of ads are considered in terms of consumer acceptance and all the factors that affect the purchasing decision of consumers. As this program continues, it is helpful to have the benefit of opinions such as yours.

Thank you, again, for taking the time to contact us.

Sincerely,

Patricia Martin
Consumer Information Coordinator

Wm. Wrigley Jr. Co.
410 N. Michigan Avenue
Chicago
Illinois 60611
U.S.A.

December 17, 1984
For the attention of William Wrigley, President

Dear Mr. Wrigley,

Our laboratories have been conducting research in order to identify the cause of a particular type of brain malfunction which is demonstrating a serious increase in North America.

We were fairly accurately able to pin down the clinical symptoms of our research, which include moronic staring through glazed eyes, loss of thought co-ordination, inability to grasp simple commands, extreme lethargy, lack of interest in communicating, complete loss of ambition, and sharply reduced speech participation.

For months we were baffled. All the information fed into our computer proved inconclusive.

Then a breakthrough! It transpired that over 98 percent of our patients were habitual users of chewing gum.

Astonishing though this at first seemed, we double checked our statistics again and again, and the evidence conclusively demonstrates that regular chewing of gum is isolated as the single cause of the gross malfunction of intellectual capacity.

We will be submitting our Paper to the World Health Organization in early course, and prior to despatching same, we would appreciate hearing your views on this alarming revelation.

Yours sincerely,

Bruce West

ANOTHER BLOW FOR
UNLUCKY FAMILY
Ted Kennedy Survives Crash

—Headline in *Ottawa Journal*,
June 20, 1964

Wm. WRIGLEY Jr. Company
WHOLESOME ✴ DELICIOUS ✴ SATISFYING

December 28, 1984

Dear Mr. West:

We're sorry and somewhat surprised to learn about your negative attitude toward chewing gum.

Exercising the mouth and jaw muscles through chewing is a natural instinct that can be traced back thousands of years, to antiquity. The ancient Greeks, no slouches where civilization is concerned, chewed the gum of the mastic tree, and the Aztecs, whose sophisticated culture in Mexico's Yucatan peninsula flourished a thousand years, raised the enjoyment of chewing chicle from the native sapodilla trees to a fine art.

Here in America, the New England colonists began making spruce gum at home 300 years ago, and gum has been commercially available for more than a century. So I wouldn't become too concerned about a world decline in intellectual capacity due to chewing gum, though we agree with you that some folks do seem to display a lack of old-fashioned common sense these days.

On the positive side, chewing gum helps relieve nervous tension, eases monotony, provides a quick and convenient pick-me-up, and is a handy, low-calorie substitute for cigarettes and fattening snacks. In fact, chewing gum was considered such a necessity that it was included in Army K-rations during World War II as a welcome "taste of home" for U.S., Canadian and British soldiers fighting in the trenches.

I hope the enclosed summary of facts will give you a fresh perspective on a quality product we've marketed proudly for ninety-two years. And please enjoy the complimentary packages of Doublemint gum we're sending you under separate cover.

With best wishes,

WM. WRIGLEY JR. COMPANY
Barbara Sadek

The Vatican
Rome
ITALY

December 30, 1984
For the attention of Pope John Paul II

Your Holiness,

As the morals of the world continue to skate downhill like a greased pig, it is refreshing indeed to listen to your iterative pontifical bringing home to us the inspired words of syllogistic rectitude.

As this planet teeters on the brink of starvation through chronic overpopulation, you sensibly ordain abstention from the use of contraceptives.

As millions of couples endure unbearable lives of relations with their spouses at no end, you persist in refusing to recognize divorce.

Truly your apostolic perspicacity is a blessing and a source of comfort and relief to all men of reason.

There are wicked cynics among us who are of the misguided opinion that an elderly celibate bachelor is not competent to be charged with responsibility for the direction of the lives of over 600 million Catholics. Naturally I do not number myself among such misanthropes. On the contrary, I feel that you should go further still, and ban the disgraceful activities which lead to birth control and divorce, namely copulation and marriage!

I enclose three dollars. Slip into something less ostentatious than your usual attire, and pop downtown incognito one night and enjoy yourself. That should hopefully silence unkind critics of your curious lifestyle once and for all!

Yours sincerely,

Bruce West
Enc.

Canadians Selling Deodorant
Witness Revolution in Lisbon

—Headline, *Toronto Star*,
April 29, 1974

The Vatican
Rome
ITALY

February 8, 1985
For the attention of Pope John Paul II

Your Holiness,

I see from my latest bank statement/returned cheques that you did indeed take my advice of the last paragraph in my letter of December 30th, as my cheque was cashed by you on January 17th!

How did you make out?

As you may imagine, I am a little disappointed that you saw fit to accept my suggestion and donation without even so much as a "thank you," or even found time to comment on the important theological issues raised in my letter.

Perhaps you will answer my concerns when your busy schedule permits, but in the meantime kindly forward a receipt for my three dollars by return of post.

Thank you.

Yours sincerely,

Bruce West

The Pentagon
Washington D.C.
20301
U.S.A.

May 21, 1986
For the attention of Caspar W. Weinberger, Secretary of Defense

Dear Mr. Weinberger,

As the U.S. Space Programme would appear to be on the brink of lapsing into a permanent "technical malfunction situation," I am compelled to offer my condolences and perhaps a word of advice here and there.

It is a cruel irony that the recent miserable failures of Satellite Launching Rockets, the Space Shuttle, Cruise Missiles over Alberta (Canada), etc., have overshadowed the more notable military successes which have made America the envy of the world!

All too soon we forget the proud achievements of your General Custer back in 1876, the defence of Pearl Harbor in 1941, the war in Vietnam, the attempted hostage rescue in Iran under President Carter, and of course the successful bombing of Libyan civilians last month on the strength of Colonel Qaddafi having conclusively been proved to have had possible connections with terrorist attacks on European airports.

But, I digress! My purpose in writing is to avail your technical staff of my valuable experience in matters relating to the problems of mechanical flight.

In my youth, I was a fanatical model aviator, and it must be admitted that I also had my fair share of "ongoing unscheduled altitude loss exingency scenarios" (crashes)!

In my case, invariably it transpired that the fault was a lack of strength and/or longevity in the rubber band driving the propellor, and, having studied the consistency of your recent losses, I conclude that this simple solution to your problems might well have been overlooked by your experts?

Accordingly therefore, I enclose a Heavy-Duty Rubber Band for your people to test for suitability, and should this prove to be the solution, I also enclose five dollars to purchase a good supply of quality bands for use on future missions!

May you soon be back on target, developing much needed sophisticated ballistics with the necessary capacity to annihilate as many people as possible.

Yours sincerely,

Bruce West
Encs.

OFFICE OF THE ASSISTANT SECRETARY OF DEFENSE

WASHINGTON, D.C. 20301-1400
PUBLIC AFFAIRS

June 12, 1986

Dear Mr. West:

We are returning under cover of this letter your check for five dollars, made payable to Secretary of Defense Weinberger, and the rubber band which accompanied it.

While we gratefully accept ideas and donations from citizens who wish to improve the defense of our nation, it is indeed difficult to accept contributions from those who ridicule it. As a result, we respectfully decline your suggestions and funds.

Sincerely,

Alice Tilton
Deputy Assistant Director

Enclosures

C.I.D.A. GUIDE TO CANADIAN CUSTOMS

FROM A DOCUMENT PUBLISHED IN 1988 BY THE C.I.D.A. (THE CANADIAN INTERNATIONAL DEVELOPMENT AGENCY): A GUIDE DESIGNED TO ADDRESS BASIC CUSTOMS IN CANADA TO FOREIGNERS WHO WISH TO UNDERSTAND OUR STRANGE WAYS.

On friendship:
Friendships among Canadians tend to be shorter and less intense than those among people from many other cultures...because they are taught to be self-reliant and...live in a very mobile society.

Canadians tend to "compartmentalize" their friendships, having their "friends at work," "friends at school," "a tennis friend," and so on.

On conversation:
In casual conversation (what they call small talk), Canadians prefer to talk about the weather, sports, jobs, people they both know, or past experience.

On relationships:
Despite the liberalization that is occurring in sexual attitudes and behaviour in Canada...men are still left to guess about the woman's attitudes in the early stages of a relationship. This is because social convention usually prevents a woman from telling a man in a direct way that she does not wish to go out with him. It is considered that such a direct message to the man will deflate his ego or hurt his feelings.

Similarly...the man will almost never tell the woman that he does not wish to go out with her. He will simply not ask her out and he will avoid paying any special attention to her when they are together in a group.

On stereotypes:
There are two stereotypes which often afflict male-female relationships involving Canadian and international students.

The first is the idea held by some international males that Canadian females are invariably willing, if not anxious, to share a bed with a male.

The second stereotype held by some Canadian females is that male international students have not interest in Canadian females other than getting into bed with them.

PICK YOUR RUT CAREFULLY
You will be in it for the
next eighty miles

—a sign near a stretch of bad
road in Alberta, mid-1950s

FROM *THE FOUR JAMESES*

William Arthur Deacon

DESCRIBED AS "THAT RARE THING IN CANADIAN LITERATURE: AN UNDERGROUND CLASSIC," THIS HYSTERICALLY FUNNY MOCK-SERIOUS STUDY OF FOUR HIDEOUSLY UNTALENTED AND UNCONSCIOUSLY FUNNY NINETEENTH-CENTURY CANADIAN POETS WHOSE FIRST NAMES WERE ALL JAMES, WAS FIRST PUBLISHED IN 1927.

James Gay: Poet Laureate of Canada, and Master of All Poets

Gay, broad and tolerant in his theological views, was a religious man in every sense. Seldom, however, has any ecclesiastical or lay writer made such an impassioned defence of the historical authenticity of the Old Testament as we find in his "Samson." The composition is doubly interesting. Without this record later generations might never have known how the Biblical strong man was once impugned, since Gay did his work so thoroughly that after publication of his "Samson," atheists never questioned the reality of his story again, but concentrated their unbelief upon Jonah. And, in using again, with even greater mastery, the rhymed prose form, Gay exhausted its possibilities and never employed it in subsequent flights.

A Few Remarks on Samson

It appears in his day he was both strong and fast, he killed
Thousands of the Philistines with the jawbone of an ass. No such
Man, we are well sure, ever lived on earth before. His wife
Betrayed him in a cruel way, caused his death without delay. His
Strength returned before too late; hundreds of his persecutors
Received their just fate. His faith was very great at the last; he
Killed more with himself than by the bone of the ass. Infidels
Say this is all a farce, Samson never killed his enemies with the
Jawbone of the ass. All those sayings spring by chance, just like
Paris, the city of France.

The next poem passes from the changeableness of the weather,
through the changeableness of man's mind and the diabolic cause of
human unrest, to the frightful reward of wickedness. In the original
printing the lines follow closely. I have taken the liberty of breaking
them into stanzas to bring out the meaning more clearly; and, as they
fall into four four-line groups, I believe I am restoring the poem to
the form Gay designed.

Canadian Climate

Canadian climate must have been changeable ever since the
    world begun,
One hour snowing, and the next raining like fun,
Our blood sometimes thick, other times thin,
This is the time colds begin.

After all, people seem strong and healthy;
Some die poor, others wealthy:
So men's minds are like the weather,
Cannot agree very long together.

This wicked spirit is around every day
To keep the minds of man astray;
The rich man's mind he does unfold,
And tells him how to make his gold;

No fear of death before his eyes,
Often taken by surprise.
O! What will be the rich man's fate?
Too late! too late, too late.

The gnomic quality of those verses is certainly reminiscent of some of William Blake's. They are quoted, however, to show the milder nature of Gay's feelings of patriotism within Canada's borders. When it is the matter of civic pride, and he is extolling his beloved city, not even the Devil can disturb the tranquility of his love:

> You travel east, you travel west, return to Guelph
>   and say it's best.

While I deny the validity of all criticisms aimed at the alleged lack of logical sequence in Gay's lines, I admit unhesitatingly the poet's marked originality. He is the least derivative of all poets. No one ever wrote like him before; and he has never been successfully imitated.

Of this originality he must have been quite aware; for when he wrote "The Elephant and the Flea," which is generally considered his masterpiece, he prefaced the poem with a note explaining that he had hit upon a theme never before treated poetically. Gay's effort is entirely satisfying; and it is safe to predict that no future poet will have the courage to attempt anything on the same subject. It stands—without predecessor or successor—unique and triumphant:

The Elephant and the Flea

Between those two there's a great contrast,
The elephant is slow, the flea very fast,
You can make friends with the elephant and gain his good-will,
If you have a flea in your bed you cannot lie still:
A flea is a small thing, all times in the way,
Hopping and jumping like beasts after their prey,
Oft dropt inside your ears—don't think this a wonder,
You will think for a while it's loud claps of thunder:
We can make friends with all beasts ever came in our way—
No man on earth can make friends with a flea;
The elephant is a large beast, and cunning no doubt;
If you offend him, look out for his snout;
Give him tobacco, it will make him ugly and cross,
A blow from his trunk's worse than a kick from a horse;
And still they are friendly, will cause no disaster,
Beg around in shows, make money for their master:
On this noble beast, the elephant, I have no more to say;
And this little black insect will have its own way.
A flea you may flatten if you know how,
But an elephant no man can't serve so anyhow.
One thing seems wonderful to your poet, James Gay—

All beasts and little animals seem to have a cunning way;
Just like the whales at sea, they seem to know their foes,
Upsets their boats in a moment, and down they goes.

James McIntyre: The Cheese Poet

The Song of Economic Salvation

Then let the farmers justly prize
The cows for land they fertilize,
And let us all with songs and glees
Invoke success into the cheese.

James McIntyre was living in Ingersoll when cheese making began there, and he witnessed the triumphant expansion of the industry in the late seventies and eighties. Then it was that the farmers, exuberant over the new-found source of wealth, were at the pitch of their enthusiasm for the enterprise. Probably more cheese is now made in Ingersoll than McIntyre ever dreamed of—and he was bold in prophecy—but the inhabitants take it more prosaically. They are busier now in scientific merchandising than in trying to make monuments that, in their assault on the eye, may capture the imagination also, and impress the world with the jubilant news of their economic salvation. Then, however, in their delirious ecstasy, it was most natural that they should have endeavoured to manufacture for display the largest cheese ever moulded by man; and history does not say they failed. This monster production weighed over seven thousand pounds. It doubtless accomplished the object of its makers; but it is doubtful whether it would have been widely remembered if it had not thrilled James McIntyre to the point of composing his immortal:

Ode on the Mammoth Cheese

We have seen thee, queen of cheese
Lying quietly at your ease,
Gently fanned by evening breeze,
Thy fair form no flies dare seize.
All gaily dressed soon you'll go
To the great Provincial show,
To be admired by many a beau
In the city of Toronto.

Cows numerous as a swarm of bees,
Or as the leaves upon the trees,
It did require to make thee please,
And stand unrivalled, queen of cheese.

May you not receive a scar as
We have heard that Mr. Harris
Intends to send you off as far as
The great world's show at Paris.

Of the youth beware of these,
For some of them might rudely squeeze
And bite your cheek, then songs or glees
We could not sing, oh! queen of cheese.

We'rt thou suspended from balloon,
You'd cast a shade even at noon,
Folks would think it was the moon
About to fall and crush them soon.

This monstrous lump of edible matter was a constant inspiration to McIntyre, for his poet's eye rightly saw it as a symbol of the glory of his community; and in another poem he explains why a big cheese represents virtues that a little cheese cannot:

In barren district you may meet
Small fertile spot doth grow fine wheat,
There you may find the choicest fruits,
And great, round, smooth and solid roots.

But in conditions such as these
You cannot make a mammoth cheese,
Which will weigh eight thousand pounds,
But where large fertile farms abounds.

Big cheese is synonymous name,
With fertile district of the Thame,
Here dairy system's understood,
And they are made both large and good.

from *Repertoire des avis linguistiques et terminologiques*

CARRÉ AU CHOCOLAT, n.m.
Petit gâteau de forme rectangulaire, aromatise au chocolat, dont la texture se situe entre le biscuit sec et le gâteau spongieux.

ANGLAIS: **BROWNIE**

—CLEMENTS

FROM MORE COURT JESTERS

Peter V. MacDonald

You wouldn't believe some of the things that tumble out of lawyers' mouths in the heat of battle—or the throes of boredom. Such situations can cause a barrister to switch off his brain for a jiffy, often with hilarious results.

Let's sift through some of the evidence:

Q. "And you are how old a woman, sir?"

Q. "Now isn't it true that when a person dies in his sleep, in most cases he just passes quietly away and doesn't know anything about it until the next morning?"

Q. "The 24th of December—was that the day before Christmas?"

Q. Were you acquainted with the deceased?
A. Yes.
Q. Before or after he died?

Q. Who else was with you in your van?
A. There was no one else.
Q. Were you alone then?
A. Yeah.
Q. And you were the driver, is that right?
A. Yeah.

Q. And the youngest son, the 20-year-old, how old is he?
A. He's 20 years old.

Q. What happened then?
A. He told me, he says, "I have to kill you because you can identify me."
Q. Did he kill you?

Q. I show you Exhibit 3 and ask if you recognize that picture.
A. That's me.
Q. Were you present when that picture was taken?

Q. Do you know how far pregnant you are right now?
A. I'll be three months on November 8th.
Q. Apparently, then, the date of conception was August 8th?
A. Yes.
Q. What were you and your husband doing at that time?

Q. Now, Mrs. Smith, do you believe that you are emotionally stable?
A. I used to be.
Q. How many times have you committed suicide?

Q. Now, Mrs. Johnson, how was your first marriage terminated?
A. By death.
Q. And by whose death was it terminated?

When you ask a Stupid Question, you're spoiling for a Snappy Comeback. For example:

Q. Could you see him from where you were standing?
A. I could see his head.
Q. And where was his head?
A. Just above his shoulders.

Before you leap to the conclusion that all lawyers are unmitigated airheads, a few words in defence of the apparent dodos we've been tuned in on. I'm a lawyer myself—I recently completed 25 years of practice—and I'll have you know that the sort of verbal wreckage recorded above is usually the result of battle fatigue or thinking ahead to the next question, or both.

A Texas lawyer, realizing he was on the verge of perpetrating one of these outrages, interrupted himself and said, "Your Honour, I'd like to strike the next question." And another Texas lawyer, cross-examining a coroner, must have wished that he'd also been able to intercept his tongue. Let's eavesdrop:

Q. Do you recall approximately the time that you examined the body of Mr. Edgington at the Rose Chapel?
A. It was in the evening. The autopsy started about 8:30 p.m.
Q. And Mr. Edgington was dead at the time, is that correct?
A. No, you dumb asshole, he was sitting there on the table wondering why I was doing an autopsy!

"Your honor, before the jury retires to reach a verdict my client wishes to present each of them with a little gift of jewelry."

—UNGER

SURE IT'S BORING, BUT IS IT LITERATURE?

CAN LIT AND OTHER LITERARY LAPSES

GERTRUDE THE GOVERNESS OR SIMPLE SEVENTEEN

Stephen Leacock

Synopsis of Previous Chapters:
There are no Previous Chapters

It was a wild and stormy night on the West Coast of Scotland. This, however, is immaterial to the present story, as the scene is not laid in the West of Scotland. For the matter of that the weather was just as bad on the East Coast of Ireland.

But the scene of this narrative is laid in the South of England and takes place in and around Knotacentinum Towers (pronounced as if written Nosham Taws), the seat of Lord Knotacent (pronounced as if written Nosh.)

But it is not necessary to pronounce either of these names in reading them.

Nosham Taws was a typical English home. The main part of the house was an Elizabethan structure of warm red brick, while the elder portion, of which the Earl was inordinately proud, still showed the

outlines of a Norman Keep, to which had been added a Lancastrian Jail and a Plantagenet Orphan Asylum. From the house in all directions stretched magnificent woodland and park with oaks and elms of immemorial antiquity, while nearer the house stood raspberry bushes and geranium plants which had been set out by the Crusaders.

About the grand old mansion the air was loud with the chirping of thrushes, the cawing of partridges and the clear sweet note of the rook, while deer, antelope and other quadrupeds strutted about the lawn so tame as to eat off the sundial. In fact, the place was a regular menagerie.

From the house downwards through the park stretched a beautiful broad avenue laid out by Henry VII.

Lord Nosh stood upon the hearthrug of the library. Trained diplomat and statesman as he was, his stern aristocratic face was upside down with fury.

"Boy," he said, "you shall marry this girl or I disinherit you. You are no son of mine."

Young Lord Ronald, erect before him, flung back a glance as defiant as his own.

"I defy you," he said. "Henceforth you are no father of mine. I will get another. I will marry none but a woman I can love. This girl that we have never seen—"

"Fool," said the Earl, "would you throw aside our estate and name of a thousand years? The girl, I am told, is beautiful; her aunt is willing; they are French; pah! they understand such things in France."

"But your reason—"

"I give no reason," said the Earl. "Listen, Ronald, I give one month. For that time you remain here. If at the end of it you refuse me, I cut you off with a shilling."

Lord Ronald said nothing; he flung himself from the room, flung himself upon his horse and rode madly off in all directions.

As the door of the library closed upon Ronald, the Earl sank into a chair. His face changed. It was no longer that of the haughty nobleman, but of the hunted criminal. "He must marry the girl," he muttered. "Soon she will know all. Tutchemoff has escaped from Siberia. He knows and will tell. The whole of the mines pass to her, this property with it, and I—but enough." He rose, walked to the sideboard, drained a dipper full of gin and bitters, and became again a high-bred English gentleman.

It was at this moment that a high dogcart, driven by a groom in the livery of Earl of Nosh, might have been seen entering the avenue of Nosham Taws. Beside him sat a young girl, scarce more than a child, in fact, not nearly so big as the groom.

The apple-pie hat which she wore, surmounted with black willow plumes, concealed from view a face so face-like in its appearance as to be positively facial.

It was—need we say it—Gertrude the Governess, who was this day to enter upon her duties at Nosham Taws.

THE PROFESSOR

Mavor Moore

The teacher has a solemn
    trust:
To pass to each new
    generation
The fine accumulated dust
Of obsolete excogitation.

One precept governs Ph.D.s—
And mere M.A.s must never
    flout it:
Our responsibility's
To teach not Life but books
    about it.

At the same time that the dogcart entered the avenue at one end there might have been seen riding down it from the other a tall young man, whose long, aristocratic face proclaimed his birth and who was mounted upon a horse with a face even longer than his own.

And who is this tall young man who draws nearer to Gertrude with every revolution of the horse? Ah, who, indeed? Ah, who, who? I wonder if any of my readers could guess that this was none other than Lord Ronald.

The two were destined to meet. Nearer and nearer they came. And then still nearer. Then for one brief moment they met. As they passed Gertrude raised her head and directed towards the young man two eyes so eye-like in their expression as to be absolutely circular, while Lord Ronald directed towards the occupant of the dogcart a gaze so gazelike that nothing but a gazelle, or a gas-pipe, could have emulated its intensity.

Was this the dawn of love? Wait and see. Do not spoil the story.

Let us speak of Gertrude. Gertrude De Mongmorenci McFiggin had known neither father nor mother. They had both died years before she was born. Of her mother she knew nothing, save that she was French, was extremely beautiful, and that all her ancestors and even her business acquaintances had perished in the Revolution.

Yet Gertrude cherished the memory of her parents. On her breast the girl wore a locket in which was enshrined a miniature of her mother, while down her neck inside at the back hung a daguerreotype of her father. She carried a portrait of her grandmother up her sleeve and had pictures of her cousins tucked inside her boot, while beneath her—but enough, quite enough.

Of her father Gertrude knew even less. That he was a high-born English gentleman who had lived as a wanderer in many lands, this was all she knew. His only legacy to Gertrude had been a Russian grammar, a Roumanian phrase-book, a theodolite, and a work on mining engineering.

From her earliest infancy Gertrude had been brought up by her aunt. Her aunt had carefully instructed her in Christian principles. She had also taught her Mohammedanism to make sure.

When Gertrude was seventeen her aunt had died of hydrophobia.

The circumstances were mysterious. There had called upon her that day a strange bearded man in the costume of the Russians. After he had left, Gertrude had found her aunt in a syncope from which she passed into an apostrophe and never recovered.

To avoid scandal it was called hydrophobia. Gertrude was thus thrown upon the world. What to do? That was the problem that confronted her.

It was while musing one day upon her fate that Gertrude's eye was struck with an advertisement.

"Wanted a governess; must possess a knowledge of French, Italian, Russian, and Roumanian, Music, and Mining Engineering. Salary L1, four shillings and four pence halfpenny per annum. Apply between half-past eleven and twenty-five minutes to twelve at No. 41 A Decimal Six, Belgravia Terrace. The Countess of Nosh."

Gertrude was a girl of great natural quickness of apprehension, and she had not pondered over this announcement more than half an hour before she was struck with the extraordinary coincidence between the list of items desired and the things that she herself knew.

She duly presented herself at Belgravia Terrace before the Countess, who advanced to meet her with a charm which at once placed the girl at her ease.

"You are proficient in French?" she asked.

"Oh, oui," said Gertrude modestly.

"And Italian?" continued the Countess.

"Oh, si," said Gertrude.

"And Russian?"

"Yaw."

"And Roumanian?"

"Jep."

Amazed at the girl's extraordinary proficiency in modern languages, the Countess looked at her narrowly. Where had she seen those lineaments before? She passed her hand over her brow in thought, and spit upon the floor, but no, the face baffled her.

"Enough," she said, "I engage you on the spot; tomorrow you go down to Nosham Taws and begin teaching the children. I must add that in addition you will be expected to aid the Earl with his Russian correspondence. He had large mining interests at Tschminsk."

Tschminsk! why did the simple word reverberate upon Gertrude's ears? Why? Because it was the name written in her father's hand on the title page of his book on mining. What mystery was here?

It was on the following day that Gertrude had driven up the avenue.

She descended from the dogcart, passed through a phalanx of liveried servants drawn up seven-deep, to each of whom she gave a sovereign as she passed and entered Nosham Taws.

"Welcome," said the Countess, as she aided Gertrude to carry her trunk upstairs.

The girl presently descended and was ushered into the library, where she was presented to the Earl. As soon as the Earl's eye fell upon the face of the new governess he started visibly. Where had he seen those lineaments? Where was it? At the races, or the theatre—on a bus—no. Some subtler thread of memory was stirring in his mind. He strode hastily to the sideboard, drained a dipper and a half of brandy, and became again the perfect English gentleman.

While Gertrude has gone to the nursery to make the acquaintance of the two tiny golden-haired children who are to be her charges, let us say something here of the Earl and his son.

Lord Nosh was the perfect type of the English nobleman and statesman. The years that he had spent in the diplomatic service at Constantinople, St. Petersburg, and Salt Lake City had given to him a peculiar finesse and noblesse, while his long residence at St. Helena,

Pitcairn Island, and Hamilton, Ontario, had rendered him impervious to external impressions. As deputy-paymaster of the militia of the country he had seen something of the sterner side of military life, while his hereditary office of Groom of the Sunday Breeches had brought him into direct contact with Royalty itself.

His passion for outdoor sports endeared him to his tenants. A keen sportsman, he excelled in fox-hunting, dog-hunting, pig-killing, bat-catching and the pastimes of his class.

In this latter respect Lord Ronald took after his father. From the start the lad had shown the greatest promise. At Eton he had made a splendid showing at battledore and shuttlecock, and at Cambridge had been first in his class at needlework. Already his name was whispered in connection with the All England ping-pong championship, a triumph which would undoubtedly carry with it a seat in Parliament.

Thus was Gertrude the Governess installed at Nosham Taws.

The days and the weeks sped past.

The simple charm of the beautiful orphan girl attracted all hearts. Her two little pupils became her slaves. "Me loves oo," the little Rasehellfrida would say, leaning her golden head in Gertrude's lap. Even the servants loved her. The head gardener would bring a bouquet of beautiful roses to her room before she was up, the second gardener a bunch of early cauliflowers, the third a sprig of mangel-wurzel or an armful of hay. Her room was full of gardeners all the time, while at evening the aged butler, touched at the friendless girl's loneliness, would tap softly at her door to bring her a rye whiskey and seltzer or a box of Pittsburgh Stogies. Even the dumb creatures seemed to admire her in their own dumb way. The dumb rooks settled on her shoulder and every dumb dog around the place followed her.

And Ronald! ah, Ronald! Yes, indeed! They had met. They had spoken.

"What a dull morning," Gertrude had said. "Quel triste matin! Was für ein allerverdamnter Tag!"

"Beastly," Ronald had answered.

"Beastly!!" The word rang in Gertrude's ears all day.

After that they were constantly together. They played tennis and ping-pong in the day, and in the evening, in accordance with the stiff routine of the place, they sat down with the Earl and Countess to twenty-five-cent poker, and later still they sat together on the verandah and watched the moon sweeping in great circles around the horizon.

It was not long before Gertrude realized that Lord Ronald felt towards her a warmer feeling than that of mere ping-pong. At times in her presence he would fall, especially after dinner, into a fit of profound substraction.

Once at night, when Gertrude withdrew to her chamber and before seeking her pillow, prepared to retire as a preliminary to disrobing—in other words, before going to bed, she flung wide the casement (opened the window) and perceived (saw) the face of Lord Ronald. He was sitting on a thorn bush beneath her, and his upturned face wore an expression of agonized pallor.

Meantime the days passed. Life at the Taws moved in the ordinary routine of a great English household. At 7 a gong sounded for rising, at 8 a horn blew for breakfast, at 8:30 a whistle sounded for prayers, at 1 a flag was run up at half-mast for lunch, at 7 a gun was fired for afternoon tea, at 9 a first bell sounded for dressing, at 9:15 a second bell for going on dressing, while at 9:30 a rocket was sent up to indicate that dinner was ready. At midnight dinner was over, and at 1 a.m. the tolling of a bell summoned the domestics to evening prayers.

Meanwhile the month allotted by the Earl to Lord Ronald was passing away. It was already July 15, then within a day or two it was July 17, and, almost immediately afterwards, July 18.

At times the Earl, in passing Ronald in the hall, would say sternly, "Remember, boy, your consent, or I disinherit you."

And what were the Earl's thoughts of Gertrude? Here was the one drop of bitterness in the girl's cup of happiness. For some reason that she could not divine the Earl showed signs of marked antipathy.

Once as she passed the door of the library he threw a bootjack at her. On another occasion at lunch alone with her he struck her savagely across the face with a sausage.

It was her duty to translate to the Earl his Russian correspondence. She sought in it in vain for the mystery. One day a Russian telegram was handed to the Earl. Gertrude translated it to him aloud.

"Tutchemoff went to the woman. She is dead."

On hearing this the Earl became livid with fury, in fact this was the day that he struck her with the sausage.

Then one day while the Earl was absent on a bat hunt, Gertrude, who was turning over his correspondence, with that sweet feminine instinct of interest that rose superior to ill-treatment, suddenly found the key to the mystery.

Lord Nosh was not the rightful owner of the Taws. His distant cousin of the older line, the true heir, had died in a Russian prison to which the machinations of the Earl, while Ambassador at Tschminsk, had consigned him. The daughter of this cousin was the true owner of Nosham Taws.

The family story, save only that the documents before her withheld the name of the rightful heir, lay bare to Gertrude's eyes.

Strange is the heart of woman. Did Gertrude turn from the Earl with spurning? No. Her own sad fate had taught her sympathy.

Yet still the mystery remained! Why did the Earl start perceptibly each time that he looked into her face? Sometimes he started as much as four centimetres, so that one could distinctly see him do it. On such occasions he would hastily drain a dipper of rum and vichy water and become again the correct English gentleman.

The denouement came swiftly. Gertrude never forgot it.

It was the night of the great ball at Nosham Taws. The whole

Susan Ryan

Poor Rushdie. He's got God on his side and Allah on his back.

neighbourhood was invited. How Gertrude's heart had beat with anticipation, and with what trepidation she had overhauled her scant wardrobe in order to appear not unworthy in Lord Ronald's eyes. Her resources were poor indeed, yet the inborn genius for dress that she inherited from her French mother stood her in good stead. She twined a single rose in her hair and contrived herself a dress out of a few old newspapers and the inside of an umbrella that would have graced a court. Round her waist she bound a single braid of bag-string, while a piece of old lace that had been her mother's was suspended to her ear by a thread.

Gertrude was the cynosure of all eyes. Floating to the strains of the music she presented a picture of bright girlish innocence that no one could see undisenraptured.

The ball was at its height. It was away up!

Ronald stood with Gertrude in the shrubbery. They looked into one another's eyes.

"Gertrude," he said, "I love you."

Simple words, and yet they thrilled every fibre in the girl's costume.

"Ronald!" she said, and cast herself about his neck.

At this moment the Earl appeared standing beside them in the moonlight. His stern face was distorted with indignation.

"So!" he said, turning to Ronald, "it appears that you have chosen!"

"I have," said Ronald with hauteur.

"You prefer to marry this penniless girl rather than the heiress I have selected for you?"

Gertrude looked from father to son in amazement.

"Yes," said Ronald.

"Be it so," said the Earl, draining a dipper of gin which he carried, and resuming his calm. "Then I disinherit you. Leave this place, and never return to it."

"Come, Gertrude," said Ronald tenderly, "let us flee together."

Gertrude stood before them. The rose had fallen from her head. The lace had fallen from her ear and the bag-string had come undone at her waist. Her newspapers were crumpled beyond recognition. But dishevelled and illegible as she was, she was still mistress of herself.

"Never," she said firmly. "Ronald, you shall never make this sacrifice for me." Then to the Earl, in tones of ice, "There is a pride, sir, as great even as yours. The daughter of Metschnikoff McFiggin need crave a boon from no one."

With that she hauled from her bosom the daguerreotype of her father and pressed it to her lips.

The Earl started as if shot. "That name!" he cried, "that face! that photograph! stop!"

There! There is no need to finish; my readers have long since divined it. Gertrude was the heiress.

The lovers fell into one another's arms. The Earl's proud face relaxed. "God bless you," he said. The Countess and the guests came pouring out upon the lawn. The breaking day illuminated a scene of gay congratulations.

Gertrude and Ronald were wed. Their happiness was complete. Need we say more? Yes, only this. The Earl was killed in the hunting-field a few days later. The Countess was struck by lightning. The two children fell down a well. Thus the happiness of Gertrude and Ronald was complete.

GREAT MOMENTS IN CANADIAN LITERATURE: THE DIARY OF SUSANNAH SULLEN

Nip 'N Tuck

VOICE-OVER: Great Moments in Canadian Literature presents: The Pioneer Diaries of Susannah Sullen.

(Lights fade up on a woman in a nightgown writing in a large leather-bound book with a feathered quill.)

SUSANNAH *(reading)*: I awoke at five o'clock this morning. How I could have slept in so late I do not know. My husband Jacob had already left for work. The rain had made the streets muddy once again. I had porridge and a biscuit for breakfast. At six o'clock I woke the children...

Wake up Todd.

Wake up Matthew.

Wake up Isaac.

Wake up Leonard. Leonard, I said wake up. Leonard was a heavy sleeper.

Wake up Elizabeth.

Wake up Cynthia.

Wake up Robert.

Wake up Ernest.

Wake up Chip.

The children had porridge and biscuits for breakfast. At seven o'clock the children began their daily chores, all except Leonard who was asleep in his porridge.

"Leonard!" I cried.

"Moose please sorry me mud chicken," he said apologetically.

Poor Leonard. He was kicked in the head by a mule when he was three. Still, he never complains. The morning passed uneventfully. Jacob came home for lunch at noon. We all gathered around the table as Jacob said Grace. Always one with a kind word, Jacob exclaimed, "This is fine porridge,

Susan Ryan

Literacy is overrated. Most people are too literal for literature. They read *Lord of the Flies* and believe that a bunch of people on a desert island will always eat the fat one. Can't be helped. *L'Étranger*, sometimes you just gotta shoot an Arab. Can't be helped. *Tale of Two Cities*, sometimes you just gotta have your head cut off for a pal. Can't be helped.

Northrop Frye

_____

We know nothing about Shakespeare except a signature or two, a few addresses, a will, a baptismal register, and the picture of a man who is clearly an idiot.

_____

Susannah. And good biscuits, too." "Moose please sorry me mud chicken," said Leonard in agreement.

After lunch Jacob went back to work at the stable, the children went back to their chores, and I went to visit dear old Mrs. Smedley.

"I brought you a pot of porridge and some biscuits, dear!!" I said, screaming into her best ear.

"Moose please sorry me mud chicken," she said smiling.

"Oh, he's fine, thank you," I replied.

The old lady always was fond of Leonard. They had so much in common. The afternoon passed uneventfully.

Mrs. Smedley bit the dust, and I went home to make dinner.

The children had finished their chores and were playing games in their room, and Jacob was let home early from the stable after having nailed a horseshoe to his hand. By six o'clock dinner was ready. The sweet smell of porridge and freshly baked biscuits filled the whole cabin. Unfortunately, neither Jacob nor the children were very hungry, so I made a plate for myself and saved the rest for tomorrow's breakfast.

The evening passed uneventfully. The children played quietly or read books, and Jacob removed the horseshoe from his hand. As the hour grew late I ushered the children off to bed.

Good night mother.

Good night Todd.

Good night mother.

Good night Matthew.

Good night mother.

Good night Isaac.

Good night mother.

Good night Elizabeth.

Good night mother.

Good night Cynthia.

Good night mother.

Good night Robert.

Good night mother.

Good night Earnest.

Good night mother.

Good night Chip.

Moose please sorry me mud chicken.

Good night Leonard.

As the wind whirled playfully outside the door, and the fire in the cabin slowly died out, Jacob and I retreated to our room and the warmth of our bed, and had relations until dawn. You see, there really wasn't that much to do in York, in 1793.

(As she finishes her entry and closes the book, the lights fade slowly to black.)

And the Warranty on His Shadow Has Expired

Warren Clements

THE COPYRIGHT ON PETER PAN EXPIRED DECEMBER 31 [1987], FIFTY YEARS AFTER THE DEATH OF AUTHOR J.M. BARRIE. TIME PASSES, EVEN FOR A BOY WHO REFUSES TO ADMIT IT...

"I'm not saying I intend to grow up," said Peter Pan, "but there's no point in closing off your options." He swilled another root beer and absent mindedly brushed Tinkerbell off his lapel. There was a barely audible thud, and the fairy's light flickered off.

"Now you've done it," snapped one of the Lost Boys, motioning to the others and clapping loudly until the light came back on. "Darned nuisance, having to applaud every time she starts dying on us."

"She does it on purpose," groused another Lost Boy. "Bit of a ham, if you ask me."

"It's the loss of copyright I'm worried about," said Peter. "I felt so young, so protected when it was in place. Even the royalties from sales of the book and play went to London's Great Ormond Street Hospital for Sick Children. Now we'll probably fall into the clutches of someone like Andrew Lloyd Webber and have everyone from Wendy to Captain Hook tarted up in furry costumes and racing around the stage on roller skates. I'll probably be shot out of a cannon."

"To be shot out of a cannon would be an awfully big adventure!" chirped a Lost Boy.

"Oh shut up," said Peter.

On his next visit to the Darlings' house in London, Peter had trouble locating Bloomsbury. The landmarks had been either changed or blocked by skyscrapers, and there was a peculiar restaurant with golden arches next to the Darling Place. When he knocked on Wendy's window, he saw an enormous poster on her wall of a man holding a guitar. Wendy was less than enthusiastic to see him.

"Oh," she said. "Peter."

"Time for spring cleaning," he said. "You promised you'd come. Second to the right and then straight on till morning, you know the way, ha ha."

Bob Edwards

———

All the world's a stage, and the majority of us sit in the gallery and throw things at the performers.

—*Eye-Opener*,
September 11, 1920

"I'm frightfully sorry, I forgot all about it," she said. "To be honest, I've rather outgrown you, and since you showed no signs of, um, developing I took up with a fellow down the street, the stockboy at Peter Punk's Record Riot."

"Oh." He looked glumly at the makeup on her bedside table. "And Michael and John?"

"Michael's heavily into computers, and John's turned out for the rugby team. I frankly don't think they'd have the time."

"Where's Nana, then, your great big nurse of a dog?"

"Father had her put down. She kept biting the mailman."

Peter sat heavily on the window ledge. He had been afraid of something like this. It was hard working in 1988, what with all the planes whizzing past him and the acid rain falling on him and Tinkerbell's habit of getting lost in the maze of neon signs and brilliantly lit office towers. He was already forgetting how to get back to Never Never Land, and wasn't sure he wanted to go anyway. The Lost Boys weren't exactly boring, but he'd grown to suspect their parents hadn't lost them by accident, and with Captain Hook gone there was no sport left in playing pirates. Even the crocodile had turned vegetarian.

"I've given serious thought to growing up, you know," he said.

"You've picked a rotten time to do it," said Wendy. "There aren't any jobs going, and the only skills you have are kidnapping young children, cutting people's arms off and corrupting minors, which is hardly the stuff of a grand curriculum vitae."

Peter subsided dejectedly on the floor. "Being a young boy is no life for a young boy these days," he said. "I'm not even sure *I* believe in fairies any more."

Tinkerbell gave a quiet gasp in the corner and fell with a thud. Peter and Wendy gave her a brief round of applause, but their hearts weren't in it.

FROM *WITH A CAPITAL T*

Mavis Gallant

In wartime, in Montreal, I applied to work on a newspaper. Its name was *The Lantern*, and its motto, "My light shall shine," carried a Wesleyan ring of veracity and plain dealing. I chose it because I thought it was a place where I would be given a lot of different things to do. I said to the man who consented to see me, "But not the women's pages. Nothing like that." I was eighteen. He heard me out and suggested that I come back at twenty-one, which was a soft way of getting rid of me. In the meantime I was to acquire experience; he did not say of what kind. On the stroke of twenty-one I returned and told my story to a different person. I was immediately accepted; I had expected to be. I still believed, then, that most people meant what they said. I supposed that the man I had seen that first time had left a memorandum in the files: "To whom it may concern—Three years from this date, Miss Linnet Muir will join the editorial staff." But

"What do you mean, you don't do Ed Sullivan? Everyone does Ed Sullivan!"

—WICKS

after I'd been working for a short time I heard one of the editors say, "If it hadn't been for the god-damned war we would never have hired even one of the god-damned women," and so I knew.

In the meantime I had acquired experience by getting married. I was no longer a Miss Muir, but a Mrs. Blanchard. My husband was overseas. I had longed for emancipation and independence, but I was learning that women's autonomy is like a small inheritance paid out a penny at a time. In a journal I kept I scrupulously noted everything that came into my head about this, and about God, and about politics. I took it for granted that our victory over Fascism would be followed by a sunburst of revolution—I thought that was what the war was about. I wondered if going to work for the capitalist press was entirely moral. "Whatever happens," I wrote, "it will be the Truth, nothing half-hearted, the Truth with a Capital T."

The first thing I had to do was write what goes under the pictures. There is no trick to it. You just repeat what the picture has told you like this:

"Boy eats bun as bear looks on."

The reason why anything has to go under the picture at all is that a reader might wonder, "Is that a bear looking on?" It looks like a bear, but that is not enough reason for saying so. Pasted across the back of the photo you have been given is a strip of paper on which you can read: "Saskatoon, Sask. 23 Nov. Boy eats bun as bear looks on." Whoever composed this knows two things more than you do—a place and a time.

You have a space to fill in which the words must come out even. The space may be tight; in that case, you can remove "as" and substitute a comma, though that makes the kind of terse statement to which your reader is apt to reply, "So what?" Most of the time, the Truth with a Capital T is a matter of elongation: "Blond boy eats small bun as large bear looks on."

"Blond boy eats buttered bun..." is livelier, but unscrupulous. You have been given no information about the butter. "Boy eats bun as hungry bear looks on," has the beginnings of a plot, but it may inspire your reader to protest: "That boy must be a mean sort of kid if he won't share his food with a starving creature." Child-lovers, though less prone to fits of anguish than animal-lovers, may be distressed by the word "hungry" for a different reason, believing "boy" subject to attack from "bear." You must not lose your head and type, "Blond bear eats large boy as hungry bun looks on," because your reader may notice, and write a letter saying, "Some of you guys around there think you're pretty smart, don't you?" while another will try to enrich your caption with, "Re your bun write-up, my wife has taken better pictures than that in the very area you mention."

At the back of your mind, because your mentors have placed it there, is an obstruction called "the policy factor." Your paper supports a political party. You try to discover what this party has had to say about buns and bears, how it intends to approach them in the future. Your editor, at golf with a member of parliament, will not want to have his game upset by: "It's not that I want to interfere but some

The art-loving Bishop of Truro
Kept a nude by Renoir in his
bureau.
He said, "It's not smut
That engrosses me but
Nineteenth-century chiaroscuro!"

of that bun stuff seems pretty negative to me." The young and vulnerable reporter would just as soon not pick up the phone to be told, "I'm ashamed of your defeatist attitude. Why, I knew your father! He must be spinning in his grave!" or, more effectively, "I'm telling you this for your own good—I think you're subversive without knowing it."

Negative, defeatist and subversive are three of the things you have been cautioned not to be. The others are seditious, obscene, obscure, ironic, intellectual and impulsive.

You gather up the photo and three pages of failed captions, and knock at the frosted glass of a senior door. You sit down and are given a view of boot soles. You say that the whole matter comes down to an ethical question concerning information and redundancy; unless "reader" is blotto, can't he see for himself that this is about a boy, a bun and a bear?

Your senior person is in shirtsleeves, hands clasped behind his neck. He thinks this over, staring at the ceiling; swings his feet to the floor; reads your variations on the bear-and-bun theme; turns the photo upside-down. He tells you patiently, that it is not the business of "reader" to draw conclusions. Our subscribers are not dreamers or smart alecks; when they see a situation in a picture, they want that situation confirmed. He reminds you about negativism and obscuration; advises you to go sit in the library and acquire a sense of values by reading the back issues of *Life*.

The back numbers of *Life* are tatty and incomplete, owing to staff habits of tearing out whatever they wish to examine at leisure. A few captions, still intact, allow you to admire a contribution to pictorial journalism, the word "note": "American flag flies over new post office. Note stars on flag." "GI waves happily from captured Italian tank. Note helmet on head."

So, "Boy eats bun as bear looks on. Note fur on bear." All that can happen now will be a letter asking, "Are you sure it was a bun?"

FROM CANNED LIT

Allan Gould

Richard J. Needham

I heard about a young man whose love life was unsatisfactory. So he went to the store and saw a book called *How to Hug* and bought it and took it home triumphantly, and found it to be the eighth volume of an encyclopedia.

Margaret Atwood

Probably Canada's best-known novelist, as well as Canada's less-well-known poet, Margaret Atwood was born in Ottawa, but had the good fortune to spend much of her youth with her entomologist father in a log cabin in northern Quebec. There she experienced firsthand the difficulty of survival and the terror of the bush. Her father's specialty was insects, which in his elder daughter's hands would evolve into her own expertise: men who bug women.

FROM THE HANDMAID'S TALE (1986)

It's rough times, as usual, for women. Fanatical Protestant fundamentalists have taken over the United States and established the Republic of Gilead, where, much as in the world of the 1990s, women have no rights: they can't hold jobs; they are not allowed to have money or property; and they must stay out of sight. Thanks to the pollution of the world—caused by men, natch—there has been a growing sterility, so handmaids are used to bear children for important men—just like today! These uteruses on two legs are given the names of the men who use them: for instance, Ofmordecai, Offarley, Ofpierre—you know.

Our heroine is Offred (since no reader would ever believe a name like Offarley), who must present herself regularly to the commander for sex—one reason this book will never make the Grade Nine Required Reading List in Saskatchewan. Much of the book is taken up with Offred thinking of the good old days, when she had a daughter and when sex was actually fun, even though it was still with men. Things get really sexy when we read how the commander loves to play board and card games with Offred, when all he should really be doing is making non-erotic love to her, just as in most other Canadian novels. Meanwhile, the commander's wife, Serena Joy, is concerned that Offred has not become pregnant, so she fixes her up with the commander's chauffeur, Nick, who actually makes love for fun(!), an idea that had yet to catch on in Canada when the novel was written in the mid-1980s. Offred escapes to Canada, which as the ten million Canadians in Florida at this very moment will be pleased to verify, is no place to escape to, even to get away from the Republic of Gilead. The book ends with a hilarious epilogue in which historians, meeting more than a century after the book takes place, discuss the book in literary terms, ignoring the brutal mistreatment of women during Offred's time. Just like historians and literary critics in the 1990s.

Pierre Berton

FROM ALL HIS BOOKS PUT TOGETHER (1926–PRESENT)

It was bitter cold in the Klondike, but the men could tell that it was cold, without even knowing it in Fahrenheit or centigrade. As their toes began to turn green and fall off, they would stare at one another

Allan Gould
FROM *THE GREAT WIPED OUT NORTH*

———

The highlights of CBC-radio have been many:

The speech from the Throne in both English and French in 1937.

Farm broadcasts in French in 1938.

Six weeks of non-stop coverage of the visit by King George VI and Queen Elizabeth in 1939, as well as the first farm broadcast in English. (You *had* to be there.)

The first provincial school broadcast in Nova Scotia and British Columbia in 1940. The opening of the Alaska Highway—live!—in 1942. (You *didn't* have to be there.)

The first fishermen's broadcasts in the Maritimes, in 1946. (You didn't want to be there.)

Endless coverage of Princess Elizabeth and the Duke of Edinburgh's four-week royal tour in 1951. (*They* didn't want to be here.)

and mumble, "Cold enough fur ya?" But the railway *would* be completed, no matter how many more delays took place. Cornelius Van Horne wasn't about to let those workmen stop his dream, in spite of any idiots in Ottawa who might come along more than a century later and drive a last spike into the railroad's heart.

Of course, if the church really *wanted* to stand for something, it would, though from the way it has been going, it will stand for anything. But the bullets kept flying, forcing the underarmed farmers to take cover behind their bales of hay; the "f—ing Yankees"(to quote directly from the countless letters mailed at this time) weren't about to be stopped. It wasn't the Dionnes who were at fault, of course. It was the good doctor, and a Depression-era public longing for everything they could read about the five obnoxious little twits.

Then the world seemed to explode, as the longest and most ferocious artillery barrage in human history burst upon the surprised Germans, initiating the Battle of Vimy Ridge. Who knew then that this was a stupid, useless, bloody war? Naturally, it wasn't Queen Victoria's fault. Albert, as always, had been breaking wind during the royal dinner, mortifying everyone within three blocks and gassing half the people in the room.

Hollywood has always had this idiotic way of looking at Canada, which is justifiable in retrospect, since there has rarely been a more idiotic country. The men shivered, the men froze, the men cursed, but they were determined to work their way into the bowels of the Arctic at last, knowing they were a lot safer there than in the bowels of Victoria's consort. They knew in their heart of hearts that anything, yes, anything, was possible in the secret world of Og.

There are many good reasons why we act like Canadians, not the least of which is that we can never seem to get enough green cards to allow all of us to work in the States. And if there is anything more smug than a Protestant/capitalist member of the Liberal or Conservative party, I haven't yet met him. Sadly, their numbers are legion, and it's a damned shame that they weren't all wiped out at Vimy or scalped by Tecumseh in 1813. My countless children gathered around our boat, anxious to continue our glorious journey up, or maybe it was down, the dangerous river and hoped against hope to be immortalized in their beloved father's writing, while not having to be shot at by Americans or Germans, or not having to freeze their little buns off somewhere in the frozen northern wastes. The recipe for *poulet à la canadienne* begins like all others from that special part of French Canada: steal one chicken, then sneak into the garden of an Anglo and grab some vegetables. Then find some large pot and measure out three litres of water, which you bring quickly to moil...

Robertson Davies
THE COMPLETE PLOT OF *THE DEPTFORD TRILOGY* IN ONE PARAGRAPH

Percy Boyd Staunton, a.k.a. Boy, throws a snowball with a stone hidden inside it at his ten-year-old Deptford friend, Dunstan Ramsay, who is really called Dunstable, but the names are already confusing enough. Ramsay ducks, making the snowball hit Mary Dempster, who is pregnant by her husband, who is a minister but not Catholic, so it's okay. The accident pushes Mary into early labour, but she and her infant, Paul Dempster, are nursed back to health by Dunstan's mother, who cautions the new mother against ever getting stoned again while pregnant. Dunstan alone knows that Boy (and a naughty boy he was, too) had thrown the snowball, but he never lets anyone know because of his decency, and sense of honour, not to mention Boy's threats to cut his little throat. But as Mary Dempster sinks into insanity—often the only sensible way to escape a small Ontario town—Dunstan feels profound guilt. He feels even worse when the crazed Mary is discovered making whoopie with a bum in a pit outside town, shocking and horrifying the townspeople and moving her sensitive, kindly minister husband, Amasa Dempster, to do the only proper thing an Ontario religious leader can do to a promiscuous, lunatic wife: tie her to a bedpost with a rope. Still, there is some goodness even in the corrupt and the insane, as any follower of Canadian politics knows so well, and when Dunstan's brother Willie nearly dies, it is Mary Dempster who nurses him back to health, without even asking for his provincial insurance number. Along comes the Great War, which really wasn't so great (see Timothy Findley's *The Wars*), and Dunstan wins the Victoria Cross, which is only one of many crosses he has to bear. Never forgetting the woman who got stoned in his place, Dunstan sends money to help her after her husband and aunt die, and after her son Paul vanishes, only to return many hundreds of pages later in another guise—but we're getting ahead of ourselves. Eventually, Mary Dempster dies in a Toronto hospital for crazy people. Boy Staunton, in the meantime, has returned from the war (see Findley) and makes big bucks expanding in his father's business (see Peter C. Newman), forming a major corporation, while keeping his friendship with Dunstan and occasionally assisting with a little insider trading. Boy marries the childhood sweetheart of both of them, Leola Cruikshank, who bears his beautiful children and lives with him in a magnificent mansion. This inevitably means that she chooses to try to kill herself and ends up dying of pneumonia, being a Canadian who just can't stand such success. Boy's daughter Caroline goes ahead and marries a wimp, while David becomes a successful lawyer, which means that he must become a drunk and try Jungian analysis in Zurich, since it obviously worked so well for Robertson Davies. Dunstan, on the other hand, has come back from the war missing a leg, something that pretty well rules out the 1920 Olympics, but there is at least some good news awaiting him upon his return to Canada: both his parents have died in the flu epidemic, leaving the readers with at least two fewer characters to keep track of. It is clear that Dunstan must escape from his home town, if only on one leg, which now seems inevitable. He obtains his M.A. in history and begins to teach at Colborne College, a prep school near Toronto, where, inevitably, Boy is governor, since it's a small world and this is a small country in spite of its large geography. Indeed, Dunstan actually gets to teach David Staunton, proving that this really is a small world. It's a small continent, too, for as Dunstan travels across Europe and spends

Allan Gould

The National Film Board has had decades of impact upon Canadians in movie theatres.

What Canadian has not rushed out of his or her house to see the latest Oscar-nominee, raced through traffic, and parked illegally in front of a movie theatre, only to discover that a 45-minute, NFB study of a grain of wheat sprouting in Northern Saskatchewan was just beginning?

What Canadian has not tossed and turned through an hour-long NFB documentary on the Golden Boy statue atop the Winnipeg City Hall?

What Canadian has not thrilled to a 90-minute, partially animated cartoon of time-lapse photography of an iceberg floating off Baffin Island?

What Canadian has not been stunned by the leftist interpretation of that sprouting Saskatchewan grain of wheat, the pinko aspect of the Golden Boy atop the Winnipeg City Hall, and the communist leanings of that Baffin Island iceberg?

some time in Mexico, he keeps running into Paul Dempster, the son of crazy Mary and the same kid who was from his mother's womb untimely ripp'd, all because of that damned snowball back in the first line...(etc.)

Marshall McLuhan
A TYPICAL LECTURE

"Good morning, students. Today's lesson, as you know, is on James Joyce, about which we should rejoice. Not like the villain in last night's "Gunsmoke," who was shot down in the street, not to mention in the heart. How many of you saw that episode? Only four? The rest of you fail. Which is fine, really, because young people today are after jobs, not careers. Education is *not* what you want, even though the word comes from the Latin word *ducare*, meaning to lead. But lead to what? TV and rock music, along with the political resurrection of Richard Nixon, is what's really important, so why sit in a classroom at all? Indeed, the city itself is a classroom without walls, as are movies, radio and TV, which is why "Gunsmoke" is so important. And speaking of important writers, have you done your reading of E.M. Forster, or have you only connected—that's a literary joke, folks—with Orwell, who created Orwellian material, while Forster couldn't see the forester through the trees. Not that trees are relevant anymore, since they once were basic to the publication of books, which are no longer read because of the rise of electronic media. Anyway, take out

–MACKINNON

your T.S. Eliot—no relation to George, who wasn't even a guy, anyway—and open to anywhere you like, since individual pages have become obsolete. Yes, uh, Mr. Marchand, I believe?"

Young student in back: "Will this be on the exam?"

You get the idea.

YOU BLANKET ME LIKE IMPENDING DOOM

Al and George

You blanket me like impending doom.

You smother me like an infant heir.

Like a report card I am held back

by your overdue fines.

Your thirst for cruelty is insatiable.

Your head is a carton of hate.

Like the moon you have a prehistoric dark side

and your Sea of Tranquillity is equally dry.

Satan has first draft choice on all your children.

Your birthstone is asphalt.

A drunk carnival ride operator could count your

virtues on his remaining fingers.

Your brain capacity has a daily limit.

You are as clumsy as Victorian surgery.

A playground face you made as a child has stuck.

My patience is an exhaust pipe you greedily suck.

You are as inspiring as network television.

Your name spelled backwards is bullshit.

Every apartment you lived in has burned to the ground.

We were born on the same day yet you always forget my
   birthday.

On top of everything else

I THINK YOU DO IT ON PURPOSE.

THE CRITIC

Mavor Moore

The critic is the public's friend.
From lofty summits we descend
To answer the eternal question:
Is it Art or Indigestion?
Without our taste (the keenest
   known)
You would be forced to use
   your own:
And it takes years to learn the
   knack
Of finding hay in a needle-stack.

FROM *SARAH BINKS*

Paul Hiebert

Sarah Binks, the Sweet Songstress of Saskatchewan, as she is often called, no longer needs any introduction to her ever growing list of admirers. In fact, it may be asked why another book should be added to the already voluminous and continually growing literature which deals with the work of this great Canadian. We already know about her life—we know about her tragic death. We know about her early struggles for recognition and her rise to fame. We know about the honours that were showered upon her, culminating finally in that highest award in the bestowal of the Saskatchewan people, the Wheat Pool Medal. But what is not known, or at least what is so often overlooked, is that quite apart from the Saskatchewan for which Sarah speaks, she was pre-eminently a poetess in her own right, that in a life so poor in incident and surrounded on all sides by the pastoral simplicity, if not actual severity, of the Municipality of Willows, she developed a character so rich and a personality so winsome and diverse. There is, too, a profound personal philosophy which speaks to us quite apart from the sweep and beauty of the prairies with which she is associated. It is this theme which the Author has developed. It definitely strikes a new tone.

From Shakespeare's "England, my England," to a Saskatchewan wheat farm may seem to be a far cry. But that same patriotism, that same confidence and joy in his native land which is the heritage of all poets, is also Sarah's. And when she cries out in a sudden awareness of her own gumbo stretch, "The Farmer is King!" or when she sings in full throat "The Song of the Chore," or hymns the joy of "Spreading Time," or discusses with deep understanding but with impersonal detachment as in "To My Father, Jacob Binks," the fine economic adjustment between the farmer and the cut-worm, we know that she speaks for the Canadian West in the language of all poets at all times. It is this which has given her the high place in the world of literature and in the hearts of her countrymen.

But there is much more to Sarah Binks than being the Laureate of Saskatchewan. Sarah was not only the expression of her day and age, she was also the product of her immediate environment. She was the product of her friends, of her books and of the little incidents which shaped her life. She was the product of the Grade School, of her neighbours, of Mathilda Schwantzhacker, of Ole the hired man, of her grandfather the philosophical herbalist, of William Greenglow who taught her Geology, of Henry Welkin who took her to Regina. From all of these Sarah emerges as a character, as a personality and above all, as a woman...

From *Childhood and Early Life*

Little remains of the old homestead. The house itself has been torn down by souvenir hunters, one of the barns leans drunkenly and the other is about to fall. Gophers play on the site of the little corral where Sarah kept the calf, wild roses grow where once were beans and potatoes. In the coulee, now dry, that ran behind the house, a meadowlark has built its nest. It may have been that Sarah, with the prophetic eye of the poetess, visualized this scene when, in her later years, she wrote those famous lines, now inscribed in bronze over the gateway of St. Midget's, entitled "Ode to a Deserted Farm":

How changed and bleak the meadows lie

And overgrown with hay,

The fields of oats and barley

Where the binder twined its way!

With doors ajar the cottage stands

Deserted on the hill—

No welcome bark, no thudding hoof,

And the voice of the pig is still.

The west was still the West in the days when Jacob and Agathea Binks first homesteaded the N.E. Sec. 37, Township 21, R.R. 9, W. To the east lay Oak Bluff, the end of the steel. To the west stretched the boundless prairies of the North West Territories, in which, to quote Sarah's own words, "The hand of man hath never trod." Here was the home of the coyote and the gopher, the antelope still flaunted his lack of tail to the western wind, and the pensive mosquito wandered unafraid. A region rich in historical interests and traditions, of tales of Indian fights with their squaws, of squaws with the Mounted Police. Willows was then Wallows, and the very name, Oak Bluff, was derived from an old Indian word, or combination of words, indicating that at that spot the white man had been frightened or, to use the Indian term, "bluffed" at a conference between Chief Buffalo Chip and Colonel MacSqueamish, the outcome being described by the chief in the Cree dialect as being "oke," meaning very good, or excellent...

Professor R. Ambush has called attention to the fact that the date of April 1st bears the entry "caff," and that this refers to the date on which Sarah's pet calf was born and that those poignant lines of "Calf" could not have been written before this date and were probably written soon after since it had not yet received a name:

Oh calf, that gambolled by my door,

Who made me rich who now am poor,

That licked my hand with milk bespread,

Oh calf, calf! Art dead, art dead?

LITTER CHOOR

FROM CANAJUN, EH?

Mark Orkin

Being largely preoccupied with keeping warm, the early Canajans did not take to reading and writing for a long time. The appearance of the first daily newspapers in the 1830s, however, marked a turning point. Now for the first time people had something to wrap the garbage in. From there is was but a hop, skip and stumble to CanLit. Those who held that Canajans were only interested in beer and hockey had to eat (and drink) their words. As McLoon may have said, "Your Canajan is but a slob, the weakest in nature, but he is a thinking slob." When recently the average income of Canajan writers grew to almost $3,723.57 a year (seasonally adjusted) it was apparent to even the dullest observer that Canada had become a force to be reckoned with in world litter choor.

The fact that they could never earn a living kept Canajan writers from selling out. In that way personal and national integrity were preserved. It was the Canajan way. Although a lot of quite good stuff got written, the majority of readers brought up on Hollywood and Hugh Ess

Oh calf, I sit and languish, calf,
With sombre face, I cannot laugh,
Can I forget thy playful bunts?
Oh calf, calf, that loved me once!

With mildewed optics, deathlike, still,
My nights are damp, my days are chill,
I weep again with doleful sniff,
Oh, calf, calf, so dead. So stiff.

...But if Sarah's formal education was neglected, if her acquaintance with the great authors was a mere nodding acquaintance, she learned all the more from the big school of nature. Nature to her was something alive, and the life of the farm, wild as well as domestic, acquired in her eyes a character and a personality. The lowly blade of grass and the stately horse were equally objects of her sympathetic speculations. She understood the grasshoppers and held them in contempt, whereas the gophers, whose inclusion in the primordial curse had, according to Jacob Binks, been omitted only through some oversight on the part of the Creator, were to Sarah a constant source of humorous amusement. For the perennial calf she had a womanly affection, and its stupidity enthralled her. She was keenly aware of sky and field. She loved the hot sunlight of the afternoon and the feel of the wind on her cheek. One need only read "My Garden" and "The Bug" to realize how deep is Sarah's sympathetic understanding of nature.

My Garden
A little blade of grass I see,
Its banner waving wild and free,
And I wonder if in time to come
'Twill be a great big onion;
We cannot tell, we do not know,
For oft we reap and didn't sow;
We plant the hairy coconut,
With hope serene and sturdy—but
We cannot tell, for who can say,
We plant the oats and reap the hay,
We sow the apple, reap the worm,

We tread the worm and reap the turn:
Too much, too much for us this thought,
With much too much exertion fraught;
In faith we get the garden dug—
And what do we reap—we reap the bug,
In goodly faith we plant the seed,
Tomorrow morn we reap the weed.

The Bug
In a little nook, a nooklet,
There beside a babbling brooklet,
Sits a little bug, a beetle,
Browsing in a little volume,
Reading in a brand new booklet,
Studying the spinal column,
Learning where to put his needle,
Get me with his little hooklet.

The Song of the Chore
I sing the song of the simple chore,
Of quitting the downy bed at four,
And chipping ice from the stable door—
Of the simple chore I sing:
To the forty below at break of day,
To climbing up, and throwing down hay,
To cleaning out and carting away,
A paean of praise I bring.
Oh, it's time to milk or it's time to not,
Oh, it's time for breakfast and time I got
The pot of coffee in the coffee pot—
I sing of the chore, "Hurray!"
Oh, it's time for this and it's time for that,
For mending unending and tending the brat,
And it's time to turn in and put out the cat,
Tomorrow's another day.

network shows continued to prefer Mare Can bestsellers. Since publishers proved only too willing to oblige, the flowering of Canajan letters turned out to be a branch plant.

—CLEMENTS

BETHUNE

Double Exposure

TOD (*from control room*): Okay, everybody. Places please. We're ready to roll on our next sketch.

GARY (*also from control room*): Could we have a slate, please?

TOD: Yes, Gary. This is "The Making of the Sketch on the Making of the Movie, *Bethune, The Making of a Hero*"...Take One. Cue the music and Bob Sharples...

(*Music: from* Rambo *album, side one, cut four, "The Game."*)

SHARPLES: Double Exposure Presents, "The Making of the Sketch on the Making of the Movie, *Bethune, The Making of a Hero*."

TOD: Cue the sound effects!

(*Sound effects: large, angry, Chinese crowd.*)

TOD: Cue Bob as Donald Sutherland!

BOB: I did not come to China to cut off arms and legs.

(*Sound effects: heavy sawing with hand saw.*)

TOD: Hold it! Hold it! Can we stop, please?

(*Cut music and effects.*)

Those sound effects are too loud, Gary!

GARY: Well, they're Chinese sound effects. I just can't control them.

TOD: Well, do what you can, Gary.

GARY (*sullen*): You're the boss.

TOD: Yes, I am. Okay, take two, please!

GARY: Slate!

TOD: Sorry...This is, "The Making of the Sketch on the Making of the Movie, *Bethune, The Making of a Hero*"...Take Two. Let's have the music and Sharples...

(Music: same as above.)

SHARPLES: Double Exposure Presents, "The Making of the Sketch on the Making of the Movie, *Bethune, The Making of a Hero*."

(Sound effects: same Chinese crowd but quieter.)

BOB: I did not come to China to cut off arms and legs.

(Sound effects: hand saw again.)

(Sound effects: studio door opens.)

LINDA: Hey! Hey! What's going on here?

BOB: What do you mean? I'm trying to do Donald Sutherland.

LINDA: Yeah, but I wrote the original script for this sketch. Who changed it?

BOB: What do you mean?

LINDA: Tod?! Stop the music, could you?

(Sound effects and music stop.)

When I wrote it, I didn't hear the saw actually cutting off limbs. That's gross!

BOB: Well, Tod and I...We...thought it would be funnier if we had limbs being sawed off.

LINDA: Fine! Then write your own script! I'm no longer involved with this project!

(Sound effects: door slams shut.)

BOB: Oh, Geez!...Am I in trouble, Tod?

TOD: I've never seen you two argue before...Yeah...I think an apology is needed here.

BOB (*sigh*): Okay. Cue the music and Sharples.

(Music: same as above.)

SHARPLES: Double Exposure Presents, "The Making of the Apology about the Making of the Sketch on the Making of the Movie, *Bethune, The Making of a Hero*."

(Sound effects: angry Chinese crowd again.)

BOB: Linda! I'm sorry about re-writing your script.

LINDA: Oh. Well...It's okay, but next time...

(Sound effects: phone rings in studio.)

(Cut music and sound effects.)

TOD: Studio 25, Tod Elvidge speaking.

(*Sound effects: funny little phone voice for five seconds.*)

I see...yes...alright.

(*Sound effects: phone hang up.*)

TOD: It's Donald Sutherland. He's upset 'cause you've taken him out of the sketch. Why don't you write him back in. At least make the gesture.

(*Music: same as above.*)

SHARPLES: Double Exposure Presents, "The Making of the Gesture After the Making of the (*Start fading here.*) Apology for the Making of the Sketch on the Making of the Movie, *Bethune, The Making of a Hero.*"...

–MAYES

FROM HULL TO ETERNITY

CANADIAN POLITICS

FROM *JOSHUA THEN AND NOW*

Mordecai Richler

The gentlemen of the William Lyon Mackenzie King Memorial Society, piling into two cars, leaving Montreal at 6:30 a.m., had arrived for their Annual Day. Portly, moon-faced Seymour Kaplan was there, Max Birenbaum, Bobby Gross, Leo Friedman, Jack Katz, Eli Seligson and Morty Zipper, all from Montreal. Momentarily they would be joined by Lennie Fisher and Al Roth, both now living in Toronto, Mickey Stein, who was doing research in social studies at Harvard, Benny Zucker from UCLA, and Larry Cohen, who had just joined the Treasury Board in Ottawa. All of them had been pimply teenagers together at FFHS and were, for the most part, still striving.

Louis St. Laurent

Socialists are Liberals in a hurry.

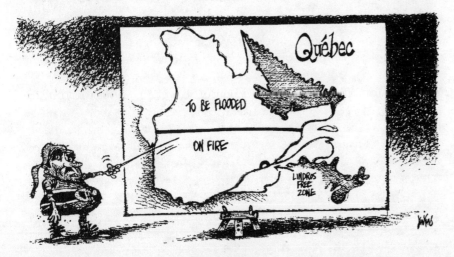

QUÉBEC EXPLAINED.

–JENKINS

"What do you get when you cross a federal politician and a pig?"

"Nothing at all. There are some things that a pig just *won't* do."

Everything possible. Joshua had already booked a private dining room, large enough to accommodate their society, at the Chateau, and he counted on Seymour, Keeper of the Artifacts, to decorate it appropriately.

As usual, the oak-framed photograph of Mackenzie King wearing his checkered tweed suit with cap to match, one hand caressing his Irish terrier Pat II, would be seated in the place of honour, to be toasted again and again. Another framed photograph of their cunning chipmunk would show him seated in his study, contemplating a painting of his beloved mum. Hanging on the wall would be a framed *Time* magazine cover of ice-skater Barbara Ann Scott, Canada's sweetheart of yesteryear, and a film still of Montreal actor Mark Stevens from *I Wonder Who's Kissing Her Now*. There would be an action photograph of Maurice "The Rocket" Richard, and another of Johnny Greco in the ring with Dave Castilloux. A Shirley Temple doll, a Betty Grable pin-up, and—a real collector's item, this—a Lili St. Cyr poster from the old Gayety Theatre. An Al Palmer gossip column from the defunct Montreal *Herald*, demanding, between gutsy paragraphs, WITH BUTTER NEARLY FIFTY CENTS A POUND, WHY NOT MARGARINE? would be in evidence. They would also have a tape of an old Foster Hewitt "Hockey Night in Canada" broadcast. There would be records by Kay Kayser, Harry James, Tommy Dorsey, Bing Crosby, the Ink Spots, Artie Shaw, Nat King Cole, Glenn Miller, Spike Jones, Mart Kenney and His Western Gentlemen, and, of course, Deanna Durbin. Yo-yos would be available for their annual after-dinner competition. Copies of *Sunbathing*, *The Police Gazette* and *Justice Weekly* would sit on the sitboard, as would a bottle of Kik-Cola and a sufficient number of Mae West bars for everyone. Nor would they be without stills of Bogart, Lana Turner and John Garfield. Or their prized photograph of Igor Gouzenko, the Russian embassy clerk turned God-fearing informer, wearing a pillowslip over his head for a press conference. Also, a newspaper photograph of their favourite among extant hockey players, the aging Flopper, then still tending the nets for the perfectly dreadful Boston Bruins.

All these artifacts, and more, in everlasting memory of William Lyon Mackenzie King.

Ostensibly bland and boring, William Lyon Mackenzie King, the prime minister of their boyhood, Canada's leader for twenty-one years, was the most vile of men. Mean-spirited, cunning, somewhat demented, and a hypocrite on a grand scale, Wee Willie was born on December 17, 1874, in Berlin, Ontario. His mother, Isabel Grace Mackenzie, was the thirteenth child of William Lyon Mackenzie, the first mayor of Toronto and leader of the Upper Canada rebellion in 1837. At the age of seventeen, Willie went on to University College at the University of Toronto and from there to the University of Chicago. He had begun to keep a diary. And he was already a confirmed Gladstonian. Which is to say, a horny little fellow, bent on the salvation of prostitutes by day, he did in fact bend over them by night, forking out as much as $1.25 a trick, not counting gratuities. In 1900, at the age of twenty-five, he was called to Ottawa to organize the

BACK BENCH

-HARROP

Allan Gould
FROM *THE GREAT WIPED OUT NORTH*

The Canadian Senate is too important to be destroyed.

Does anyone realize what it would cost the Canadian people to build a *new* senior citizens' home in such a marvelous location?

newly created Department of Labour. He became the department's first deputy minister. It was that same year, on Thanksgiving Day, that he espied his blessed Kingsmere, the little lake in the hills on the Quebec side of Ottawa, some eight miles from Parliament Hill. King was first elected to Parliament as a Liberal in 1908; a year later he entered Sir Wilfrid Laurier's cabinet as minister of labour. His beloved mother died in 1917, but Wee Willie was soon to commune with her spirit nightly by means of a crystal ball. In 1919, he was elected leader of the Liberal Party. Two years later he became prime minister for the first time.

Mackenzie King already owned a cottage on Kingsmere Lake in 1920. Two years later he increased his holdings, and an estate at Kingsmere was created, King calling his house "Moorside." Another five years passed before he became "owner of house, barns, woods and another 100+ acres of land." The same year the perspicacious King also purchased an adjoining lot, in order to prevent "a sale to Jews, who have a desire to get in at Kingsmere & who would ruin the whole place," possibly by opening a kosher delicatessen.

Ah, Kingsmere, where Wee Willie was to create an artificial ruin, instantly time-honoured, the "Abbey ruin," which he thought was "like the Acropolis at Athens." King diligently added to his ruins during the thirties, but he didn't make his prize catch until 1941. On the dark day following the bombing of Westminster Hall, King sent a cable to Canada House in London. Blitzed London. The cable was SECRET AND MOST IMMEDIATE. It arrived at 10 p.m. and was promptly decoded. The prime minister wanted to know if Lester B. Pearson, then with the Canadian high commissioner's office in London, could immediately prevail upon the British to round up a few stones from bombed Westminster for his ruins at Kingsmere. An embarrassed Pearson put through the request and, to his surprise, it was not met with indignant refusal. On the contrary. Historic stones were shipped safely via submarine to add a new élan to Wee Willie's ruins.

It was in 1938 that King, now a confirmed spiritualist, first met Adolf Hitler and quickly recognized something of a kindred spirit, another leader profoundly devoted to his mother's memory and the value of *Judenfrei* real estate. I believe, he wrote in his diary, the world will yet come to see a great man, a mystic, in Hitler. He "will rank some day with Joan of Arc among the deliverers of his people, and if he is only careful may yet be the deliverer of Europe."

"Yes, but he's the only leader we've got."

—ARNOULD

In 1924, friends of King gave him a dog, an Irish terrier called Pat, which he soon took to be a living symbol of his mother. Kneeling in prayer before his mother's portrait in 1931, "little Pat came up from the bedroom and licked my feet—dear little soul, he is almost human. I sometimes think he is a comforter dear mother has sent me, he is filled with her spirit of patience, and tenderness & love." Pat died in his arms in 1941, even as Willie sang aloud to him "Safe in the Arms of Jesus." "I kissed the little fellow as he lay there, told him of his having been faithful and true, of his having saved my soul, and being like God." Fortunately, another Irish terrier, Pat II, soon came into his life, and before going to bed, King and his little angel dog often used chat together about the Christ child and the animals in his crib. Of Pat II's death, on August 11, 1947, the prime minister of Canada wrote, "I felt as if he had died for me, that my sins might be forgiven me." His dog's death put him in mind of Christ's crucifixion. Pat II was buried near what King called "the Bethal Stone" at Kingsmere.

King's obsession with the hands of the clock seems to have begun in 1918; he regarded it as auspicious if the hands were together, as in twelve o'clock, or in a straight line, as at six o'clock. By 1932 he was attending seances and consulting mediums in Canada, the United States and England. He also went in for table-rapping, wherein it was revealed to him in 1933 that he had been predestined to become prime minister, the fate of Canada being in his hands. Leonardo da Vinci appeared at King's little table, as did Lorenzo de' Medici and Louis Pasteur, who was good enough to prescribe for little angel dog Pat's heart condition. Another visitor to King's table, the spirit of Sir Wilfrid Laurier, assured him that President Roosevelt loved him. "He will treat you like a prince." However, when Roosevelt and Churchill came to Canada for the Quebec conference during World War II, they wouldn't let Wee Willie anywhere near the big table, and only grudgingly allowed him to have his photograph taken with them. To be fair, however, Roosevelt proved to be a lot nicer after his death. He appeared before King, begging him not to retire, if only because, said the late president, he had the wisdom that Churchill lacked, as well as "the caution and the integral honesty that holds a country together." From time to time Willie's mum would appear to "my own dearest boy, my pride and joy, best of sons." Once she went on to introduce President Roosevelt to him. "Frank, as I call him." This time out, Frank pleaded with King to take a real rest, "knock off for at least a year." He also said that it was vital that King should write his memoirs, including "the most important chapter, your firm faith in a future life, that you have evidence of it."

William Lyon Mackenzie King, the longest-serving prime minister in the history of the Commonwealth, survived both his dearest loves in this world, Pat I and Pat II, and passed on to the Big Kennel in the Sky on July 22, 1950. Just as he died, thunder and lightning and torrents of rain came on without any warning. The rain fell only at Kingsmere, not in Ottawa.

King, who always presented himself as a man of very modest means, earned $7,000 a year when he first became a minister in 1909. On his retirement in 1948, his pay and allowances totalled $19,000 annually. And yet—and yet—miraculously, perhaps—he died leaving a fortune of over $750,000, and this did not include the Kingsmere estate, which he left to the nation.

Their Annual Day in honour of the scheming old fraud began, quite properly, at Kingsmere, the Jews getting in to ruin the whole place at last, with a champagne breakfast on the site of the "Abbey ruins." From there they moved on to pay their respects to Pat II, at the Bethal Stone, where they sang "Safe in the Arms of Jesus," but in Yiddish, this version being the inspiration of Mickey Stein.

Then they adjourned to Laurier House. ...

As they imbibed still more champagne, they turned to the serious business of the society. Joshua rose to read aloud the letter he had written to Clarence Campbell, President of the National Hockey League:

"Dear Sir, The undersigned represent a group of respectable businessmen, civil servants, professionals, and artists who convene once a year to celebrate the memory of that great political leader and statesman, William Lyon Mackenzie King—"

"Gentlemen," Seymour bellowed, raising his glass, "I give you Mackenzie King."

Everybody at the table stood up and raised his glass.

"—We are not a political group, but come from all parties—"

"Except the Communist Party, it goes without saying, Comrades."

"Hear! Hear!"

"—and we have only one motive: patriotism."

"Gut gezukt."

"Each year, in order better to perpetuate the late great one's memory, we try to come up with a suitable trophy or award. One year it was a dog show prize (see enclosed advertisement from *Dogs in Canada*) for the hound that best personified Pat II's godliness and bore the most striking resemblance to Mr. King's beloved mum, Isabel Grace Mackenzie. Another year, honouring yet another deeply felt interest of the late great one, it was the Mackenzie King Memorial Hooker Award, offered to two prostitutes—one English- and one French-speaking, each award worth $500—for bringing the most intense religious fervour to their work. "This year," Joshua continued, "we intend to dig deeper into our collective pockets. We take great pleasure in offering the National Hockey League a trophy, sweetened, as it were, by a purse of $1,000: The William Lyon Mackenzie King Memorial Trophy."

Everybody thumped the table, and yet another toast was proposed to the late great one.

"This trophy, to be presented at the end of each season, would go to the player who, in his efforts on ice, most exemplified the undying spirit of Mackenzie King.

Tory re-election slogan

–KRIEGER

William Lyon Mackenzie King

When Professor R. McGregor Dawson left the University of Toronto for Laurier House in 1951 to write the official biography of Mackenzie King, he intended the work to comprise two volumes...Encountering his friend D.G. Creighton, Dawson raised the question of what titles he should choose.

"You called your biography *Macdonald, The Young Politician,* and *Macdonald, The Old Chieftain.* Do you have a suggestion?"

"Well, McGregor," snorted Creighton, "I suppose you could call them, *King, The Young Son-of-a-Bitch,* and *King, The Old Son-of-a-Bitch.*"

—from *Canadian Political Anecdotes*

"Obviously, the player we have in mind would not be a high scorer, a natural star, but rather a plodder who overcomes with effort and cunning a conspicuous lack of talent, intelligence or grace. In the nature of things, he would have to be a player who has been in the league for at least ten years, unnoticed, unheralded, but persevering. The fellow we have in mind spears when the referee has his back turned, trips an opposing player if he can get away with it, but unfailingly backs down from a fight. Preferably, he would be a man who respects his mother more than the coach, and has a firm faith in the world-to-come. If he is on the ice when a goal is scored for his side, he argues for an assist on the play. If he is on the ice when a goal is scored by the opposition, he promptly disowns responsibility. Above all, he is a vengeful winner and a sore loser. He has no close relationships with any of his teammates. Loyalty is unknown to him. Forced into a quick decision on ice, in the heat of play, he neither opts for the possibly inspired but risky choice nor stands tall and resolute on the blue line. He avoids making any decision whatsoever, heading for the safety of the bench. All the same, when many a more talented player has retired, legs gone, or has been removed from the fray in his prime through injury, our Mackenzie King Memorial Trophy winner will still be out there skating. Skating away from trouble. Persevering.

"Your Canadianism undoubted, your patriotism proven in two world wars, we hope, Mr. Campbell, that you will give this award every serious consideration. Should more information be required, or a meeting be considered advisable, we are, sir, at your service. Respectfully, Joshua Shapiro, Secretary, The Mackenzie King Memorial Society."

CARRYING THE TORCH

Bill Bissett

what happend whn th kebek govt
decided they didint want royal english
shit on kebek soil

th queen sd i will
dock my barge thn in th st. lawrence

th kebek govt sd we dont want
royal shit in th st. lawrence eithr
to polute our undrwatr life

aftr all th queen is not th
mafia that we know uv

th queen sd we do not
have chemicul toilets
th kebek govt refusd
to purchase chemicul toilets
for buckingham palace

so ottawa
had to dew that an they
sent designs to queen elizabeth
uv possibul flushing units

th queen sd if ths
is what they dew in canada thn
we do not want to b on ther fukan
stamps

so ottawa has set
up a millyun dollar reserch
teem to provide adequate
shit disposal units for th royal
familee 900,000 uv ths mony
has gone alredy to le farge cement
co.

bcoz uv th serious rumor
alredy sent thruout th land
that th royal family

fr sure is into
heavy shit

Simon Rakoff

I was beaten up the other day because of a tattoo; not a real tattoo. I fell asleep on the bus against my newspaper.

I woke up with a picture of Mulroney on my face.

JOHN DIEFENBAKER
FROM *A FUNNY WAY TO RUN A COUNTRY*

Charles Lynch

John Diefenbaker told a story about when, as a young politician, he was admitted to the federal penitentiary at Prince Albert to address the inmates. Not that they were able to vote, as he explained, but at least they might provide an audience, not an easy thing for a Tory to get in Saskatchewan in those days.

"It is good to see so many of you here," was his opening line.

"Considering all the other things you could be doing," he went on. Titters in the audience.

—PETERSON

"The other places you could be...

"I want your support in my work, as you have my support in yours. I know you have gone through a lot to get where you are."

By this time, roars from the crowd of convicts.

Things went from bad to worse, and Diefenbaker wound up with a flourish that, as he himself said, finished him off.

"Let men of conviction work together for liberty, equality and freedom in this great Canada of ours!" Loud cheers.

GLORIOUS AND FREE
FROM *AIR FARCE*

Dave Broadfoot

INTRO: At a time when our country is rife with political controversy...when more politicians than ever are desperately looking for *solutions*. . .Air Farce is pleased and proud to introduce a politician who's always ready with a whole new set of *problems*. The Member for Kicking Horse Pass, David J. Broadfoot.

(Music: Maple Leaf play-on. Out, when Dave in place.)

DAVE: As we hover here on the brink of the future...drowning in debt...wallowing in drugs...choking on pollution...losing our ozone...industries collapsing...country falling apart... bigotry our only growth industry...it's important that we maintain a positive attitude towards our future.

All we need to do is get our imaginations going again. Instead of worrying about alienation between the public and the police, we should be building our police stations and donut shops under the same roof.

Where's the imagination in our Armed Forces? Our Navy has its budget cut and now they can't decide which ship to spend their money on. I say "Frigate!"

What about immigration? People are getting all worked up about undesirables being let in to the country. It's too late. That mistake was made by the Iroquois. For the past 100 years the definition of a Canadian has been "a person who can make love in a canoe." For a new citizen, that should be the only test. Standing up.

We must use our imagination.
Some people are doing that.

Quebec politicians produce unilingual signs.
Ontario politicians produce unilingual cities.
This is the way Canadians compete!

The mayor says, "Let's declare our town unilingual!"

Kenny Robinson
Comedian

————

The Stephen Lewis report [a study on race relations between blacks and the police, presented in June 1992 to the Ontario government by the former NDP provincial leader] is bullshit! There *is* no racism in Canada...unless, of course, you are an Indian, Paki, Nigger or Chink. If you are white and don't *parlez vous français*, you will get along just fine with most Canadians you meet.

—DEWAR

FROM *ZINGER AND ME*

Jack MacLeod

Dear Mrs. Thornton,

I have had a problem about voting for Mr. Diefenbaker. I know he is a grand old man, a stalwart Canadian, and our local favourite son. But when he endorsed Claude Wagner as the Conservative leadership candidate, does that mean that a vote for Mr. Diefenbaker is a vote for French Canadian Catholic separatism and bilingualism? I am very concerned that a vote for the Tories and Mr. Diefenbaker locally might encourage those frogs in Quebec not to speak white. Is multiculturalism the same as bilingualism? Has our Mr. Diefenbaker become associated with a Papist plot, and are we likely to be obliged to write to our Wheat Pool in French?

Mrs. R.T., Meadow Lake

Dear Mrs. R.T.,

This column cannot presume to tell you how to vote, but rest assured that a vote for Mr. Diefenbaker is not necessarily a vote for Popery or bilingualism. You have only to listen to The Chief speaking French to realize that Louis Riel was well and truly hanged, that Mr. Diefenbaker has little in com-

The councillors say, "Who will this help?"
The mayor says "Nobody!"

The councillors say, "Let's do it!!!"

We need to be imaginative as never before. There are a lot of diseases sweeping this country today. And they're all *mental!*

We have people suffering from linguaphobia. The abnormal fear that if you speak more than one language, your tongue will fork itself.

Many of these sufferers belong to a self-help group called APEC: Alliance for the Preservation of English in Canada. The APECers know that six million North Americans speak French. Two hundred and seventy-five million North Americans speak English. Having a majority of only 269 million has the APECers panicked.

Ron Leitch. The head. The APECer head...got the idea for APEC from a book called *Bilingual Today, French Tomorrow*, written by a man who became a looney before the dollar bill did.

The book claims Quebec is a breeding ground for the eventual take-over of all of Canada.

Can you imagine that???

Rocket Richard going coast to coast forcing all of us to put Grecian Formula in our hair! Beautiful school teachers from Quebec going around, shoving the French tongue down our throats!

Frightening! Frightening!!

Exciting...but frightening.

We have other people suffering from homophobia: the abnormal fear that in the middle of the night, gay people are going to break into your home and restyle your hair!

Then there are the sad people who have the dreaded gynaphobia.

The abnormal fear of women. The hardest disease of all to understand. Because so many of us are born of women.

Nearly all of us! Only a *woman* can give birth.

Oh, yes...I hear the misogynists saying "Only a man can write his name in the snow!" That's another issue for another time.

My mother...was a woman!!
She carried me for nine months.
My bank manager...is a man
He wouldn't carry me for *one* month!!!

The country I see today is a place filled with uncertainty.

The country I see today is a country divided.

The country I see today is...the U.S.S.R.

Soon to be known as "Republics R Us."

There is no way you can compare what's going on over there with what's happening in Canada.

Over there, the different language groups still talk to each other!!

mon with Claude Wagner, Duplessis or Voltaire, and that no bilingual civil servant could ever understand or pay the slightest attention to anything said by Dief in French. Or in English, probably.

The purity of our language will remain inviolate, except as it may be used by many recent high school graduates who appear to speak or write no known language.

–MAYES

LOOKING FOR A JOB IN QUEBEC

Radio Free Vestibule

(Music: information show theme.)

ANNOUNCER: Good evening and welcome to Looking For a Job in Quebec. Tonight, we look at the job interview: a crucial part of any job search. We have here Mr. John O'Leary.

JOHN: Hi. How are you?

ANNOUNCER: Mr. O'Leary here is a unilingual Anglophone applying for a bilingual job. Now, he has an interesting approach to overcoming this obstacle.

(Sound effects: busy office sounds.)

BOSS: Hi, Mr. O'Leary, pleased to meet you. Sit down please.

(Sound effects: sits down.)

Kenny Robinson

The cops keep killing these black kids. You never hear about Canadian cops shooting Greek kids, do you? I guess that's because they know that if they did, they'd never get another free doughnut and coffee.

BACK BENCH

–HARROP

Boss: Now, I want you to know one thing here: you have to be bilingual for this job.

John (*with fake French accent*): Ah, I am bilingual but my English is a little rusty so if you don't mind, I'd like to do the interview in English so I can practise.

Boss: I don't think you should worry. Your English sounds fine.

Announcer: Bluffing is an acceptable part of any interview. However, once you begin, it can get quite sticky.

Boss: There's one thing is occurring to me right now, Mr. O'Leary. You seem very French yet you have a very Anglophone name. Why is that?

John: It's pronounced "Thibodeau."

Boss: Thibodeau? Really?

John: It's a very unusual spelling.

Boss: Okay. Well, why don't we do the rest of the interview in French?

John: Well, I much prefer to practise.

Boss: No, no, no. I want to make you as comfortable as possible.

John: No—

Boss: *Pourquoi avez-vous choisir de faire application à notre compagnie?*

John: *Oui.*

Boss: *Non, vous n'avez pas compris la question. Pourquoi avez-vous choisir notre compagnie parmi tout les compagnies? Donnez moi vos raisons.*

John: *Il y a des oiseaux...dans ma fenêtre...avec des petites cautchou...et ce numero...et Capitaine Crouche...il y a des éléphants dans ma frigo...pamplemousse?*

Boss: *Pamplemousse,* huh?

John: *Deux pamplemousses.*

Announcer: Be sure to join us next week when we look at Tips on Moving to Toronto.

(*Music: theme.*)

WHAT IS LIFE BUT A PROCESSION?

Roch Carrier

AN EXCERPT FROM *HEARTBREAKS ALONG THE ROAD*, A SATIRE OF
DUPLESSIS-ERA QUEBEC AND A CANADIAN CLASSIC. LITTLE OPPORTUN
WAS CRIPPLED WHEN HE WAS HIT BY A CAR AND THEN CURED WHEN
HE WAS HIT BY A CAR AGAIN. IN THIS SCENE HE HAS JUST DIED AFTER
FALLING IN A VAT OF FRENCH FRY OIL.

The altar boy whose soutane was too short, who was carrying the
processional cross, emerged from the church.

At the foot of the hill, a fiery tree was swaying in the night. Was
it a house? Whose house was on fire? Who was the good Lord striking with such a scourge? All those who had been unable to get into

"What's the difference between
a dead skunk in the middle of
the road and a dead Canadian
politician?

"There are skid marks *in
front of the skunk."*

WITH APOLOGIES TO DAVID LOW

–KING

the church left the places on either side of the street that they'd selected and held, for which they'd waged war. They ran towards the flames. They jostled, they pushed, they restrained one another. Old men and old ladies were hurrying as fast as the children; the sick, the infirm, those with weak hearts or sick lungs were running as fast as everyone else.

Seeing the deserted street and a column of fire and a plume of sparks at the bottom of the hill, the altar boy hesitated, uncertain what to do. Emerentiènne Gousse, the eldest Daughter of the Virgin, ran down the aisle towards the choir, and her cane and the metal taps on her shoes made it sound as if she had three feet. She summarized the tragedy to the sexton, Théophile Labbé, who rushed off to whisper something in the ear of Curé Fourré, who was already sitting under the canopy, at the side of the Local Riding Minister who was worried because the Minister of Roads and Bridges was late. Curé Fourré turned pale, staggered and, to keep from falling, leaned against one of the poles that held up the canopy. He inhaled and exhaled several times, finally regained his balance, then held out his arms in a papal gesture.

"My dear, my very, my most very dear brethren, God has just wrought another miracle in our parish. When He took young

-QUESTION-
HOW MANY COMMISSIONS DOES IT TAKE TO CHANGE A LIGHT BULB?

-ANSWER-
A COMMISSION HAS BEEN APPOINTED AND WILL REPORT AN ANSWER IN ONE OR TWO YEARS.

—MALLETTE

Opportun away from us, letting him be struck by a car, we all grieved and found it hard to understand the good Lord's will. Then he gave young Opportun back to us by having him hit by a car again; we rejoiced, not really understanding the good Lord's will, though we thanked Him here in this church. Now I have just learned that the good Lord has taken young Opportun from us yet again. I don't think the good Lord can give him back this time, despite His infinite powers; this time again, we do not understand the good Lord's will. We do not understand the good Lord, but we are going to thank Him with the grandiose procession He has allowed us to organize."

The Local Riding Minister emerged from under the canopy and, like Curé Fourré, held out his arms in a papal gesture.

"The new road I'm going to give you, thanks to the Right Party's cooperation, will bear the name of the little saint from this village who rose up to Heaven in a spectacular bonfire. The road will be called Chemin Opportun. That's the name we'll put on all the maps. If the Opposition came to power I don't know what they'd call our new road...That's why I'm officially baptizing the road with Opportun's name here and now."

Curé Fourré swooped in front of the Local Riding Minister, raised himself to his full biretta-ed height and extended his arms in a magnificent gesture that displayed the broad sleeves of his alb in all their splendour. This move caused the Local Riding Minister to disappear behind him.

"My dear, my very, my most very dear brethren, only the Church, whose humblest apostle I am, has the power to baptize. And so I baptize the new road, to be built thanks to the Right Party's generosity, to which we will all be grateful. I baptize that road to the future the Chemin Opportun."

At these words, the church trembled. No violence; it was shaken gently. The Curé, the Minister, the faithful and the altar boys thought they were about to see an appearance by God Himself. They saw nothing. Everything was once again as quiet as if the church had never trembled on its foundations. People shot questioning, astonished looks at one another. Some of the women were upset.

"Most very dear brethren and sisters," Curé Fourré assured them, "the soul of our sainted Opportun has just passed through our church, which is located on the road that leads to the good Lord."

"Is the Minister gonna try and tell us the Right Party built that road?" shouted the disrespectful logger Uguzon Dubois, a non-believer from the Opposition.

Curé Fourré's face turned red with rage at the infidel who had once again broken the silence in this holy place. As a priest of God his role was only to forgive and he took pains to do so. He dropped his dry, pointed chin onto his flat chest to collect his thoughts. The Local Riding Minister spoke:

"The Right Party builds roads where the good Lord wants 'em, when He wants 'em. The good Lord wants the Chief of the Right Party to build a road right here in Saint-Toussaint-des-Saints, for the populace, old and young. When the Opposition was in power—for too

Simon Rakoff

I have a theory about how Brian Mulroney became Prime Minister. I think it's because we once elected Joe Clark, the chinless idiot. We looked at Mulroney and said, "Look at this guy's chin; he must be a genius!"

Harland Williams

Getting things done with the government is like a dog chasing his own tail. You just keep going around in circles until you finally come to an asshole.

long—the good Lord asked them to build roads for the people too, but the Opposition didn't listen to the good Lord's voice. It didn't build any roads and it didn't build any bridges. The Opposition doesn't follow the voice of God, because there's too many communists in the Opposition: communists that don't even respect the House of God, that shout insults at established power and show no respect for the holy tabernacle that contains the body of Christ."

There were sputterings of applause. Curé Fourré didn't take offence at this unaccustomed tumult in the House of God. He thanked God that the Minister had gone into politics and not the priesthood. Compared with such a priest, who knew how to stir up a crowd, Curé Fourré would have cut a pale figure with the bishop. The Minister listened to the applause and thought again of the Minister of Roads and Bridges, who was very late.

The Minister of Roads and Bridges, who was to honour the important procession with his presence, had kept to the schedule that was drawn up. At the appointed hour, his airplane had taken off from the Capital. He had brought along a secretary, an adviser and some boxes of personal letters on which he was supposed to inscribe his signature. The Minister of Roads and Bridges reminded the voters of all the blessings the Right Party had sown in the Appalachian Region. When he was handed the letters to sign, the Minister pushed them away, saying, "Put my personal signature there yourselves; yours are realer than mine." He settled back in his seat, stretched his legs and fell asleep. He was very likely dreaming about politics, which gave him so many splendid opportunities to live high off the hog. He was smiling as he dreamed, as he did in the publicity photos that showed him shaking the hands of women voters clustered about him. He sighed. He snored. The clouds were draped in soft pink evening

–MAYES

light. The airplane followed the river that was like a slack blue road, then it turned south and flew over flat fields that rose suddenly into rugged hills. The land raged like a sea. The hills, which rose higher and higher, were covered by an even harsher forest. Here and there, a rent in the forest showed houses scattered along roads that zigzagged through fields, circled hills and crept between the houses clustered around a church like chicks around a hen. Steeples rose in the sky like tall pointed trees without branches. The functionaries signed his electoral messages. They said nothing, but they were thinking that the Minister of Roads and Bridges was less adroit than the Local Riding Minister. Throughout their careers as servants of the State, they could not recall a Minister ever organizing a procession in honour of a local saint to inaugurate construction of a segment of road. True, such a tactic could be effective only in a backward region. Whenever they talked about political strategy, one of the functionaries was in the habit of declaring that what was effective in backward regions should work in the Capital, too.

Allan Gould
FROM *THE GREAT WIPED OUT NORTH*

Barbara Amiel is the only right-wing Canadian outside of hockey who gets any attention in this country.

FROM *SEX AND SECURITY*

Dave Broadfoot

When young activists from our universities give advice, it is called participatory democracy. Well, there is another unsung group of young activists, some of whom are not quite dry behind the ears, but who are dying to get their feet wet. They are—many of them—keen, intelligent, idealistic, informed, sometimes eloquent, often incompetent, and frequently dumb—which, as you know, is only one step away from being deaf. They are the back-bench Members of Parliament, and they also believe in participatory democracy. That is why you are likely to see them chewing their lower lips to shreds in sheer frustration, waiting for a chance to be heard.

Few of these Members feel they have done anything significant since voting to raise their own salaries. They have discovered that the world belongs, not just to Youth, but to Older Youth. And my advice to the two predominant Older Youths is: if you sincerely want to start a dialogue with Younger Youth and reach across that yawning generation gap, there is no better place to begin than in the House of Commons.

I know from personal experience the frustration of a young Member waiting to be heard. I still remember the excitement of making my own maiden speech, now immortalized in the annals of Hansard:

MR. BROADFOOT (*Member for Kicking Horse Pass*): Mr. Speaker...

SOME HON. MEMBERS: Shut up. Get her. Siddown you clown.

MR. BROADFOOT: Mr. Speaker...

Richard J. Needham

Three statements which no-body, but nobody, believes:
1) The cheque is in the mail.
2) Of course I will respect you as much in the morning.
3) I'm from the government and I've come to help you.

SOME HON. MEMBERS: Oh, oh!

AN HON. MEMBER: Here she goes again.

MR. BROADFOOT: Mr. Speaker, am I to be permitted to speak?

AN HON. MEMBER: Coward!

MR. SPEAKER: Order! I think I should call the attention of the House to the fact that the Honourable Member for Kicking Horse Pass has the floor. There are many extraneous conversations going on in this chamber. I appreciate that members have much to talk about aside from the matters before the House, but the House will soon be in recess, and I suggest that those conversations can best be carried out at that time.

MR. BROADFOOT: Thank you, Mr. Speaker. I appreciate that the Hon. Members want to get out to breakfast...

AN HON. MEMBER: *Mange la merde!*

SOME HON. MEMBERS: Hear, hear!

MR. BROADFOOT: But I'm sure they can wait till I've spoken...

AN HON. MEMBER: Schmuck!

MR. BROADFOOT: Mr. Speaker, there is a crisis in my riding...

AN HON. MEMBER: Not as big a crisis as when they counted the ballots...

SOME HON. MEMBERS: Ha, ha, ha...Hear, hear!

MR. SPEAKER: Order please.

MR. BROADFOOT: Thank you, Mr. Speaker. My purpose in speaking today is to bring to the attention of the House...

AN HON. MEMBER: Liar!

MR. BROADFOOT: Who called me a liar?

SOME HON. MEMBERS: Ha, ha, ha.

AN HON. MEMBER: Greenhorn!

MR. BROADFOOT: What I am determined to make clear today, and it happens to involve my constituents...

AN HON. MEMBER: Fuddle off!

MR. SPEAKER: It now being nine o'clock a.m., I do now leave the chair. The House is in recess.

FIRST POLITICAL SPEECH

Eli Mandel

first, in the first place, to begin with, secondly,
in the second place, lastly

again, also, in the next space, once more, moreover,
furthermore, likewise, besides, similarly, for example,
for instance, another

then, nevertheless, still, however, at the same time,
yet, in spite of that, on the other hand, on the contrary
certainly surely, doubtless, indeed, perhaps, possibly,
probably, anyway, in all probability, in all likelihood,
at all events, in any case

therefore, consequently, accordingly, thus, as a result,
in consequence of this, as might be expected

the foregoing, the preceding, as previously mentioned

as already stated

Irving Layton

In Pierre Elliott Trudeau,
Canada at last produced a
political leader worthy of
assassination.

CANADIAN CROWD CONTROL

—GABLE

THE TWENTIETH CENTURY MUST HAVE BELONGED TO SOMEONE ELSE

CANADIAN IDENTITY

Briane Nasimok

I just got signed to star in the Canadian version of the movie *Fame*. It's titled *Total Obscurity*.

BORN ON THE FIRST OF JULY PROMO

———

Royal Canadian Air Farce

(Music: movie tension under.) ·

ANNOUNCER (*voice-over*):   Coming soon. The most exciting and controversial war film released all week. It has action like you've never seen.

(Music: out.)

CANUCK: Come on, give me your best shot.

(Sound: machine gun fire, about five seconds.)

CANUCK: You missed, nya-nya.

ANNOUNCER: It has intrigue.

(Music: something sultry.)

SEXY: Well, soldier. I'm waiting. Tell me what you really want.

CANUCK: I'll have the corned beef and the french fries.

(Music: out.)

ANNOUNCER: It's full of Canadians.

CANUCK: How's it going, eh?

(Music: tension in and under.)

ANNOUNCER (*voice-over*):   It's the movie that proves Canadians can make movies as patriotic as Americans. It's...

(Music: "Born in the U.S.A. in and under.")

ANNOUNCER (*voice-over*):   *Born on the First of July*. A Canadian War Picture. The gripping story of a Canadian soldier faithfully serving his country in peace-torn Cyprus. Then, one unforgettable and tragic night, an event happens that forever changes his life. He cuts his lip in a bizarre drinking accident. He must spend the rest of his life trying to cope with his handicap.

CANUCK: Damn it, eh. I *can't* use a straw. It hurts when I suck.

(Music: to tension.)

ANNOUNCER (*voice-over*): Don't miss this important Canadian film, starring Eric Malling as Canadian War Hero and army veteran, Private Kevin. Also starring Hana Gartner as his best friend, Stan. And Al Waxman as the wacky third battalion.

(Music: "Born in the U.S.A.")

ANNOUNCER (*voice-over*): *Born on the First of July.* It's so Canadian. A co-production of the National Film Board, Telefilm Canada, the Alberta Film Development Corporation, TV Ontario, the Egg Marketing Board, Jerry the Accountant and Arnie the Dentist.

ANNOUNCER (*continued*): *Born on the First of July.* Based on a Canadian true story, well sort of.

Nominated for an Oscar, an Emmy, and sixty-five Geminis, and runner-up in "America's Funniest Home Videos."

Born on the First of July, opening in theatres on Friday. Available on video cassette the following Monday.

(Playoff.)

Two Canada Post employees are playing basketball with first class parcels.

One picks up a parcel marked FRAGILE.

"What do I do with *this* one?" asks one worker to his friend.

"Oh, those we throw under-handed."

THE U.S. OR US—WHAT'S THE DIFFERENCE, EH?

Eric Nicol

A Canadian is defined as an American with the spark plugs removed. Conversely, an American is a Canadian who found his ID.

Citizens of the United States put a high price on their Americanism. Canadians are reduced to clear. Previously frozen.

Canada is dependent on the United States for its culture, its economy, its defence and its baby alligators. In contrast, the only thing that the States really needs from Canada is water. Some U.S. senators believe that if a way can be found to rid Canada of its impurities (the Canadian people), the country has a tremendous potential as a reservoir.

Is this a sound basis for free trade?

That is the question being debated since Prime Minister Mulroney made it clear that his meetings with President Reagan were not just a crush but the beginning of a meaningful relationship. According to the polls of public opinion, most Canadians favour free trade with

−DEWAR

the U.S. Anything they can get for free, they'll take. But how much of this enthusiasm stems from the novelty of seeing a Canadian prime minister go to the States to hug another man? May this not be backlash against the previous PM, Pierre Trudeau, who made no attempt to conceal his preference for women?

Your authors have analyzed the options for Canada as follows:

1. Go for free trade with the U.S. (Also known as Amway Anschluss.) Free trade means removing all duties except taking out the garbage. It is the opposite of protectionism (spray or roll-on). By imposing duties on imports, protectionism protects the jobs of the country's workers who are being overpaid to turn out inferior products, i.e., most of our immediate family.

    The problem for Canadians is that, even if free trade with the U.S. increases their income, they will use the extra money to leave the country. Canada has a frightful imbalance of tourist trade with the States. At any given moment, most of Canada's gross national product is climbing into a bus bound for Las Vegas. For free trade to work, millions of Americans must spend their winter holidays in Canada, possibly as an alternative to capital punishment.

2. Keep Canada poor but honest. Are Canadians prepared to pay the price for free trade, namely, losing their identity, and if so how would they tell that it was gone?

    French Canada will be the first to notice that increased sales of their maple syrup are offset by the fact that the maple trees now belong to the United Fruit Company. It will take the English-speaking provinces longer to realize that they have been absorbed by the U.S. Newfoundland may never find out...

When Is an American?

The average European, Asian or alien from outer space views Canadians as Americans because they inhabit North America. Yet Mexicans too are North Americans, and nobody calls them Americans unless he wants a taco shoved up his nose. What shapes the Canadian character to fit into the blender?

Canadians who wish to be distinguished from Americans have asked that citizens of the neighbouring republic (the U.S.A.) be called Usasians. Or Statics. Neither name has caught on. It is said that you can always tell an Englishman, though you can't tell him much. In contrast, you can't tell a Canadian, though he's dying to hear.

Canadians don't help matters, the way they tell themselves. The francophones refer to two-thirds of the population as *les maudits Anglais*, while the anglophone resents "the French" for trying to shove their tongue down his throat (a French kiss).

Thus "American" means the highest common factor, "Canadian" the lowest common denominator. The world regards the States to be a whole that is greater than the sum of its parts. Canada doesn't add up.

The superior cohesiveness of Americans results from the fact that immigrants to the U.S. left the old country of their own accord, whereas immigrants to Canada were sent there, by relatives who needed their room to store vegetables.

The Pilgrim Fathers were Quakers feeling their oats. A spirited group of émigrés, they were ready to talk turkey with the Indians and replace tobacco by lighting up a witch. But very few of the early settlers to Canada considered themselves to be pilgrims. If Canada was the promised land, they soon learned the difference between land promised by God and by the CPR.

Canadians still might have achieved a sense of unity had they enjoyed the advantage of a bloody revolution, in order to achieve their independence. The best that Canada could manage was a couple of minor rebellions, led by men who were either crazy or members of parliament, or both. Louis Riel, though he has made a comeback in recent years as a national hero, never caught on like George Washington because he lost so much of his impact after he was hanged. Also Canada had no charming little story about young Louis chopping down his father's cherry tree and later admitting that the axe was to blame.

George Washington is revered in the U.S. because he was a soldier who fought against the English. John A. Macdonald killed a lot of Scotch, but only as a civilian.

Nor has Canada had a great civil war, to create an emotional bond as well as Confederate money. In Canada, brother has never had to fight against brother, unless they were drafted by different hockey teams. A Canadian novel about the struggle between the North and the South would be titled Gone with the Whiff.

In terms of civil strife, the closest that Canada has come to the Burning of Atlanta has been René Lévesque smoking three packs a day.

Les Québécois waited too long to put the mayor of Montreal in a Renault and have him ride through the province shouting "The British are coming! The British are coming!" The British were already there. All the French could do was change the street signs into French and go back to bed.

The only war that Canada has fought on its own territory (the War of 1812) was against the Americans. Apparently 1812 was not a good year for wars. Nobody said anything memorable. The British troops sacked Washington, but they were professionals and referred all requests for interviews to their agent in London.

Are there enough United Empire Loyalists left in Canada to resist union with the States? To give their lives, if necessary? Not if it jeopardizes their American Express card...

Apparently what the Canadian sees in the mirror is not just an American who has had a bad night.

It follows that symbiosis of the two peoples is too complex a phenomenon to be dismissed without examination of the survival rate of the African bird that finds its food amid the teeth of the crocodile. How conscientious is Uncle Sam about flossing? Is the Canada goose fast enough on its feet?

Allan Gould
FROM *THE GREAT WIPED OUT NORTH*

———

Canadians say "À Mari Usque ad Mare," which means from "From Sea to Sea."

Americans sing "From Sea to Shining Sea."

But then, *everything* they do down there is glitzier.

Northrop Frye

What is resented in Canada about annexation to the United States is not annexation itself, but the feeling that Canada would disappear into a larger entity without having anything of any real distinctiveness to contribute to that entity: that, in short, if the United States did annex Canada it would notice nothing except an increase in natural resources.

What's so special about a Canadian, besides the bronze halo?

1. *Canadians are more modest than Americans.* They don't expect to win the gold medal for anything. For Canadians, the streets of Heaven are paved with bronze. When Canada produces a world champion, the people assume:

   a) He or she was born in another country and has been a Canadian citizen for ten days.

   b) The Russians were not competing.

   c) The Canadian team had the wind behind them.

   d) The other contestants had been drinking/failed the dope test/been taken hostage by terrorists.

   e) All of the above.

   Canadians believe that Canada is a nice place to live, but they wouldn't want to visit there. They rarely boast that Canada is the best country in the world, in case someone asks why. Canada produces less raw jingoism than any other land except Tibet. Chauvinism is restricted to the provincial level, where it is displayed on licence plates ("Beautiful British Columbia," "La Belle Province," etc.). Canada is too big to have developed an ego that covers all ten provinces, the territories, and the mayor of Montreal.

2. *Unlike the Americans, Canadians have a great aptitude for remaining neutral.* Canada is a nation of referees. They are trusted by the entire world, when it comes to blowing the whistle. The Canadian salute is one arm held straight up above the head to indicate a penalty. When the UN flag is attached to the arm, Canadian soldiers may ride in a jeep between combatants who are confident that these peacekeepers are backed by massive reserves of disinterest.

   In contrast, Americans can't resist taking sides. Being impartial makes them nervous. They are naturally adversarial. Even their baseball umpires indicate a strike or an out by punching the air belligerently.

   Americans are so determined to be the Good Guys that they will stop at nothing. They are prepared to kill for human rights. The American says "My country, right or wrong." The Canadian: "My country, but what are the other options?" The statistical probability of a public-opinion poll asking the question "Are Canadians too noncommittal?":

   Yes 10%

   No 10%

   No opinion 80%

3. *The U.S. is the more virtuous nation, but Canada is decent.* Evidence: the States have been quicker to restore capital punishment. Americans place such a high value on human life that they will kill someone who takes it. Although most Canadians favour the death penalty, parliament is waiting for the States to develop a humane method of execution that won't require the services of a member of the Canadian Medical Association.

   Americans show more enterprise in exporting freedom. They are blessed with a surplus of liberty that they are anxious to share with other countries, by force if necessary. Canadians, however, produce only enough human rights to meet their own needs. They are happy if Amnesty International gives them a B-minus. Both countries are generous in their foreign aid, but Canadians are less influenced by whether the applicant people are starving to the right or to the left.

   Since Vietnam, Americans have spent much time searching their conscience for possible flaws. They worry about soul erosion. Not so the Canadian. Not being charged with the moral leadership of the Free World, he can devote more time to feeling guilty about morning breath.

4. *Canadians are less volatile than Americans.* It is said that the Canadian is more thoughtful than his city cousin. However, there is no scientific evidence that he is thinking. He may just be standing there, or more likely sitting there, possibly lying there, without any measurable mental activity.

   Canadians see Americans as prone to spontaneous combustion. To Americans, Canadians are proof that the rule "Everything in moderation" can be carried to excess. As cold-blooded as a vertebrate can get and still suckle its young, Canadians are ideal candidates for cryogenic intergalactic space travel, requiring a minimum of adjustment to being frozen bodily for release at a more convenient time.

   For their part, Canadians fear that union with the U.S. may leave them with a lowered resistance to hysteria. They accept the article of faith that God saw that the world needed a Valium, so He created Canada.

   As for the Americans who have considered the absorption of the northerners into their nation, they feel some apprehension about taking 25 million tranquillizers without knowing the possible side effects.

The Ten Can-Commandments

For Canadians who want to stay that way even unto Eternity, the ten commandments are:

1. Thou shalt not make unto thee any graven image, except it hath the Queen's head on one side and a whole beaver on the other.

Richard J. Needham

———

The ghastly thing about postal strikes is that after they are over, the service returns to normal.

2. Thou shalt not take the name of the Lord in vain, but shalt remember what comes after "God save our gracious Queen..."

3. Remember the sabbath day, by shopping in Canada.

4. Six days shalt thou labour, unless told otherwise by a wholly independent Canadian labour union.

5. Honour thy father and thy mother, that thy days may be long in the house after thou hast failed to make it in the States.

6. Thou shalt not kill. Canada is underpopulated as it is.

7. Thou shalt not commit adultery, by sleeping with thy U.S. Cabbage Patch doll.

8. Thou shalt not steal, or have income from American investments.

9. Thou shalt not covet thy neighbour's house, thou shalt not covet thy neighbour's swimming pool, nor his lower unemployment rate, nor his Declaration of Independence, nor his large pepperoni pizza.

10. Thou shalt not believe that there is a good reason why Canadians are taken for granted, dull, wimperialist and possessing the spirit of wallpaper paste...

So shalt the choice for Canadians be this: to go to Hell in the comfort of thy neighbour's limo, or be proud and independent enough to make the descent in a handbasket of genuine Inuit design.

For truly the lion and the lamb shall lie down together, but do the twain getteth up?

A CANADIAN IS SOMEBODY WHO

John Robert Colombo

Thinks he knows how to make love in a canoe

Bets on the Toronto Maple Leafs

Enjoys Air Canada dinners, desserts and all

Distinguishes between Johnny Wayne and Frank Shuster

Attends the concerts of Anne Murray and Liona Boyd

Boasts that Donald Sutherland comes from New Brunswick

Possesses "a sound sense of the possible"

Is "sesquilingual" (that is, speaks one and a half languages)

Has become North American without having become

Either American or Mexican

Knows what the references in this poem are all about

ATHABASKA DICK

Robert Service

When the boys come out from Lac Labiche in the lure of the
early Spring,

To take the pay of the "Hudson's Bay," as their fathers did
before,

They are all a-glee for the jamboree, and they make the
Landing ring

With a whoop and a whirl, and a "Grab your girl" and a rip
and a skip and a roar.

For the spree of Spring is a sacred thing, and the boys must
have their fun;

Packer and tracker and half-breed Cree, from the boat to the
bar they leap;

And then when the long flotilla goes, and the last of their pay
is done,

The boys from the banks of Lac Labiche swing to the heavy
sweep.

And oh, how they sigh! and their throats are dry, and sorry
are they and sick:

Yet there's none so cursed with a lime-kiln thirst as that
Athabaska Dick.

Dave Broadfoot
FROM *RENFREW: SAN FRANCISCO*

We climbed up onto the cable
car and checked out every single passenger.

There were Chinese peo-
ple, Japanese, Korean, Vietnamese, Filipino, Greek, Italian,
Irish, Lebanese...

What were all these Cana-
dians doing in San Francisco?

Broodle
FROM *CANAJUN, EH?*

———

Mark Orkin

Savage, cruel. As in: "I tellya, Rick, the Leafs' lass game was sumpm broodle."

He was long and slim and lean of limb, but strong as a stripling bear;

And by the right of his skill and might he guided the Long Brigade.

All water-wise were his laughing eyes, and he steered with a careless care,

And he shunned the shock of foam and rock, till they came to the Big Cascade.

And here they must make the long *portage*, and the boys sweat in the sun;

And they heft and pack, and they haul and track, and each must do his trick;

But their thoughts are far in the Landing bar, where the founts of nectar run:

And no man thinks of such gorgeous drinks as that Athabaska Dick.

'Twas the close of day and his long boat lay just over the Big Cascade,

When there came to him one Jack-pot Jim, with a wild light in his eye;

And he softly laughed, and he led Dick aft, all eager, yet half afraid,

And snugly stowed in his coat he showed a pilfered flask of "rye."

And in haste he slipped, or in fear he tripped, but—Dick in warning roared—

And there rang a yell, and it befell that Jim was overboard.

Oh, I heard a splash, and quick as a flash I knew he could not swim.

I saw him whirl in the river swirl, and thresh his arms about.

In a queer, strained way I heard Dick say: "I'm going after him,"

Throw off his coat, leap down the boat—and then I gave a shout:

"Boys, grab him, quick! You're crazy, Dick! Far better one than two!

"Hell man! You know you've got no show! It's sure and certain death—'

And there we hung, and there we clung, with beef and brawn and thew,

And sinews cracked and joints were racked, and panting came our breath;

And there we swayed and there we prayed, till strength and
    hope were spent—

Then Dick, he threw us off like rats, and after Jim he went.

With mighty urge amid the surge of river-rage he leapt,

And gripped his mate and desperate he fought to gain the
    shore;

With teeth a-gleam he bucked the stream, yet swift and sure
    he swept

To meet the mighty cataract that waited all a-roar.

And there we stood like carven wood, our faces sickly white,

And watched him as he beat the foam, and inch by inch he
    lost;

And nearer, nearer drew the fall, and fiercer grew the fight,

Till on the very cascade crest a last farewell he tossed.

Then down and down and down they plunged into that pit
    of dread;

And mad we tore along the shore to claim our bitter dead.

And from that hell of frenzied foam, that crashed and fumed
    and boiled,

Two little bodies bubbled up, and they were heedless then;

And oh, they lay like senseless clay! and bitter hard we
    toiled,

Yet never, never gleam of hope, and we were weary men.

And moments mounted into hours, and black was our
    despair;

And faint were we, and we were fain to give them up as
    dead,

When suddenly I thrilled with hope: "Back, boys! and give
    him air;

"I feel the flutter of his heart—" And, as the word I said,

Dick gave a sigh, and gazed around, and saw our breathless
    band;

And saw the sky's blue floor above, all strewn with golden
    fleece;

And saw his comrade Jack-pot Jim, and touched him with
    his hand:

And then there came into his eyes a look of perfect peace.

And as there, at his feet, the thwarted river raved,

I heard him murmur low and deep: "Thank God! the
    whiskey's saved."

—RAESIDE

RED'S MAIL CALL—YUKON LETTER

The Red Green Show

HAROLD IS SITTING IN THE SMOKEY DEN IN HIS CHAIR WITH A MAILSACK BESIDE HIM AND A COUPLE OF OPENED LETTERS IN HIS HAND. HE STARTS TO TALK WHEN HE SEES RED COMING IN.

HAROLD: We have a really interesting letter today, Uncle Red. Came from the Yukon. I put the stamp in my time capsule.

RED: The Yukon—the land of the Midnight Sun. Dog sleds. Igloos. Six months of daylight. Gold Rush. Polar bears and Penguins. Quite a place.

HAROLD: Yeah oh yeah. "Dear Red, Living up here in the Yukon is real great. The only problem is the people from the South who stereotype us Northerners. They think of the Yukon as the Land of the Midnight Sun, with everyone on dog sleds, living in igloos and hunting seals for six months of daylight. Tourists ask us where the gold rush is or where they can find the polar bears and penguins. What kind of idiot doesn't know that penguins are only at the South Pole? How can we break away from these stupid stereotypes?"

RED: I think the main problem is the foreigners. They come here expecting to see nothing but snowmobiles and Mounties. When was the last time you saw a Mountie? I mean, I wonder if there even *is* such a thing as a Mountie. Have you ever seen one? Mr...did he sign his name?

HAROLD: Yeah, oh yeah. Corporal H. Benson of the Royal Canadian Mounted Police, White Horse Detachment.

RED: Oh. Sorry Corporal Benson, nothing against the Mounties, you're a great bunch of guys. You men carry on a great Canadian tradition, and Corporal H. Benson, if we do have one stereotype, let it be the Canadian Mountie in his bright red uniform. I salute you, sir.

HAROLD: The H stands for Helen.

Arsey Em Pee
FROM *CANAJUN, EH?*

Mark Orkin

Founded by Sir John, eh? in 1873, for almost a hundred years the Moundies enjoyed great P.R. They always got their man, they rode musically, and they sang like Nelson Eddy. They also could do no wrong, as witness their motto *"Maintiens le droit"* (I maintain we're right)...

—MAYES

NASH NULL ANTHUM
FROM *CANAJUN, EH?*

Mark Orkin

Just as Canajans have been much discombobulated in their quest for an eye denty, so they have been more than a little confused in their choice of a Nash Null Anthum...Here it should be recalled that "Eau Canada" is an Anglo version of an old French Canadian boat song. The only verse that anyone remembers is the first, which runs somewhat as follows:

Eau Canada! How roam a neigh tough land?

Troop ate rot love-in awl thigh suns come hand.

With glow ingots we seethe here eyes

That rue north Strachan unfree,

Ann's tendon guard, Eau Canada,

Wheeze tendon guard 'fore thee.

(Coarse)

Eau Canada, Gloria's unfree!

Wheeze tendon guard, wheeze tendon guard 'fore thee.

Eau Canada, wheeze tendon guard 'fore thee!

The committee heard much argument to the effect that the use of five tendon guards was redundant and most of them should be cut. Given the nature of partisan paul ticks, much argument ensued between those who wanted to sever all ties and those who felt strongly that the authorized version should remain intact. Still others were of the opinion that it was a bit much to expect twenty million Canajans to learn new words when they scarcely knew the old ones. After prolonged debate a compromise was reached and only two tendon guards were cut, one from the verse and one from the coarse. The last few lines of the verse and coarse were thus revised to read:

Frum faron why d'eau Canada

Wheeze tendon guard 'fore thee.

(Coarse)

God key power land Gloria's unfree!

Eau Canada, wheeze tendon guard 'fore thee.

Eau Canada, wheeze tendon guard 'fore thee!

The whole thing then went back to the Housa Comms where it was placed in the legislative hopper, never to emerge again. As a result, Canada remains without a fishle nash null anthum and one may in all good conscience remain seated no matter what the band plays.

THE STAR-SPANGLED MAPLE LEAF

Max Ferguson

Following the sale to an American company last year [1970] of Canada's major text book publisher, the 140-year-old Ryerson Press, it seems safe to assume that future generations of Canadian students should graduate without any jingoistic or chauvinistic delusions about their national heritage.

(The scene: a Canadian classroom.)

TEACHER: Quiet, children, please! Now I know you're all very excited over these new text books we've just received but let's simmer down and we'll all take our first look at these handsome, new books which we'll be using for the first time this year. This one here is entitled *A Child's Garden of Canadian Verse* and right here on page one we find a delightful poem called: "The Song My Paddle Sings."

PUPIL: But teacher, we already took that last year...it's by Pauline Johnson.

TEACHER: No, no dear. Not this one. This is by the famous American, Al Capp, and it's all about how a teacher instils the right ideas into the minds of young people by use of corporal punishment.

PUPIL: Gee, whizz. Isn't Pauline Johnson in that book?

TEACHER: Well, now, let's just browze through it and find out. Oh yes, here we are. "Pauline Johnson. An Indian poetess chiefly remembered for two things...her great-grandson Lyndon who became president of the United States and her great-nephew, Jack, who became one of America's first heavy-weight boxing champions. Now, children, I'd like to turn for a moment to our new history text. It has the lovely title *The Romance of Canada*. As you can see, it's just loaded with lovely, coloured pictures of the great events in our history. Look! Here's one showing the famous Battle of Queenston Heights with the American soldiers driving the

Allan Gould

Why is Anne of Green Gables considered the consummate Canadian Heroine, when she is imaginative and spontaneous?

Official shot of Ron and the gang just hanging out.

MUNRO UNION ART SERVICE
APRIL '85 TORONTO/CANADA

—MUNRO

—AISLIN

Canadians and the British regulars helter-skelter into the Niagara River.

PUPIL: Golly, teacher. I always thought Canada won that battle.

TEACHER: No, dear. You must be thinking about the old text we used last year. This new publisher can afford much better research techniques and a higher level of scholarship.

PUPIL: Well, is General Brock in that picture?

TEACHER: That's strange; he doesn't seem to be. It lists the names of all the important men taking part but I don't see....oh, wait a minute. It says here..."Absent when the picture was taken is General Brock who got drunk before the battle, climbed to the top of the Brock monument and attempted to show off in front of his troops by standing on his head. He fell off and fractured his skull."

PUPIL: Teacher! What about the Battle of Lundy's Lane. Is that in there?

TEACHER: Lundy's Lane. I'll check it dear...just a moment... Lane...Lane...Ah, here we are, Lane. No, it doesn't seem to be listed...let's see there's Frankie...Lois (*see* Superman)...no, I guess it isn't here. Well, let's move on to our new text in mathematics. That's one subject that never varies. The cold, unswerving, objective truth of math, unlike history or literature, always manages to withstand the blowing winds of change. Now, if you'll all have your pencils and papers ready I'll just read out a typical problem that youngsters your age have wrestled with for generations. Let's see, now. How about this one on top of page three: "In the Vietnamese village of My Lai there are 387 people. If a U.S. marine lieutenant kills 180, how many will be left to cheer the liberation of their village from the brutality of the Viet Cong?"

SCARBOROUGH BLUFFS

SECOND CITY
(by John Candy and Dave Thomas)

ANNOUNCER: And on the international scene, war between Canada and the United States has continued into its thirty-seventh day today, with still no sign of a truce. All able-bodied Canadians have been conscripted into the armed forces, and Prime Minister Joe Clark has asked them to stand on guard along the 49th Parallel.

VOICE I: Hey—pssssssssp.

VOICE 2: Where have you been? You're two hours late.

VOICE I: Sorry I'm late. I was looking for a side arm.

VOICE 2: Ya.

VOICE I: This is what I got. All the real guns, they took them early.

VOICE 2: What is that?

VOICE I: That's a mataruba or something, I don't know. No good. anyway.

VOICE 2: Well...

VOICE I: Sorry for being late.

VOICE 2: Well, here's the flag. It's your watch.

VOICE I: Ya. Thank you. Did you see anything?

VOICE 2: No, and it's a good thing too. 'Cause the guy with the bow and arrow was supposed to be here at three.

VOICE I: Well, you could have fired this, or thrown it like a spear.

VOICE 2: No, I don't think so. I don't think it would go too far. It's the only one we've got, anyway. Hey, a helmet!

VOICE I: Ya. I just got it today. It's not really that good. It doesn't have a strap.

VOICE 2: Ya. Where'd you get it? Hercules? [an army surplus store in Toronto]

OH CANADA

John Robert Colombo

Canada could have enjoyed
  English government,
    French culture,
      and American know-how.

Instead it ended up with
  English know-how,
    French government,
      and American culture.

BACK BENCH

–HARROP

Voice 1: Ya.

Voice 2: Ya. Figures.

Voice 1: Where'd you get yours?

Voice 2: Stratford.

Voice 1: Ya. I should have shopped around a little more.

Voice 2: Ya. Look, ah...

Voice 1: Maybe we can think of something else to use it for.

Voice 2: Ya.

Voice 1: If you know what I mean.

Voice 2: Hey, uh, listen, do you mind if I stick around for a while? There's really not that much to do, at home. It's kind of boring.

Voice 1: Ya. You're telling me. They're at my house again today.

Voice 2: Ya? Who's that?

Voice 1: The R.C.M.P.

Voice 2: Oh, no. Not again!

Voice 1: Ya. They took all my aluminum siding.

Voice 2: Oh no, that's terrible.

Voice 1: They said it was Alcan. It had to go.

Voice 2: Ya, ya, ya. I know they're taking all that American stuff, and I understand. The only thing that I've got now is my Electrohome Television set.

Voice 1: Well, that was Canadian, wasn't it?

Voice 2: Well, except some of the parts were American you know, and now they don't work worth a shit.

Voice 1: Ya, ya, I know.

Voice 2: I think I'm going to turn it into an aquarium, you know.

Voice 1: That's a good idea.

Voice 2: Ya.

Voice 1: Well, there's nothing to watch on T.V. since they blacked out the American programming, anyway.

Voice 2: Ya, well, I heard the other day that Canadian stuff is supposed to be pretty good.

Voice 1: No! They've got Elwood Glover and the detective series is now called "Elwood-O." And then that other boring thing, "The Streets of P.E.I."! What are they *doing*?

VOICE 2:   I know, I know. You know, they are ruining sports too, you know. They've got the Expos playing themselves now.

VOICE 1:   Ya, I heard about that. I saw the headline: EXPOS PLAY WITH THEMSELVES.

VOICE 2:   Ya, and they still manage to lose five games. I don't know.

VOICE 1:   Well, the Canadian Movie of the Week, it's on six nights of the week. I don't know how they figure it. I've seen *Duddy Kravitz* thrity-seven times now. And that American kid that's in the film? What's his name now?...

VOICE 2:   Richard Pramis.

VOICE 1:   Ya, well, they cut him out of the film! And now we've got all these Canadians talking to a hole!

VOICE 2:   They've been doing that in Ottawa for years.

VOICE 1:   Ya, well...

VOICE 2:   Ah, gee...

VOICE 1:   Do you want to listen to the radio? I heard they took your wife.

VOICE 2:   Ya. He was from Detroit. He just walked right in and pulled her ass right out of there! It was terrible. Lonelier than hell.

VOICE 1:   I lied about my wife. I told them she was from America, ya know...

VOICE 2:   Ya. Where was she from?

VOICE 1:   Chatham.

VOICE 2:   Really?

VOICE 1:   They wouldn't take her.

VOICE 2:   They wouldn't!

VOICE 1:   No.

VOICE 2:   Ah, that's a bummer.

VOICE 1:   They said there was no room in the truck.

VOICE 2:   Ya. I've seen your wife, too.

VOICE 1:   You should have seen it. It was an eighteen wheeler. A huge thing. The biggest truck I ever saw.

VOICE 2:   A lot of weight stuck in there I bet.

VOICE 1:   Ya. No room for mine, though.

VOICE 2:   Your wife's awful big, though.

VOICE 1:   Ya, I know so.

VOICE 2:   Well, you're the one who's got to live with her.

VOICE 1:   Why don't we listen to the radio?

VOICE 2:   Ya, okay, let's turn her on and see what's on.

VOICE 1:   There's really nothing to talk about.

How do you sink a Canadian submarine?
Knock on the door.

Irving Layton

Having overheard that Leonard Cohen's TV film was titled *I Am a Hotel* his oldest friend murmured:

"Praise the Lord. Here at last is one Canadian who doesn't have an identity problem."

VOICE 2: Ya, okay, well, it's not working properly.

RADIO—FEMALE VOICE (*whistles*): Now take me with you when you go. (*She sings that line.*) Hello Canooks, this is Buffalo Rose again. So, what's happening up there north of the 49th, huh? Or, eh, as you'd say. Not much, I guess, eh, Canooks, we took away everything, didn't we? I bet right now you'd love to sink your little white teeth into an Oreo cookie. Mmmmmm or how about a Big Mac? Mmmmmm we've got them all over here, Canooks. But of course you'll never taste our American goodies again. You can stick with your Vachon cakes for the rest of your lives. That is, unless you want to surrender. Come on, Canooks, lay down your arms. You'll never win. You're gonna lose anyways, Canooks.

VOICE 1: Turn it off. I can't take it any more!!

RADIO: I'm waiting for you. (*Whistles.*)

VOICE 1: Turn it off...she's right, we should give up. There's nothing to defend here, nothing at all.

VOICE 2: What do you mean? Canada's a beautiful country. Lakes, trees...

VOICE 1: Trees! What are we, a bunch of dogs? Forget it. There's nothing to defend here, nothing at all.

VOICE 2: Oh, ya?

VOICE 1: Ya.

VOICE 2: Well, I've got something at home that's worth defending.

VOICE 1: What's that?

VOICE 2: Labatt's. Let's go get a couple. Come on!

SUNDAY DRIVE
FROM *DIVIDED WE STAND*

A collective creation by the Mainstreet Collective

"A PLAY ABOUT GROWING UP 'ETHNIC' IN CANADA, AND THE FACT THAT THOSE FROM NEITHER AN ENGLISH, FRENCH, NOR ABORIGINAL BACKGROUND ARE NOW THE MAJORITY IN THIS COUNTRY," TO QUOTE ONE OF ITS AUTHORS.

(JOHN *goes centre stage and addresses audience as* OTHERS *create "car" from chairs.*)

JOHN: It's October 1970. You remember the War Measures Act. There are soldiers all over Montreal. And what does my family, the Hornofluks, do? We go for our normal Sunday drive.

(*They all get in the car.* JOHN *becomes the teenage* SON.)

BROTHER (*about five*): Look, dad! Machine guns!

(MOTHER *ducks to floor of back seat as* BROTHER *starts to shoot an imaginary machine gun all over and then at the* SON, *who pushes him in the face.*)

Sis-2 *(about twelve)* :   Let's go home, ma, I'm hungry.

Father *(with Ukrainian accent)*:   Shut up and enjoy the ride.

Brother: I feel car-sick.

Son: Look—you got to sit next to the window, so shut up.

Sis-2:   You got the front seat so you shut up.

Son: No, you shut up!

Sis-1 *(about thirteen)*:   You shut up! *(It's a free-for-all between kids.)*

Father: HEY, SHADDAP!!!!...Oooooooh.

(MOTHER *slowly rises, glancing about.*)

Sis-1:   This is boring.

Brother: Look, pa, a tank!

(MOTHER *ducks again.*)

Father: A tank! *(to* SIS-1*)* How often do you get to see a tank, eh?

Sis-1:   Every day on TV.

Father: It's like we're back in the old country, eh, Mama?...Mama?

Son: Mom, will you get up off the floor! This is embarrassing!

Mother: I don't want to look.

Father: Mama! They're not Russians! We're in Canada!

Mother: Ah, Ljubomir! We should have settled in Saskatchewan! It's so peaceful in Saskatchewan!

Father: Relax, Trudeau will never let these separatist bastards get away with it.

Brother: What's a separatist, dad?

Father: French punks who want an independent country.

Son *(the innocent incendiarist)* :   Like the Ukrainians?

Father: No! That's different. *(Hits* SON *on back of head.)*

Son: Why is it different?

Father: You're too young to understand. *(Hits* SON.*)*

Son: Well, if you explain it to me, maybe I'll understand. Why is it different?

CWICK CANADA CWIZ

(Questions)

1. What's the capital of Canada?

2. What's the automotive capital of Canada?

3. What has become of the Canadian protest movement?

4. How do they take the census in Canada?

5. What is a Canadian political cartoon?

6. What is a hard-hitting Canadian political cartoon?

7. Why is it better to shop in Toronto than in Saskatoon?

8. Why is Canada always pink on the map?

FATHER: *(Putting a muscular arm around SON's neck and kissing him on cheek)* Because I say so!

SIS-1: Can we go home? I got to pee.

FATHER: I'll stop at a gas station.

MOTHER: What? You want her to catch one of those French diseases?

SIS-2: I'm hungry!

MOTHER: I should've brought some hard-boiled eggs.

SIS-2: I don't want a boiled egg! Why can't we eat at the A&W for a change!

SON *(frantic):* NO! I got to go home!

SIS-1: Pa!!! Let's eat out!

–DEWAR

Sis-2: All my friends eat at the A&W every Sunday. Why can't we have a burger for once?

Mother: No-no-no...I've made three dozen potato perogies, three dozen meat perogies, and four dozen cherry perogies.

Father: Come on, Mama, we'll eat them tomorrow.

Son: They won't be fresh tomorrow! (*MAMA is pleased by his concern.*)

Other Children: Please Dad! Pleeeeeese!!!

Son: I've got seven book reports to hand in—

Sis-2: He's lying! He doesn't want to go to the A&W because—

Son: You shut your face, you fat Cossack!

Mother: (*Slaps SON on the head; all hell breaks out in the car, as it lurches left to right, etc.*) Your sister is not a fat Cossack! She is healthy! Not like those anemic English girls! (*FATHER slams on brakes.*)

Father: All right! Quiet! So, Mama? We go to the A&W?

Other Children: Please, Mom! Pleeeeese!!!

Mother (*hesitates; this is a big departure*)**:** OK! We go to the A&W!

(CHILDREN, *except* SON, *cheer.*)

Son (*crafty*)**:** Mom, you know how much they charge for french fries at the A&W? Sixty cents!

Mother: Sixty cents? Ljubomir turn the car around. You know how many pounds of potato fries I can make for sixty cents!

Father: Mama, what's once in ten years!

Mother: I don't want to be taken for a sucker.

Son: And you know, the cooks, for fun, they hork in the burgers before they close the buns.

Sis-1: Is that why Sarah eats there every day?

Son: I'm gonna kill you!

Father: Sarah? Who is this Sarah?

Sis-1 &Sis-2: His GIRLFRIEND!!!!!

Son: Stop the car! Stop this...

Father (*delighted, hugging him with one arm*)**:** Twelve years old, he already has a girlfriend! Ehh! He's a real Hornofluk! Hey, you got any hair down there yet?

Son: She is not my girlfriend!

Mother: What is this name...Sarah?

(Answers)

1. Mainly American.

2. Detroit.

3. He got married and settled down.

4. Take the American census and divide by ten.

5. A beaver rolling up its sleeves.

6. A beaver rolling up its sleeves and making a fist.

7. You can order direct from New York.

8. From embarrassment.

—*A quiz from the* National Lampoon, *April 1973*

(FATHER *brakes to a sudden stop.*)

FATHER: Sounds Jewish.

MOTHER (*Wails in mourning throwing arms into the air.*): AHHHHHHH! Somebody gave him the Evil Eye! You know what they say about Jewish girls?

SIS-1: She's not Jewish Ma, she's French.

MOTHER (*a moment's silence, then*): AHHHHHHHHHHHH! You know what they say about French girls?

SON: YOU KNOW WHAT THEY SAY ABOUT UKRAINIAN GIRLS?!?

MOTHER: Lies! All of them! Lies! (*Hits SON.*)

FATHER: Relax, Mama. The boy just wants to have some fun. Eh, son? You just hit them with your Ukrainian sausage and run. French, English, Jewish—boom boom! Eh boy, boom-boom! Ah Mama, you're gonna get it tonight!

MOTHER: Ljubo!

SISTER: Boom-boom!

SON: STOP THE CAR! STOP THE CARRRRRRR!

FATHER (*turning left*): OK, OK girls! No more boom-boom! We eat quiet at the A&W.

SON: No, no, I don't want to eat! Can I please have the keys to the house?

FATHER: What? You ashamed to show your family to this girl?

(*Family freezes, all looking at SON; he stands up on his chair and talks to audience.*)

SON: What would you say? All my friends hang out at that A&W...And you know how hard I fight to be one of those kids hanging out at the A&W? OK, I still get a lot of static about my name—Hornofluk. But then we talk about, y'know, sex 'n drugs 'n rock 'n roll. We hang out at that A&W in harmony...At home, though, my parents are always reminding me, right, Sarah's French, Tyrone's black, John's English. And the more my parents talk about it, the weirder it makes me feel about my parents! 'Cause I don't feel any different than Sarah or John or Tyrone. So I figure it's my parents who're different. And I don't want to be seen at the A&W with a bunch of immigrants...But no, we turn into the A&W...I slide down in my seat (*he does so; family comes back to life*) hoping none of my friends will notice us...But as we pull into the parking lot, my old man starts to whistle.

(FATHER *starts to whistle A&W jingle, and all others join in, except* SON, *who is mortified.*)

Let's all go to A&W

Food's more fun at A&W

We'll have a mug of root beer,

Or maybe two or three

Pick the perfect fries

From the burger family.

Son (*overlapping*): Oh noooooooo! (*covers face; then looks up*) Oh God, now! Take me now, please come and take me now!

Harry (*as others move chairs*): And now some words you'll never hear in an ethnic home: "It's all right son, you don't have to drive me home; I'll take a taxi."

SNAP

CODCO

(*A political panel show similar to "The McLaughlin Group." Three male right-wing panellist all called GEORGE, and one female, centre-liberal panellist called VALERIE.*)

George 1: Hello, welcome to "SNAP," the loud and thoughtful show where right-wing millionaires snap at each other in the restraining presence of a female Liberal Democrat. The border with Canada—what about it? Should we get rid of it, annex it, send in the Marines? It's right there in our front yard, George.

George 2: They drink a lot of Pepsi up there in Quebec. I think they'd welcome us with open arms.

George 3: Canadians own more real estate in California than any other race.

George 1: Canadians are not a race—They're a sub-species of Americans. FACT!

George 2: Canadians have a ravishment fantasy with the U.S. FACT!

George 3: I thought we had Canada already.

George 1: We did? How was it?

George 3: Frigid.

(*They laugh.*)

George 2: We may not have to invade now, George.

George 1: Why not?

George 2:   They have Meech Lake up there.

George 1:   What's Meech Lake?

George 2:   It's a cold bath that the Prime Minister Mulrooney poured for himself one night when he was drinking with the Provincial Leaders.

George 1:   We don't have that kind of hatred between the provinces that the Canadians have.

George 3:   That's because we don't have provinces, George.

Valerie: We had the Civil War.

George 1:   Come on, Valerie—that's history!

George 3:   Who's causing all the problems with the Meech Lake deal, anyway?

George 2:   A little guy from Newfoundland called Wells.

George 3:   Meech Well? I thought it was Meech Lake.

George 1:   I don't know if it's a lake or a well but it's a drop in the bucket in American Politics, and if they want to join America, let 'em line up with the rest of the world.

Valerie: We're very linked with Canada. Now we got the gas, the oil, the water.

George 3:   Wouldn't it be much simpler if we owned Canada outright? The whole Alaska thing would make more sense.

George 2:   Connect the dots.

George 1:   Exactly.

George 3:   How can we understand Meech Lake? *Canadians* don't understand it. One side is speaking English, the other side French.

George 2:   It's the Tower of Babel again.

George 3:   The leaning Tower of Babel.

George 1:   Is it leaning our way?

George 3:   Well, if they don't swallow Meech Lake, Canada will break up and join the U.S.

George 1:   You mean voluntarily?

All: No fun. No fun.

George 2:   I want to go in with guns.

Valerie: Canada is a free and sovereign country. We can't just invade it.

George 2:   You know, I'm so *tired* of Liberal Democrats telling us who we can and cannot invade. I mean, are we free or not??

GEORGE 1: Who's *free*-er—us or them?

GEORGE 2: We are.

GEORGE 1: Then we're free to invade. Let's go.

(*They pick up guns and helmets from under their chairs and put them on.*)

GEORGE 1: Hold those defence cuts.

VALERIE: Just a minute. Let's just think about this for one moment.

GEORGE 1: What do you mean "think"? Are you an American or a Canadian?

VALERIE: American.

GEORGE 3: Then accept Jesus.

GEORGE 2: Worship the Flag.

(*George 1 tossing first-aid kit.*)

GEORGE 2: And keep your mouth shut. And that, Valerie, is the sweet taste of freedom.

(*They get up to leave.*)

GEORGE 1: (*shouts*): We'll be back.

—BADEAUX

TWO, FOUR, SIX, EIGHT, WE ALL WANT TO SEPARATE

CANADIAN CITIES AND REGIONS

FROM *MALICE IN BLUNDERLAND*

Allan Fotheringham

(PUBLISHED IN 1982.)

DRIVE CAREFULLY
YOU MIGHT HIT
AN ANGLICAN.

—*Controversial church sign
seen in Manitoba*

Ottawa is rather like Detroit: those who dump on this year's model of tin are thought of, in truth, as having a small essence of treason in their souls.

I argue about this with my friends and journalistic colleagues, Charles Lynch and Doug Fisher, settled inhabitants and chroniclers of the upper-middle-class capital of the world. *Of course* it's a comfortable town for those who wish to spend the rest of their lives there, cosseted by the parks, theatres, skating canals and bicycle paths paid for by the unwashed of Moncton and Kamloops. That's the point—why it is such an unreal, artificial place for the dispensing of governmental wisdom. The residents have a vested reason (the journalists included) for maintaining Ottawa's privileged anthill, prepared even to endure the loathsome climate so as to be members of what, perforce, is an exclusive club: i.e., excluding *all* Canadians not privy to the perks.

It is Canada's own Brasilia, its own Canberra, artificially created enclaves, hermetically sealed from the realities that a politician getting on the subway or trying to hail a taxi in London, Paris or even Washington, must endure. In Ottawa one bicycles, mentally as well as physically. There are designated paths for both. One never freelances.

There have been transplants to Ennui-on-the-Rideau who have been around for years, still wandering around in a daze, their minds stuffed with bafflegab and their mouths filled with persiflage—and vice versa. The first rule that must be remembered is that Rockcliffe matrons, who run the town, speak only to cabinet ministers who speak only to Pierre Trudeau, who speaks only to God or himself—whichever comes first to mind. I was once at a black-tied dinner of men of staggering intellect, which someone described as the greatest meeting of minds since Pierre Trudeau dined alone.

But I digress. It is impossible to buy a tank of gas in Ottawa after dark. I have encountered towns where they roll up the sidewalks at sundown (a wise man advised that you should never order a martiniin a town that still has a high school band—and Ottawa still qualities) but the capital puzzles in that it assumes no one *drives* after dark. There may be a message there. The gas jockeys of the town, emulating the swivel servants, rush home, when the sun hits the deck, to watch reruns of Desi and Lucy, the most intellectual thing to hit town since they began to show the recreations of Mackenzie King's seances.

(There is a certain justice of the Supreme Court of Canada who, noting the law of the land stipulates that Supreme Court judges must reside within forty miles of Ottawa, says that is his own personal definition of "capital punishment.")

The prime architectural boast is the Chateau Laurier, which looks as if it were designed by a group of Walt Disney animators who got stoned one night on strange mushrooms. The bellhops are so old they are mistaken for senior citizens and are often helped onto elevators by little old ladies. The CBC has its local radio headquarters in the loft, proving that there are indeed bats in the belfry.

The uniqueness of the cuisine of the town has to do with the arrival—on any important feast day or national holiday—of a fleet of "chip wagons" that descend from the Quebec hills and other unknown depths of the boondocks. These are broken-down buses, looking as if they should be in the graveyards where elephants go to die, with the sides blow-torched out of them, dispensing hot french fries to otherwise deprived gourmands of the capital.

It has not yet been proven that the quality of thought coming out of Ottawa is directly related to the amount of greasy chips that are consumed, winter and summer, man and child, but it is understood that a Carleton University professor is researching a paper on it. He has received a government grant and hopes to be finished, with graduate student help, by 1986.

The locals boast grandly about the Gatineau Hills across the Ottawa River in Quebec. These are mildly undulating mounds of earth that would elsewhere be classified as topographical bumps. The local avid skiers can descend them at approximately 12.5 mph for up to 200 yards, and it is considered a great thrill. Any town raised on the oratorical delights of Mackenzie King and Allan MacEachen is easily thrilled.

One does not want to paint too truthful a picture, but truth must be observed. Ottawans think hot-tubs are located in bathrooms. Condominiums are thought to be a New Brunswick birth control device.

It is the only city in the world where rush hour starts at 3:30, the indexed-pension people fleeing the office early to hit Desi and Lucy.

Q. What is black and blue, and floats in the bay?

A. A mainlander who tells Newfie jokes.

Briane Nasimok

I knew I was in for an exciting time when my plane landed at the Charlottetown International Airport and Game Reserve. I landed at 4:30 and my cab got stuck in the Rush Minute. The cars were bumper-to-bumper...both of them.

"What's the difference between herpes and a condo in Calgary?" "You've got a *chance* to get rid of herpes."

Men wear three-piece blue suits in July. Mandarins wear six-piece minds all year round. The Canadian flag on the Peace Tower goes up and down like a toilet seat as senators die off.

Ottawa (bland on the outside, comatose on the inside) has all the verve of a glass of champagne that has been left standing for two days. I have two favourite vignettes. Sparks Street, the former main drag of this swamp town, has been turned into a pedestrian mall in vain hopes of injecting some humanity into what is basically and irrevocably an inhumane ambience. Scattered sculptures and fainthearted fountains speckle this attempt at pseudo-Rome, and the idea is that a casual, free-flow of pedestrian traffic through what could be a brick Omaha will transfuse a touch of joy into a purse-lipped city.

At each narrow cross street there is a traffic light—designed for the *cars.* But the pedestrians—*Ottawa* pedestrians, conditioned to *obey*—stand dutifully, watching absentmindedly the usually empty two lanes of traffic and refuse to travel the further twelve steps of their casual stroll until the unrelenting red light (their master, their guide, their Ottawa mind-gauge) tells them it's okay to proceed.

Only in Germany have I seen such blind, unblinking obedience at the street level. It is not learned. It is *conditioned.* Ottawa has ways to make you conform.

The second delightful indicator is the elevator of the Booth Building, 165 Sparks Street. It leads to the National Press Club and a vast clutch of the Ottawa offices of important newspapers, magazines and radio networks. It being Ottawa-run, the numbers on the elevator buttons keep falling off. The repairmen, being Ottawa-run, have lazily patched things up: the "odd" panel reads "1-3-4-6" and the "even" panel, "2-3-5-8."

Strangers enter the elevator, puzzle, and ride up and down for ten minutes searching for their destinations. Little old ladies break out in tears. A sometimes resident of an office up the street, I have watched this tableau with interest for more than a year. The botched-up buttons remain and no one—the tough journalist tenants upstairs who overthrow governments and destroy cabinet ministers—complains. It's accepted. This is Ottawa. You can't get there from here.

THE BEAUTIFUL BANKS OF TORONTO

Al and George

There's Florence! City of the Renaissance!
Paris! City of romance, and existentialism!
New York! City of Gershwin and David Letterman
and
TORONTO!...A world class city.

CHORUS:

Oh, I wish I was back by the beautiful banks of Toronto
Toronto with all its charm
There's bus lanes, half-finished highway
and automobile alarms

The police are really friendly
When they're not shooting blacks
Toronto's a fun city
IF YOU HAVE FUN PAYING TAX

If culture's what you're after, there's the CN Tower
and the SKYDOME, where the BLUE JAYS PLAY
If history's your pleasure, there's the Flat Iron Building
and...SAM THE RECORD MAN.

In Toronto you can always get a loan
When you don't need one
and give money to the homeless
'cause one day you might be one
for real estate is costly in that Toronto place
'Cause Canada has 25 million people

ALL CRAMMED INTO SUCH A SMALL SPACE

TORONTO always says that it's a world class city
You know, like someone who says "I'm really weird."
Only when they say, "I'm really weird," they're not really
weird
They're just annoying.

I'm going home to my girl in Toronto
and meet her on the mezzanine level of her
American-owned multi-national
and go down to the underground shopping concourse
and sup in the food court...NOW THAT'S WORLD
CLASS!

CHORUS:

Oh I wish I was back by the beautiful banks of TORONTO
With all the lovely money I adore
Only all that lovely money isn't my money
...'cause I'm a Canadian!

LET'S GO NOW!

C.I.B.C.
ROYAL BANK
BANK OF NOVA SCOTIA
BANK OF MONTREAL
CANADA TRUST
And last but not least...AMERICAN EXPRESS.

Allan Gould
FROM *THE GREAT WIPED OUT NORTH*

———

The Globe and Mail is Canada's most influential newspaper—it carries a good selection of articles from the U.S.'s national newspaper, the *New York Times.*

The trial of the bank robber in Newfoundland goes on for several weeks. The jury returns after several days.

"Have you reached a verdict?" asks the judge.

"We have. We find the accused *not guilty*," states the foreman.

"Your honour?" asks the Newfoundlander who has just been acquitted.

"Yes?" asks the judge.

"Does this mean that I get to keep the money??"

TORONTO—THE WORLD-CLASS CITY THAT NEVER WAS

Jim Cormier

How did Toronto fit into world history? Here's a telling list, contrived by selecting pivotal events in Metro history and placing them in context of other important events that occurred in other major centres of the earth the same year.

1884: German physician Arthur Nicolaier discovers tetanus bacillus...Rodin sculpts *The Burghers of Calais*...Gold is discovered in Transvaal...The Toronto Bald-headed Men's Association is formed.

1892: Émile Zola publishes *La Débâcle*...Gladstone becomes the Prime Minister of Britain...Diesel patents his first internal-combustion engine...Toronto voters reject the operation of streetcars on Sunday by a vote of 14,287 to 10,351.

1907: The first Cubist exhibition is staged in Paris...Joseph Conrad's *The Secret Agent* is published...Britain's 31,550-ton S.S. Lusitania is launched...Toronto City Council, by a vote of 15-8, decrees that tobogganing in city parks on Sunday will forthwith be illegal.

1913: Neils Bohr formulates his theory of atomic structure...D.H. Lawrence publishes *Sons and Lovers*...Albert Schweitzer opens his hospital in Lambarene, French Congo...Toronto Railway Company streetcars are first equipped with illuminated route signs.

1925: Russian botanist N.I. Vivilov postulates the theory of gene-centres...Hindenberg is elected president of Germany...F. Scott Fitzgerald publishes *The Great Gatsby*...The Toronto Transit Commission issues its first "tear off" transfers.

1942: President Roosevelt freezes wages, salaries and prices to forestall inflation...Waksman and Schatz discover streptomycin...Sartre publishes *L'Être et le Néant*...The first female conductor appears on the TTC.

1958: The "beatnik" movement, originating in California, spreads throughout Europe and America...Boris Pasternak wins the Nobel Prize for Literature... The U.S. artificial earth satellite Explorer I is launched from Cape Canaveral...Toronto telephone subscribers are first able to use direct distance dialling to reach various parts of Canada and the U.S.

1964: Pope Paul VI makes a pilgrimage to the Holy Land...Saul Bellow publishes *Herzog*...The Museum of Modern Art opens in New York...Parking control officers, affectionately known as Green Hornets, make their first appearance on Toronto streets.

1969: Mrs. Golda Meir becomes Israel's fourth Prime Minister...The Woodstock Music and Art Fair draws 300,000 youths from all over America...U.S. astronaut Neil Armstrong becomes the first man to walk on the moon...TTC fares increase from 25 cents to 30 cents; tickets/tokens from 5/$1 to 4/$1.

1976: *One Flew Over the Cookoo's Nest* wins five Oscars...U.S.S.R.'s Soyuz spacecraft docks successfully with the orbiting Salyut space station...American scientists detect a new atomic particle known as "upsilon"...The TTC establishes the "exact fare" system.

1980: The U.S. boycotts the Moscow Olympic games...A major Picasso retrospective is staged at New York's Museum of Modern Art...Insulin produced by genetically engineered bacteria is first tested in diabetic human patients...The new TTC Metropass is introduced at $26 a month.

1982: The centenary of Stravinsky's birth is celebrated by the New York City Ballet and the Metropolitan Opera Ballet...The space shuttle Columbia completes its third and fourth trial flights...Leonid Brezhnev dies to end an era of Soviet history...Beer goes on sale for the first time at the CNE stadium.

Did you hear about the tragic Christening that took place in Newfoundland last week?

They had to hit the child five times before the champagne bottle finally broke.

OUR POLITICIANS PLUNDER. WE LIKE THEM THAT WAY.

Ray Guy

A St. John's radio chat show recently ran a poll on the status of politicians in local society. I believe that they ran a notch ahead of child molesters, but gave considerable ground to grave robbers and pussy cat garrotters. We prefer them that way.

In Newfoundland politics is one thing and government is another. Here in the land of the rising scum, a politician is someone who, once all his relatives have been sated, shares some of his plunder of "The Gum'mint" purse with his constituents. "The Gum'mint," on the other hand, is a demi-divine creation composed vaguely of royal governors, the Church and the better classes of St. John's. It has nothing to do with the price of trimmed navel beef or potholes in the roads. Once it was used to issue postage stamps and hang people, but it doesn't even do that any more.

A long history of colonial rule, an interval of quasi-government, sixteen years (1933-1949) of government by appointed commission followed by Smallwood provided no firm grounding in civics. Perhaps the closest we get to a concept of "The Gum'mint" is like the one in E. J. Pratt's epic of the scrimmage between the whale and the giant squid. You know the two brutes are down there somewhere in the depths locked in mortal combat but you're not about to go down there and referee the match. No more than you would dream of concerning yourself with the mighty submarine plungings and thrashings of "The Gum'mint."

At certain intervals the two monstrous combatants heave themselves up into the daylight to crash out of sight again beneath the waves. It is one of the most thrilling sights in nature. It's called an election. During the brief interval in which God's ferocious handiwork presents itself to human view you place your bet on the monster that seems to be getting the upper hand. This is called voting. To ensure that the Tory leviathan and the Liberal kraken don't rise too close and upset your dory you pour a constant stream of tribute money into the mysterious deeps. This is called paying taxes. It works like a charm. That's pretty well "Gum'mint." Politicians may be like the barnacles, limpets and sea lice sticking to the great carcasses, but that's about the only perceived connection.

This peculiar blind spot makes our merry band of legislators the happiest and luckiest dogs in creation. True, they're considered the lowest of breeds but they're actually *expected* to be rogues, pilferers and artful dodgers. "They're all alike!" is the cheerful description of politicians you'll get from most Newfoundlanders. All pots calling kettles black and the other way around. How came this unique outlook?

In 1933 when Newfoundland went bankrupt and all semblance of democratic government was suspended, a royal commission was set up by the dear old mother country to see what the bloody hell had been going on here. There'd been political corruption on a grand scale. The national budget hadn't been balanced in twelve years and the civil service was compared to the Mexican army: "Very little pay but unlimited licence to loot." The prime minister escaped a howling mob by scuttling over a back fence. One of his acolytes was, need it be said, the young Joey Smallwood. My Lords Commissioners, when they started rooting around in the shambles, were aghast.

Why was it, they asked, that in Newfoundland politics the sediment always rose to the top? An answer was that the Newfoundland public doted on political skullduggers. If your honourable member was a dab hand at lining his own pockets it was a fair bet he'd be just as agile at plundering the public purse on behalf of his loyal constituents. Or, rather, "The Gum'mint" purse, a mysterious fountain with no visible plumbing connection to taxation. After 1949, federal largesse from Ottawa boosted this odd concept of government into the rosiest of clouds. And so, by the maxim that people get exactly the kind of government they deserve, all Newfoundlanders were condemned as rogues and scoundrels.

There's pitifully little to disprove this nasty notion. Several times during the twenty-three-year reign of Joey Smallwood, even he feared it might be necessary to appoint an opposition since only three or four warm bodies had been elected to it. Smallwood came to us with Canadian goodies and the operating manual bequeathed to him by that prime minister, one of his idols, who'd skedaddled over the back fence. He was followed by Moores who found the Smallwoodian formula too seductively workable to pitch out. With a great flourish, Moores brought in corrective legislation but a recent royal commission discovered the obvious—as generalissimo of the northern branch of the Mexican army, Moores had in some ways topped Smallwood.

Those who'd hoped for some political novelty to brighten their golden years had them dashed by the coming of Peckford. He's an almost perfect Smallwood clone...

When, in 1949, Newfoundland ceased to be even a semblance of a nation some fellow at the ceremonies in the ballroom of the Newfoundland Hotel cried out (for, by golly, though stupid we are passionate little buggerinos): "God help thee, Newfoundland!" The departing royal governor was heard to sniff: "God helps those who help themselves."

There's another election in the wind, but no hopes are held for a first-class spectacle. The Liberal squid has most of its tentacles in splints and can do little but squirt while the Tory whale has become so bloated it can barely heave its blubber against a mild tide.

Pity us, with not even a half-decent show to lighten our predicament. But what sympathy can we expect from you bunch west of the Cabot Strait who've done your best to ruin the only industry we had going here—bilking the feds. Your milk of human kindness must have turned to plain yoghurt; otherwise you would not have started sending scoundrels to Ottawa who can run rings around our rogues.

SOME CANADIAN CITIES
FROM *THE GREAT WIPED OUT NORTH*

Allan Gould

Montreal

Canada's most sophisticated, exciting, cultured city, no matter what Toronto and Vancouver say. Thanks to former Mayor Jean Drapeau, Montreal was, or is now, the home of a magnificent subway, glorious superhighways, Le Place des Arts, Expo '67, the 1976 Summer Olympics, the World Trade Centre, the CN Tower, Buckingham Palace, the Taj Mahal, L'Hermitage, the Pyramids, the Louvre, the West Edmonton Mall, the Mosque of Omar and the Great Wall of China.

Well, *most* of them.

In every way, Montreal is a world-class city. Its Metro has been described as the most comfortable and quietest subway system in the world. And with its employees on strike for most of each year, it is getting quieter all the time.

Montreal is the city that nurtured such giants of Canadian literature as A.M. Klein, Irving Layton, Mordecai Richler, Leonard Cohen and several decent gentile writers, as well.

The city even boasts a professional hockey team, unlike Toronto, and once even had a winning football team, until it went to that 110-yard playing field in the sky, in 1987. It also has a professional baseball team, the Expos, which draws as many as five thousand fans a

"What is the difference between Calgary and yoghurt?" "Yoghurt has culture."

game to its grandiose, unfinished, unsafe, never-to-be-paid-for Olympic Stadium, which has 58,367 seats.

From its seaport on the St. Lawrence Seaway to its many tens of thousands of former residents who now live in Toronto; from the cross on the top of beautiful Mount Royal to the double-cross at the core of its handsome City Hall, Montreal is a city like none other in the world: with its Francophone culture and its Anglophone bankers, this is the place to be. And thanks to a separatist provincial government that was in power in the late 1970s and early 1980s, the housing is extremely affordable as well.

Montreal! The city that never sleeps (because there's too much racket down on St. Catherines Street). A city unique on the planet Earth, in that until recently, knowledge of the French language was not considered an asset.

Montreal! Where the sun never sets, even though Sun Life set off for Toronto over a decade ago.

Montreal! Where the bagels are hard, the civic politicians are even harder, and the Secretary General in charge of Administration can earn over $120,000 a year.

And so can anyone else, if he's a guy, pretty smart and knows people in the right places. (Knowledge of English remains an asset.)

Montreal! It might not have the world's tallest free-standing tower like Toronto, but its taxes are far higher.

Montreal! Where a white cop can kill an innocent black and be declared just as innocent by a jury of his white peers.

Montreal! Where its major street, named after an Englishman who fought for French rights, could be changed overnight to the name of a French-Canadian who fought against English rights.

Montreal! The city with a great past. (For future, see **Toronto.**)

Vancouver

The third largest city in Canada and one of the most beautiful places on earth. The only reason why Vancouver's population is not closer to twenty million than half-a-million is that it rains in the city for approximately 415 days each year. Another reason is that the good citizens of the province in which it is tragically located, British Columbia, have a tradition of electing men who are politically to the right of Kurt Waldheim, with memories to match. (With occasional socialist inter-regna. Go figure.)

Still, any city that can boast a semi-professional hockey team (the Vancouver Canucks), a non-retractable domed stadium (B.C. Place), an exquisite university (U.B.C.), another school of presumably higher learning (Simon Fraser), a glorious park named Stanley, and a lovely symphony orchestra often nicknamed Former, as well as such electrifying and electronic personalities as Jack Webster (who always sounded as if he were trapped in a Glasgow closet) and Laurier LaPierre (who managed to break out of a Canadian one in the last decade), cannot be all bad.

Indeed, for a mere half-a-million bucks or so, a person can purchase a nice little cottage in North Vancouver, and for a mere one or two hundred dollars more, one can fly down to San Francisco and see *real* professional baseball and football, as well as hear a thriving symphony orchestra and discover what sane politicians are like.

Still, if one wants thrills and chills, Vancouver is the most logical place in Canada to find them: the thrilling skiing down Grouse Mountain; the chilling nude beaches on Howe Sound; the gentle swoops and sudden dives of the Vancouver Stock Exchange.

Most important, Vancouver stands out as the western-most point a Canadian can move on the mainland without having to tread water. And since it rains all the time in the city, both visitors and residents end up treading water, anyway. After Vancouver, with a handful of tiny exceptions, there is only Japan and China, and the businesses of both of those countries already own much of the Canadian city's economy, already. So if a person can't "make it" in Vancouver, it's either poverty, despair, or a move to the United States, where success is not scorned or mocked. Then again, it rains more than 350 days a year in Seattle, so what's the use?

Windsor

One of the tragic Canadian border towns of the United States, much smaller than its older sibling, Detroit, and miserably lacking in the latter's murder rate, crime rate, racial tensions, slums, corruption, and, most important, cheaper gasoline. For the last reason, the vast majority of Windsor's approximately 200,000 citizens pour over the Ambassador Bridge or through the Windsor Tunnel each day to purchase inexpensive gallons instead of Canada's overpriced litres. After "filling it up" in the larger, American city, Canadians usually bring back what they so often miss in their own country: two-dollar bottles of wine, pornography and the occasional scars from a mugging.

Although Windsor residents are essentially decent souls, the rest of their Canadian compatriots often look down upon them, partly because they know full well that if they were *really* good at their work, they could have landed a job in Detroit; but mainly because, in their ignorance, Windsor residents have tended to root for the Detroit Tigers over the years, when now that Toronto has its own baseball team, and a good one at that, they have a moral, religious and patriotic obligation to shift their allegiance 250 miles to the northeast.

And they'd better.

The other problem with Windsor is more topographical than spiritual: the city lies immediately to the *south* of Detroit, a fact that has utterly confused its Canadian population over the years. Still, tens of thousands of Windsorites continue to pour across the Detroit River every single day of the year, earning them the affectionate nickname "moistbacks."

Two Newfoundlanders are walking along the beach in their province. One suddenly covers his eyes and moans, "It's so sad!"

"What is?" asks the other.

"Oh, I know that it's normal and natural, but it still always upsets me."

"What's normal and natural? And what upsets you?" asks the other Newfoundlander.

"Oh," sobs the first Newfoundlander, "It's just a dead seagull."

The second Newfoundlander looks up into the sky. "Where?? Where?? Where???"

A woman is mugged in a parking lot in Moncton and her purse is stolen. She rushes to the police department, where they take down all the information and then escort the victim to a darkened room. Suddenly, a curtain is pulled up, revealing ten men standing on the stage in front of her.

The Newfoundlander in the line-up promptly points to the woman in the audience and screams, "*That's her!!!*"

THE SPADINA-CHINA SYNDROME BLUES
FROM *TORONTO, TORONTO*

Mark Shekter and Charles Weir

TWO ELDERLY JEWISH MEN LAMENT THE LOSS
OF THEIR OLD STOMPING GROUNDS.

(Music: Minor key, plaintive rhythm.)

WHEN I WAS A LITTLE BOY
SITTING ON MY FATHER'S KNEE
HE'D SAY "YOU DON'T HAVE TO GO TO ISRAEL
HERE'S THE NEW JERUSALEM, YOU SEE."

HOW WE WORKED ALL NIGHT AND DAY
MAKING CLOTHES FOR LITTLE PAY
BUILDING WITH OUR HEARTS
A PROMISED LAND
IF MESSIAH CAME
YOU KNOW HE'D WANT TO STAY

CHORUS:

WHAT HAVE THEY DONE TO SPADINA?
WHAT ARE THESE NAMES CHUNG-LING?
WHEN YOU ARE LOOKING IN A WINDOW
YOU SEE PIGS AND SQUIDS
AND EVERYTHING!

MOSES TOOK OUR PEOPLE OUT
TOLD US WHAT THE LAWS
WERE ALL ABOUT
YOU SHOULDN'T EAT A SHRIMP
WITH LOBSTER SAUCE
IT'S GONNA MAKE YOUR TONGUE
AND TEETH FALL OUT

SO WE LIVED THE WORD OF GOD
BEING CHOSEN WAS VERY HARD
EVERY DAY IN SHUL
WE'D SING OUR THANKS
THEN IN THE EVENING
SIT AND PLAY OUR CARDS

CHORUS:

> WHAT CAN YOU EAT ON SPADINA?
> WHAT IS THIS DISH: RICE-FRIED?
> WHEN YOU ARE LOOKING FOR A BAGEL
> YOU GET A COOKIE
> WITH A MESSAGE INSIDE.

What do they call a beautiful woman (or handsome man) in Regina?

> A tourist.

NOW WE'RE GETTING KINDA OLD
WEARING SWEATERS
SO WE DON'T GET COLD
TELLING OUR GRANDCHILDREN
'BOUT THE GOOD OL' DAYS
BEFORE THE CHOICEST
PROPERTIES WERE SOLD.
SO HERE WE SIT
MIT TEA AND A BUN
TALKING 'BOUT
THOSE TERRIBLE THINGS THEY'VE DONE
TRYING TO FIGURE OUT
WHAT IS GOD'S PLAN
FROM OUR CONDO
UP ON STEELES AND YONGE.

CHORUS:

> WHERE ARE THE JEWS ON SPADINA?
> WHY HAVE THEY DONE THIS THING?
> LOOKING OUT THE WINDOW FROM SHOPSY'S
> YOU SEE CHINAMEN AND EVERYTHING.

WHERE ARE THE JEWS ON SPADINA?
THE FUTURE IS LOOKING DARK.
NOT ONLY HAVE WE
LOST OUR BUSINESS
BUT THERE ISN'T ANY PLACE TO PARK!

How can you tell that a woman from Alberta is classy?

Her tattoo is spelled correctly.

Toronto Song

Three Dead Trolls in a Baggie

A COMEDY TROUPE, IT IS RELEVANT TO NOTE, FROM EDMONTON.

Joe and Wes:

I hate the Skydome and the C.N. Tower too
I hate Nathan Phillips Square, and the Ontario zoo
'cause the rent's too high and the air's unclean
and the beaches are dirty and the people are mean

and the women are big and the men are dumb
and the children are loopy 'cause they live in a slum
and the water is polluted and the mayor's a dork
and they dress real bad and they think they're New York
In Toronto
Ontario ho ho

Wes: Actually I hate all of Ontario.

Joe: Yup. Me too.

Joe and Wes:

I hate Thunder Bay and Ottawa
Kitchener, Windsor, and Oshawa
London sucks, and the Great Lakes suck
and Sarnia sucks and Turkey Point sucks

Joe (*simultaneously with Wes's next part*):

Beaverton sucks and Moosonee sucks
South Hampton sucks and Guelph sucks too
Peterborough, Scarborough, Stratford suck
Georgian Bay Islands, and Uxbridge suck
Mississauga sucks and Point Pelee sucks
and Brighton sucks and Belleville sucks
Gravenhurst sucks and Stirling sucks
and Long Point sucks, Wallaceburg sucks

Wes (*simultaneously with Joe's previous part*):

I took a trip to Ontario
to visit Brian Mulrooney
he beat me up and he stole my pants
and he put me in a tree
I went to see the Maple Leafs
and got hit in the head with a puck
I don't know how they did it 'cause
I was in the bathroom at the time

Joe and Wes: Ontariooooooooooooooooo wo wo wo...sucks

Wes: Geez ya know, now that I really think about this,
I think I hate all the provinces and territories
in Canada!

Joe: Except Alberta!

Wes: Oh yeah, I love Alberta, there's so many rocks
and trees and dirt and cows and stuff...But

Both:

> I hate Newfoundland 'cause they talk so weird
> and Prince Edward Island is...too small
> Nova Scotia's dumb 'cause it's the name of a bank
> New Brunswick doesn't have a good mall
> Quebec is revolting and it makes me mad
> > Ontario sucks, Ontario sucks

Joe: Manitoba's population density is 1.9 people per
square km.

Wes: Isn't that stupid?

Joe and Wes:

> Saskatchewan is boring and the people are old
> and as for the Territories...they're too cold!
> and the only good thing about the province of British
> Columbia
> > is that it's right next to us!
> > 'cause Alberta doesn't suck
> > but Calgary does

–GABLE

MOOSE-ALANEOUS

THINGS THAT DIDN'T FIT ANYWHERE ELSE

Howie Mandel

Two guys walk into a bar... which is really stupid, because you figure that the first guy walks right into it, the second guy would have seen it.

THIS AND THAT

Paul Dutton

It's not what I said, but what I meant to say about what I had to say that should be said about what I meant was this: to say what I meant about what I said I had to say that what I should have said was "I meant to say it's not what I said but what I meant." It's not what I meant, but what I said should be said about what I meant to say. I mean I said what I meant. I said "what" but what I meant was "this"—I mean what I said was "It's not what I said but what I meant to say about what I said that was what I had to say about this." I mean, I meant to say that—and what I meant to say about that is this. Not that "that" is "this," but let's say it is, and what I mean to say is that this is what I meant: "that." In other words, this.

Frank Peppiatt

IN THIS GANGSTER SKETCH WRITTEN FOR "THE PERRY COMO SHOW" IN 1962, PAUL LYNDE AND DON ADAMS WERE HEADS OF RIVAL GANGS. DON HAS JUST SHOT PAUL, WHO TURNS TO HIM AND LAUGHS.

PAUL: You can't hurt me, Big Al. I took the real bullets out of your gun and put in blanks.

DON (*laughs*):   I knew you put in blanks, so I put the real bullets back in.

PAUL: I knew that you put back the real bullets, so I put back the blanks.

DON: I knew that you knew that I knew that you knew, so I put back the real bullets!

PAUL: But I knew that you knew that I knew that you knew that I knew so I put back the blanks!

DON: HA! But I knew that you knew that I knew that you knew that I knew that you knew (*Counts on fingers.*) that I knew that you knew so I put the real bullets back in.

PAUL: I didn't know that! (*Clasps his heart.*) I'M DEAD!!

Stevie Ray Fromstein

——

I've got to be more assertive. When I get into a taxi, I say, "Wherever you're headed."

TURVEY IS ENLISTED
FROM *TURVEY*

——

Earle Birney

Private Turvey reporting, and would the gentlemen kindly remember he's just a Body, and so are all the other Joes, and they never really lived, and they got phony names and outfits. And he's sorry about some of their language but the real guys talked a lot worse, and he hopes there ain't any sailors present.

Number eight was a drawing of an envelope addressed to Mr. John Brown, 114 West 78th St., New York, N.Y. It had a New York postmark but no stamp. The squeaky sergeant had told them to draw in the missing part of each picture. Turvey licked his pencil point and tried to recall whether King George had a beard.

He had finished the stamp, except for one edge of perforation, when he remembered the American postmark. It ought to be George Washington. There was no eraser on the pencil he had been given. Turvey was in the midst of a leisurely probe of his trouser pockets when his head, coming up, was transfixed by the sergeant's amber stare. It was a stare of suspicion; it leapt in a straight beam from the sergeant's highstool, over the hunched and shirted backs of the other recruits, unmistakably and directly to him. Turvey blushed, made a show of scratching his behind, and returned to picture Eight.

Implanting a careful X over the implausible head of George, and an arrow to the margin, he began a profile which in spite of himself grew into the head of the sergeant. He shouldn't have put in the Adam's apple. Turvey was laying pencil to tongue again, wondering if the remaining eight pictures in Test One would be as tough, when, like the sudden shriek of chalk on a blackboard, the sergeant's voice scratched the heavy air:

"Lay down your pencils. Turn over the page and fold under. You are about to begin Test Number Two."

Turvey tried to go more quickly but the camel held him up. It was two-humped and had a guy riding it backwards. The sergeant had, with a precise maidenly firmness, made it very clear to them that in each set of four pictures, one and one thing only was wrong, and to be crossed out. Since in the other three a man rode an animal frontwards, the camel picture must be wrong. Still, should you ride

Richard J. Needham

Broadly speaking, people are honest and won't steal anything that is red-hot or embedded in concrete.

an elephant with your feet tucked under its ears? Or a horse with no knee-joints in its forelegs? The broad-beamed youth at the next barrack room table broke wind suddenly and the roomful of silent sweating men stirred in sympathy, squirmed on the pitted benches, sighed as in dreams of anguish. But Turvey continued to regard the little parade of riders; the more he examined them the more he was convinced they were all wrong. All except the camel, maybe. If you rode a camel backwards you could see better. And you had the rear hump to hang on to; it was more pointed; you could get a grip on it. Turvey was neatly crucifying the mahout and his elephant when the gopher voice of the sergeant piped again, and they were in Test Number Three. When it came to the arithmetic questions, Turvey remembered what Mac had said and was careful not to go too fast. Besides, he had caught a fair glimpse, through the dusty window beside him, of a girl in the backyard of a store—no, it couldn't be—yes, and unbelievably, in a bathing suit, like a butterfly from the garbage can.

Once the O-testing was over, Turvey began to think his second day in the army much more enjoyable, though he hadn't found any Kootenay Highlanders yet. Yesterday he had stood in long dispirited line-ups before attestation clerks and then naked before staccato doctors. Now, though they had been filed out of the testing room into a big hall where he couldn't discover a window with a view of the girl, there was a lull. He got friendly with two Icelanders and had won a dollar-twenty from them shooting craps in a corner of the lavatory before he heard the bawling of his name and it was his turn to sit down before the Personnel Corporal in a dark corner of the bare hall.

He was a bulky balding chap whose questions came out tonelessly between sucks on a rooty pipe. Turvey was surprised at the number of large stiff papers the corporal had with TURVEY, THOMAS LEADBEATER already typed at the top. And now he was starting to fill out a new one in a big sloping hand, pronouncing each word as he traced it, much as if his arm were phonographic.

"Born thirteenth May nineteen-twenty-two Skookum Falls B.C...white, single, next-of-kin Mr. Leopold Turvey Skookum Falls brother. No glasses righthanded. Ussssp?"

Turvey would not have ventured to halt the flow of the voice and bulbous pen if he had not decided that the last suck of the corporal's pipe was meant to be a question mark.

"Lefthanded, sir...except for hockey."

The corporal's pen wavered and his pipe hissed mildly.

"Wut about a rifle?"

Turvey smiled ingratiatingly. "Anyway you like, sir."

The corporal pouted his lips at the tip of his pipe and put a curvaceous R in the corner of the big sheet. "Dont call a corporal 'sir,' callum 'corporal.'" The voice was almost expressionless but Turvey detected a purr and decided he had said the right thing.

"Completed grade nine Kuskanee High at sixteen wotcha chief occupation civil life?"

Turvey thought carefully. "Well, I was chokerman in the

Kootenays once. Just a two-bit camp." The corporal looked blank. "Then I was a bucker in Calgary."

"You mean you was a bronco-buster?" The edge in the corporal's voice betrayed a hint of unprofessional surprise.

"No, s—, no, corporal, on a bridge. You know—holdin a bat under the girder for the riveter. I was a sticker, too." The corporal kept his eyes on the form, nodding as if he had known all along, but his bald head pinkened slightly and his pen halted. "That's fine. How long you, uh, stick?"

"At stickin? Not very long. I got to missin rivets with my bucket and a hot one set a big Swede on fire and he complained to the strawboss. Then I rode the rods east and sorta bummed. Then I was scurfer in a coke plant. And I was a pouncer once, for a while."

The corporal twisted his ear as if he were having trouble hearing. His face had become a mask of distrust. Turvey felt sorry he had mentioned pouncing and he added apologetically:

"In a hat factory, Guelph. You know—sandpaperin up the fuzz on fedoras. Then I come to Toronto to join the Air Force, cause the war had started, but they wouldnt have me 'cause I hadnt matric and couldnt see enough green at night or somethin. So my pal Mac and I hit the freights to Vancouver to get in the Kootenay Highlanders but they was filled up. Then in Victoria we worked house-to-house gettin moths out of pianos. Then—"

But the corporal had taken the pipe out of his mouth and was holding it at a monitory angle, and his voice was a growl:

"Dont try no smart stuff here. I ast you wut cher *chief* occupation was. Wut did you do longest?"

Turvey thought rapidly. There was the time he was a popsicle-coater, and then assistant flavour-mixer, in that candy factory. But he quit after, what was it, four months? Got tired of the vanilla smell always on his clothes. Wanted to get east anyway and try the army again. The corporal was staring sullenly at his forms. What happened then? O yes, the army turned him down because he had a mess of hives and his front teeth were out and his feet kind of flat. So after a while he landed that tannery job. How long was he there? Gee, almost a whole winter!

"Wet-splittin."

The corporal's eyes rose, speckled and malevolent, but they saw only a round face beaming with the pleasures of recall and the tremulous smile of the young man anxious to please.

"I ran a machine scrapin fat off hides. Eastern Tannery, Montreal."

The corporal laid his pipe down (it had gone out), wrote "Machine Operator," and asked hurriedly:

"Any previous military experience?"

"Well, we started cadets in Kuskanee High but we never got rifles. But I was in the Boy Sc—"

"That's all. Wait on a bench atta back till the officer calls you, next man!" The corporal looked past him, mopped his veined head with a khaki handkerchief, and whanged his pipe spitefully against the table leg.

DRIVE SLOW AND
SEE OUR CITY

DRIVE FAST AND
SEE OUR JAIL

—*common road sign in Canada*

THE GROUND HOG

The Red Green Show

It is Spring.
The groundhog comes out of
  his hole
and sees a shadow.
It is the shadow of my right
  front tire.
That means Winter will last
  another
six weeks.
But not for him.

POEM#19

It is Winter.
A time to pause.
The driveway is half shoveled
  out.
But I lay down the shovel
And I pause to enjoy this
  moment.
After all, this is my first heart
attack.

THE BALLAD OF JUAN GOMEZ

Nip 'N Tuck

(Enter Benny, the sociology major, followed by Juan, an emaciated little man in shorts and undershirt, who gnaws on a greyish root and generally looks pathetic.)

BENNY: Juan Gomez is very poor. He has never owned a TV, a telephone, a silk nightie, or any turquoise jewellery. How awful. Juan is the fourth son in a family of fourteen. By Mexican tradition this means he must chop wood for the family.

There is no wood in the hot Mexican desert. Still, Juan goes out every day and chops sand. Juan's brother, Miguel, the carpenter, resents Juan. His sand tables do not sell well in the village, and blow away in the high wind. Juan's aspirations for an education are bleak. Every day he must walk forty-three miles to school. By the time he gets there, classes are over. Juan does not eat well. Sometimes food is so scarce that in order to survive Juan is forced to pick dirt and gravel from the tread in his sneakers. This is not a balanced diet. And it hurts to pass gravel.

The situation has become so desperate that many of these poor unfortunates choose to become wetbacks and swarm into our country where they breed in bathrooms and cause unrest. And because they get treated so badly we can't eat things like lettuce and grapes...food of which I am very fond. So please, help these people to attain a better life in their own country. Send money, left-overs, or trees to me, BENNY THE SOCIOLOGY MAJOR, Box 1400, N.Y.U., N.Y.C., N.Y.

Please, help more than Juan—help many.

CATS

Marla Lukofsky

(Holding a cat up to the camera.)

Some people think this is a cute face.
I don't.
You see, I'm a dog lover and cat owners are constantly trying to convince me otherwise.
Cat owners say: "Marla, you should get a cat. They're so intelligent."
A cat strolls across the room and steps into its litter box.
"See how smart she is," they say.
Geez. It couldn't be the smell helping them out, could it?

Am I a genius because I can find the Ladies' Room at Simpsons? (Actually they are pretty hard to find.)

Cat owners say: "But Marla, cats are so clean!"

Sure. Look at them. They spend all day licking themselves.

If I did that, I'd get arrested.

Cat owners say: "But Marla! Cats are so independent! I don't have to walk them. I don't have to play with them. They do their thing and I do mine."

Sure. But would your cat drag you out of a burning building? No. A cat would say, "Good luck on the fire escape, buddy. I hear that last step is a big one."

Why, I even read an article in the *National Enquirer* that said, DOG OWNERS ARE OUTGOING, AFFECTIONATE AND POPULAR, WHEREAS CAT OWNERS ARE SELFISH, OPINIONATED NON-CONFORMISTS.

If it's good enough for the *National Enquirer*, it's good enough for me.

But I must give equal time to cat lovers. After all, dogs *do* things that some people may find mildly unpleasant, and I'm willing to discuss them.

Dogs...sometimes...bark.

What do Canadian jazz musicians play, when asked to perform "Take the A Train"?
"Take the Train, Eh?"

EAT ME WHEN I DIE

Nip 'N Tuck

(Cheesy lounge singer seated at a large white piano. Slight smattering of applause.)

LOUNGE SINGER: Thank you. Thank you very much. You're nice people. Y'know, I was over at Ron DuMaurier's place the other night. Does anybody here know Ron? We got any industry people with us?

(Sound effects: applause.)

Terrific! Well, for those of you who don't know, Ron is the man who produced my last album, did a terrific job on it too, I think, but hey, enough of that stuff. No, I was over at Ron's place, as I say, and when I was there Ron told me this beautiful story of this Inuit family—that's Eskimo people, y'know. It was the story of this man and his two children, and the man's mother, the children's grandmother. About how they were stranded up North there, which is where those people hang out y'know. And they had no food or anything like that for the longest, longest time. And the mother was dying...so she told them, "Hey, look, when I die, eat me," y'know. Well she did die, and they did eat her. But because of that, those other three people were able to live—know what I mean? I dunno, to me it seemed like a really beautiful gesture.

Lorne Elliott

———

I tried studying philosophy for a while, and came to the conclusion, if a tree falls in a forest and nobody hears it, maybe it's because a passing philosopher cushioned its fall.

———

(Lounge singer starts to play the piano.)

And I think if he could, that man might have said it something like this...

(Singing.)

It was cold so cold
Oh that endless winter night
The wind was blowing hard
We struggled on with all our might
The children they were hungry
They had no food at all
Mama had the answer
I heard her fading call

CHORUS:

Why don't you eat me when I die
Though I'll be gone the rest of you
    can surely carry on
So eat me everyone
The children can't go hungry
I don't like to hear them cry
I'm fading fast I'll never last
So eat me when I die
 I told her—hush your foolish talk
We'll make it through this drama
But when the wolf bayed at the moon
The spirits took my mama
The gentle woman's soul lives on
Her body in our trust
We're all better people now
There's a bit of her in all of us

(Enter two female backup singers.)

CHORUS:

Why don't you eat me when I die
Though I'll be gone the rest of you
    can surely carry on

So eat me everyone
The children can't go hungry
I don't like to hear them cry
I'm fading fast I'll never last
So eat me when I die

FROM *DIEPPES OF DESPAIR*

Larry Zolf

The total failure of the Canadian Army raid on the French casino town of Dieppe in mid-August 1942—thousands of Canadians dead, thousands wounded, thousands captured—hit the North End of Winnipeg pretty hard. First of all, Hitler's Fortress Europe had not been given even a glancing blow. Lying dead on the beach at Dieppe, his body twisted in half by a direct pillbox hit, was the ever-popular Selkirk Avenue Boulevardier—Feivel "Fish" Feinstein. Captured by the Germans at Dieppe was he of the dazzling smile, the great ladies' man and ballroom dancer, Bindel "Bones" Bakalinsky. Missing in action at Dieppe was the Talmud scholar and pool shark, Tevye "Tools" Treyfus.

Soon talk began to sweep the neighbourhood that Mackenzie King had pushed for the Dieppe raid to bloody the Canadian troops and scare the Frogs into enlisting. Others said some British or admiral was riding to glory on the backs of the Winnipeg boys dead at Dieppe. Everybody was asking the question "Why Dieppe? Why now?" and the answers were coming fast and furious.

At a special meeting of Emma's Enemas of the People Anarcho-socialist Reading Club, Esther Dvorkin, chairwoman, was busy introducing the main guest of the evening. Actually, Sarah Strydance needed no introduction at all. Sarah Strydance was Canada's grand dame of feminism, Canada's most famous suffragette, Canada's most famous elocutionist, Canada's most famous writer.

It was Sarah Strydance's suffragette rallying cry: "To every petticoat a vote, to every Lothario a goat" that first lit up the bald prairie for women's suffrage and women's rights. When Sarah and her cohorts released fifty-six goats onto the floor of the Manitoba Legislature—one goat each for each of the fifty-six members of the all-male Manitoba Legislature, the women's suffrage issue was truly galvanized. Manitoba soon led the nation in the petticoat vote and in goat droppings.

Sara's novel, *A Woman's Place*, was about a totally just, totally fair, all-female Utopia in darkest Africa which is visited two or three times a year—at the most—by very friendly and not bad-looking male baboons from a neighbouring island. The baboons satisfy the feminists, harvest all the crops, wash all the piled-up dirty dishes and heaps of dirty laundry—and do all the necessary shopping. The feminists outlawed drinking, smoking and chewing gum in their Utopia. The baboons secretly do all three things.

The women of the Utopia have no particular love of country or sense of patriotism; they owe allegiance only to their fellow sisters. The baboons, on the other hand, have a flag of their own—a baboon, sitting on a dung heap, and about to place a forty-eight starred crescent on top of his head— which they daily salute and run up the flag pole. They also have an anthem entitled: "Oh, Say Can You See the Baboon That Is Me!"

Richard J. Needham

If you really want to make the world a better place, you could start by moving to the back of the bus.

Susan Ryan

As Einstein said, "Great souls will always encounter violent opposition from mediocre minds." And so will anyone who goes around saying that.

The baboons are also secretive and clannish, and take care of each other financially. One of the baboons operates an illicit liquor still. The other baboons help him to distribute the sour mash among unsuspecting and emotionally unbalanced feminists in the Utopia.

The baboons worship the feminists and desperately imitate their customs, their habits, their way of doing things. But this worship is not reciprocated. The feminists refuse to meld or merge with the baboons. The Utopia remained half-baboon, half-feminist, two solitudes, each going their separate ways.

A Woman's Place was rapidly embraced by feminists, baboon lovers, and by Utopians—from Marxists to Jehovah's Witnesses everywhere. Their mania for the Strydance novel spread like a contagion among more general readers. *A Woman's Place* was hailed by the critics as a landmark in Utopian writing. Sarah Strydance's sensitive portrayal of the baboons as innocent and xenophobic victims of the sisterhood of a superior species won her the Rin Tin Tin Award of the Rights of Animals League in Cincinnati, Ohio.

In a moving ceremony in New York City where each guest sat at the head table and wore a Tarzan suit draped over the shoulder, and fitted snugly at the crotch, everybody banged jungle clubs on their tables in approval as Sarah Strydance won the Survival award of the Charles Darwin Society. Sarah, said the Darwin Society, was "the fittest writer in America."

A Woman's Place was also praised by the *New York Times,* "No longer is Sarah Strydance issuing a wild cry from out of the Tundra, nor is she passing on a searing insight through the tangled web of the Canadian bush. This time it's women and baboons—in darkest Africa. But the Strydance voice is the same—the most mesmerizing Canadian female voice since Mary Pickford. It is a voice that will both soothe and arouse the ancient passions that still afflict both men and women—and, in the case of *A Woman's Place,* baboons as well."

Finally, Canadian nationalists viewed *A Woman's Place* as more than a feminist fantasy or just another animal story. They viewed *A Woman's Place* as a metaphor for Canadian-American relations and suggested that intrusions from American baboons into Canada should be limited by law to a maximum of three visits a year.

Sarah Strydance was in her late forties. Sarah's legs were short and stumpy and her posterior was far larger than the posteriors of the average member of the Methodist Mothers of Manitoba. Sarah's frizzy brown hair was parted down the middle and hung in a mess of ringlets down to her shoulders. Her face was narrow but pert; her eyes were small, alive. Her thin lips were pressed into a quirky half smile that delineated a high degree of self-satisfaction plus an enormous willingness to share the dazzling insights and abstractions she had so carefully accumulated over the years. Oh, Sarah loved to teach, to instruct, to revise, to correct. She was willing to listen to anyone—anyone who worshipped her, agreed with her, swore fealty to her, or who would introduce her gushingly—as Esther Dvorkin, chairwoman, was now doing.

"The Jewish women of Winnipeg," said Esther Dvorkin, chairwoman, "have no greater friend, no greater guide to living the correct Canadian way than Sarah Strydance. Everyone knows of her writing skills, of her crusade for women. Sarah is probably the greatest Methodist Mother of Manitoba—of them all. A close friend of J.S. Woodsworth, a great socialist and a great feminist—ladies, I give you Sarah Strydance, O.B.E., Order of the British Empire!"

Sarah Strydance's message to the members of Emma's Enemas of the People Anarcho-socialist Reading Club was stark in its simplicity. The emancipation of women was being halted, said Sarah, by the pervasive spread of demon rum. Women were too battered by drunken husbands and drunken lovers to be able to picket and demonstrate for women's rights. Demon rum, said Sarah, had stopped socialism dead in its tracks. The workers were too drunk to strike or act class consciously. There were not enough houses, shoes, shirts and socks to shelter and clothe the hungry and the poor because the workers were too drunk to build or make these necessary goods.

Then came Sarah's bombshell. "It was Bronfman and his whiskey barons and the bootleggers they control," said Sarah, "who brought this unwanted war with its Dieppes of despair upon us in the first place. It is Bronfman, the whiskey barons and their bootlegger's allies who are stopping us from winning the War now. Dieppe didn't just happen! It was made to happen! It was Bronfman and the whiskey barons who debauched our Canadian boys before they ever embarked for Dieppe. Our boys," said Sarah Strydance, jabbing her delicate forefinger in the air above her pretty little head, "were too damn drunk with Bronfman liquor to capture Dieppe. That's the real story, ladies!"

The ladies of the Emma's Enemas Reading Club were seized by a mixture of emotions. Sam Bronfman, after all, was once a neighbourhood boy, and now his name had been taken in vain. Emma's Enemas were socialists, sisters, wives and mothers and their fellow socialist sister and mother, the widow Sarah Strydance, had just given them the first explanation of the Dieppe fiasco that made some sense. A resolution moved by Esther Dvorkin, seconded by Fette Feige, condemning Samuel Bronfman and the whiskey trade for all the sins of the country and for the ghastly fiasco at Dieppe was carried unanimously.

Isaac Dvorkin, the editor of the *Jewish Streetfighter* was in a foul mood. That morning Isaac had lost one of his many battles with Menachem Shtarker, his paper's ace reporter. The head on Shtarker's story stayed in the paper: "Streetfighter Editor's Wife Champions Prohibitionist-Feminist Attack on Samuel Bronfman." Sam Shandelman, a Bronfman fixer, had phoned Dvorkin that morning to tell him there would be no more "Jewish Man of Distinction" and Universal Mattress advertisements in the paper in the future. There would also be no more free Seagram's V.O. rye for the Streetfighter's annual summer picnic in Kildonan Park.

But what made things even worse was that Esther, under the Strydance influence, had thrown all the V.O. bottles out of the house.

Susan Ryan

I love meeting moral relativists, people who say there is no right or wrong, it's all just point of view. Mother Teresa, Ted Bundy. Same difference. I kick them in the shins, real hard. When they howl, I say, "What's wrong? *I* enjoyed that."

Bob Edwards

When Solomon said there was a time and a place for everything he had not encountered the problem of parking his automobile.

—*Eye Opener*, July 1, 1922

Esther was also hinting at leaving Isaac altogether unless Dvorkin did something about "Bronfman and the whiskey barons. If Bronfman stays in business, we will have a Dieppe every day—and Hitler will be here in Winnipeg tomorrow!"

"Esther, you don't really believe Bronfman got the troops drunk before Dieppe?"

"Why not? Bronfman's had this city half drunk day in and day out—ever since I first arrived here!"

[Yes, Ms. Strydance *is* unmasked as a fascist by the end of the story.]

MIRACLE ON CENTRAL AVENUE

Frank Macdonald

There is a God. The manifest proof of His existence is most often experienced by individuals who are left speechless by the serene beauty of the universe. Only rarely are His good works performed before a host of witnesses, but it has happened. The biblical evidence can be confirmed in the story of the loaves and fishes. In desperate circumstances the Lord intercedes to influence the outcome of a worthy cause.

On Wednesday afternoon of last week the power failed, putting our fragile existence on hold. At 3:00 p.m. kettles stopped boiling, cash registers quit and restaurants were caught with nothing but a menu of cold cuts. Empty cars parked beside crippled gas tanks at the garages, banking facilities had to let their customers keep their money a little longer, and newspaper computers crashed. The town of Inverness marked time, while the non-electric clocks ticked on.

At 4:00 p.m. no flicker of electricity pulsed into the empty outlets. At 5:00 p.m. expectations were sinking in the sweltering heat of the hottest day of the year. A mild anxiety gripped the community as the rooster tugged the worm on the face of the clock that read 5:30 p.m. The power failure was reaching its critical point although there was no visible evidence of panic in the streets. But it could be felt, like the desperate lurking of something sinister in a midnight graveyard. A large entourage of cars cruised back and forth over Central Avenue, the drivers sweating and parched and praying behind the sun-baked windshields.

At 5:55 p.m. on Wednesday evening, June 16th, 1988, the Lord said "Let there be light!" the miracle unlocking the door of the Inverness liquor store for five brief minutes. The spiritual devotion of this community has been largely under-estimated, but the joint offering of rosaries, hymns, letters to Jimmy Swaggart and meditations upon the belly of the Buddha turned the ear of heaven nostalgic for the days when whole wedding parties cheered the trick of turning water into wine.

Only five or six cars belonging to the truly faithful had parked in front of the liquor store all afternoon, those who had not seen but believed. At 10 seconds past 5:55 p.m., a cheerful multitude swarmed into the parking lot like a congregation late for Easter Mass. Stress, anxiety and doubt evaporated like mist under the magnificent presence of the sun, the celestial symbol of the light at the end of the dark tunnel of existence.

No fire, accident, drowning or circus has drawn so many in so few seconds. Eighty-year-old women sprinted down the sidewalk, conservative middle-aged men squealed into the parking lot like teenagers on hot rods, and relieved youngsters with amorous plans for a warm summer evening wondered if a shopping cart full was enough. They came out of restaurant kitchens, down telephone poles and on crutches to pay homage to the miracle. Even teetotallers were compelled to participate for the sheer joy of sharing the five-minute moment.

At 6:00 p.m. it was over. The key turned in the lock according to scripture and verse of the Nova Scotia Liquor Control Act. The fervent crowd dispersed with whatever they could carry or consume, but more than one of the gratefully blessed was heard to utter, "I was thirsty and you gave me drink."

HOW TO BEHAVE IN THE COMPANY OF GIANTS
FROM *THE BIGGEST MODERN WOMAN OF THE WORLD*

Susan Swan

Do not ask, "How's the weather up there?" or talk about good things coming in small packages.

Do not speak in a loud voice like Gulliver, who remained small when he appeared big.

Do not trick giants into being measured. Giants lie about their height: as a way of pleasing the world; out of politeness; sometimes through fear or humility.

Do not bribe giants to exhibit themselves unless you have left them no other way to make a living.

Do not expect giants to carry you when you can walk.

Do not make giants perform rescue operations when there is nobody to save.

Do not climb to the top of a giant's head to make yourself feel important.

Do not boil giant flesh for bones to make bridges, even in your imagination.

Do not kill giants and steal their treasures.

Do not bring giants gifts or take them out to the park because it is be-nice-to-a-giant week.

Bob Edwards

Meanwhile, the meek are a long time inheriting the earth.

How to Behave in the Company of Dwarfs

Do not try to breed dwarfs.

Do not put dwarfs in choker collars and ask them to run naked through your apartment.

Do not serve dwarfs in cold meat pies as a way of improving a dull dinner party.

Do not exhibit dwarfs in boxes or sell their bodies to the College of Surgeons before they die.

Do not handle dwarfs in your lap or against your breast unless you have carnal inclinations.

Do not say "Hi Pygmy!" to a dwarf.

Do not wipe your hands on the hair of dwarfs sitting beneath banquet tables.

You can nominate dwarfs for the legislature; dwarfs have sharp wits and make excellent counsellors of state.

Do not make dwarfs fight turkeys for your amusement.

Where to See Giants

The American Museum.

The Roman games at the Coliseum.

Civic parades, where giants are stuffed and mounted on floats.

Any schoolyard, where there is sure to be one giant who may not grow tall enough to work for P.T. Barnum.

Where to See Dwarfs and Midgets

The American Museum, picking on giants.

Wrestling in teams in European sporting events.

Holding bridles in civic processions.

QUEEN OF ALL THE DUSTBALLS

Bill Richardson

Once, not very long ago, and not so far away,
Lived a man called Bob, who, at the dawning of each day
Vowed to rid the world of grime and keep it all pristine.
He'd dab his dainty wrists and lobes with Vim and Mr. Clean,
Then don his starched and ironed jeans and freshly laundered shirt:
And stride into the germy world to vanquish filth and dirt.
No spill nor stain nor stinking drain would valiant Bob deter:
He'd fight them with his trusty sponge and mop Excalibur.

He had a potent vacuum he could use for heavy jobs:

And any guy would die to have a crevice tool like Bob's.

So long so wide so true so tried, imbued with lasting power,

The kind of tool to make you drool and run a chilling shower.

(But that's enough of all this stuff, I'll get myself in trouble:

You'll say I'm sick if I inflict more rude *entendre doubles*.)

Let's harken back to Bob and to the story that's at hand:

His mission was to purge the scourge of dirt throughout the land.

He'd travel through the countryside and challenge every mess:

He had a thousand solvents to alleviate distress.

If gallant lords or damsels couldn't cope with rampant dustballs.

They never had the slightest doubt that it was Bob they must call.

A breathless runner one day came, his ruby lips were trembling.

"How now brown cow?" asked noble Bob, no need of fear dissembling.

"Oh master Bob," the runner sobbed, his eyes all wild and feral,

We have construed, oh fearful news, our nation is in peril!

I do not sing of petty things, like cash or constitutions,

But rather of a dustball that's demanding restitution.

No, not some pallid ball of dust that lurks beneath the bed,

No tiny hallway tumblewood," the frightened runner said,

"No, this is one mad mama, with a mean gleam in her eye,

She's Yukon cold and twice as big again as PEI!

She's called you names like Git and Twit and Nit and even Slob:

She's Queen of all the Dustballs and she's out to get you, Bob!"

"Oh is that so? Ho ho! Ho ho!" cried Bob, "Well let her threaten!

That dusty yob has not met Bob, nor faced his fearsome weapons!

My faithful mop Excalibur will end her grisly rule:

The dreadful wretch won't soon forget my mighty crevice tool!"

So out Bob strode along the road, cheered on by gladsome crowds.

He swaggered full of confidence, erect, correct, and proud.

As David slew Goliath and as Beowulf offed Grendel,

Bob was preened to meet the queen and prove she could be handled.

Stevie Ray Fromstein

So the cop pulls me over. And he says to me, "You have any idea how *fast* you were going?"

So I said, "You're the fascist pig; *you* tell *me*."

Well, I didn't...use those *exact* words. I think what I said was, "No sir, I *don't*."

Lorne Elliott

Psychologists say that we only use 10 percent of our mental capacity. I thought that was clever, and then I thought, if that's true, whoever said that, there's a 90 percent chance that he's *wrong*.

He smelled her ere he saw her, and he gasped at what he saw:

A tangled mass of glinging dirt around a gaping maw.

She had a tumbling swagger and she had a vicious sneer:

She pulsed and loomed and then she boomed: "Hey Bob! Get over here!

I see you've brought some toys along in order to defeat me:

Is that your famous crevice tool? Or are you pleased to meet me?"

"Oh foul wretch!" big Bob kvetched, "from what dank grave exhumed?

Now leave our land, no man will stand to hear his tool impugned!"

So fell they to. I know that you have never ever seen

So grim a sight as was the fight of Robert and the Queen.

He dashed her with Excalibur, she countered every charge,

Their vicious words were clearly heard from here to Lake Labarge.

He doused her with ammonia, and she uttered piercing shrieks.

She filled his lungs with dust and dung, till Bob, once strong, grew weak,

From brute to wimp, all wilted, limp, he spent his warrior lust:

She showed no ruth but proved the truth that man's no match for dust.

Bob will never more be seen. His mission has been squelched.

His only sordid epitaph was when the dust queen belched.

My tale is done. The moral is one that's very plain to see.

Dust is how you started out, and dust is what you'll be.

—CLEMENTS

INDEX: THERE IS NO INDEX

Stephen Leacock

Readers of books, I mean worthwhile readers, like those who read this volume, will understand how many difficulties centre round the making of an index. Whether to have an Index at all? Whether to make it a great big one, or just a cute little Index on one page? Whether to have only proper names, or let it take in ideas—and so on. In short the thing reaches dimensions that may raise it to the rank of being called the Index Problem, if nothing is done about it.

Of course one has to have an Index. Authors themselves would prefer not to have any. Having none would save trouble and compel readers to read the whole book instead of just the Index. But the reader needs it. Otherwise he finds himself looking all through the book, forwards and then backwards, and then plunging in at random in order to read out to a friend what it was that was so darned good about Talleyrand. He doesn't find it, because it was in another book.

So let us agree, there must be an Index. Now comes the trouble. What is the real title or name of a thing or person that has three or four? Must you put everything three or four times over in the Index, under three or four names? No, just once, so it is commonly understood; and then for the other joint names, we put what is called a cross-reference, meaning, "See this" or "See that." It sounds good in theory, but in practice it leads to such results as—*Talleyrand, see Perigord*...and when you hunt this up, you find—*Perigord, Bishop of, see Talleyrand*.

The same effect can be done flat out, with just two words, as *Lincoln, see* Abraham...Abraham, *see* Lincoln. But even that is not so bad because at least it's a closed circle. It comes to a full stop. But compare the effect, familiar to all research students, when the circle is not closed. Thus, instead of just seeing Lincoln, the unclosed circle runs like this, each item being hunted up alphabetically, one after the other—Abraham, *see* Lincoln...Lincoln, *see* Civil War...Civil War, *see* United States...United States, *see* America...America, *see* American History...American History, *see* also Christopher Columbus, New England, Pocahontas, George Washington...the thing will finally come to rest somehow or other with the dial pointing at *see* Abraham Lincoln.

But there is worse even than that. A certain kind of conscientious author enters only proper names, but he indexes them every time they come into his book, no matter how they come in, and how unimportant is the context. Here is the result in the Index under the Letter N:

Napoleon—17, 26, 41, 73, 109, 110, 156, 213, 270, 380, 460. You begin to look them up. Here are the references:

Page 17—"wore his hair like Napoleon."

Page 26—"in the days of Napoleon."

Page 41—"as fat as Napoleon."

Page 73—"not so fat as Napoleon."

Page 109—"was a regular Napoleon at Ping-pong."

Page 110—"was not a Napoleon at Ping-pong."

Page 156—"Napoleon's hat."

Pages 213, 270, 380, 460, not investigated.

Equally well meant but perhaps even harder to bear is the peculiar kind of index that appears in a biography. The name of the person under treatment naturally runs through almost every page, and the conscientious index-maker tries to keep pace with him. This means that many events of his life get shifted out of their natural order. Here is the general effect.

John Smith: born, p.1; born again, p.1; father born, p. 2; grandfather born, p. 3; mother born, p. 4; mother's family leave Ireland, p. 5; still leaving it, p. 6; school, p. 7; more school; p. 8; dies of pneumonia and enters Harvard, p. 9; eldest son born, p. 10; marries, p. 11; back at school, p. 12; dead; p. 13. takes his degree, p. 14...Suppose, then, you decide to get away from all these difficulties and make a Perfect Index in which each item shall carry with it an explanation, a sort of little epitome of what is to be found in the book. The reader consulting the volume can open the Index, look at a reference, and decide whether or not he needs to turn the subject up in the full discussion in the book. A really good Index will in most cases itself give the information wanted. There you have, so to speak, the Perfect Index.

Why I know about this is because I am engaged at present in making such an Index in connection with a book on gardening, which I am writing just now. To illustrate what is meant, I may be permitted to quote the opening of the book, and its conversion into Index Material:

As Abraham Lincoln used to say, when you want to do gardening, you've got to take your coat off, a sentiment shared by his fellow enthusiast, the exiled Napoleon, who, after conquering all of Europe, retaining only the sovereignty of the spade in his garden plot at St. Helena, longed only for more fertilizer.

As arranged for the Index, the gist, or essential part of this sentence, the nucleus, so to speak, appears thus:

Abraham Lincoln: habit of saying things, p.1; wants to do gardening, p.1; takes his coat off, p.1; his enthusiasm, p.1; compared with Napoleon, p.1.

Coat: taken off by Abraham Lincoln, p. 1.

Gardening: Lincoln's view on, p. 1; need of taking coat off, for, p. 1; Napoleon's enthusiasm over, p. 1; *see also* under spade, sovereignty, St. Helena.

Napoleon: his exile, p. 1; conquers Europe, p. 1; enthusiastic over gardening, p. 1; compared with Lincoln; retains sovereignty of spade, p. 1; plots at St. Helena, p. 1; longs for fertilizer, p. 1; *see also* Europe, St. Helena, fertilizer, seed catalogue, etc., etc. ...

That's as far as I've got with the sentence. I still have to write up *sovereignty, spade, sentiment, share, St. Helena,* and everything after S. There's no doubt it's the right method, but it takes time somehow to get the essential nucleus of the gist, and express it. I see why it is easier to do the other thing. But then sin is also easier than righteousness. See also under Hell, road to, Pavement, and Intentions, good.

SORRY—I KEPT MEANING TO INCLUDE THIS ONE,
BUT NEVER COULD GET AROUND TO IT...

PROCRASTINATION

Bill Carr

I'm here today to confirm the rumours. What people have been saying about me is true. I've come forward on behalf of thousands of others to tell our story. I am a procrastinator.

It's true. I put off till tomorrow what I could do today.

You see, I have a theory. If it's bleeding, put a band-aid on it. If it's not, don't pick it.

I have a friend who gets up every morning, makes a great huge list of things to do, and then extinguishes his day doing them. Yuck. I'll admit, there are things which have to be done, and I've made a list of them: eating, sleeping, loving, and brushing your teeth. Other than that, everything else is optional.

I honed my procrastination skills while at university. I felt that you shouldn't study on Monday because Monday was the beginning of the week and you don't want to leap into anything.

I didn't study on Tuesday because I found it was such a short day anyway.

Wednesday, I took a mid-week break.

Thursday was really the beginning of the weekend.

Then, thank God it's Friday, and nobody studies on Friday.

Saturday is a play day.

And Sunday is a day of rest.

See, procrastinators are happy people. We don't have ulcers, we have smile wrinkles. We would worry about things, we really would. We just never get around to it.

Someday, procrastinators will rule the world.

Maybe tomorrow.

Or the day after.

Whatever.

LIST OF CONTRIBUTORS

Page numbers indicate page on which piece begins.

Three Dead Trolls in a Baggie: 254
Torgov, Morley: 128
Tremblay, Michel: 44
Unger, Jim: 69, 103, 133, 171
Walker, George F.: 150
Ward, Norman: 8
Waxman, Martin: 113
Wayne and Shuster: 86
Weir, Charles: 252
West, Bruce: 155
White, Nancy: 29, 68
Wicks, Ben: 45, 182
Williams, Harland: 4, 7, 15, 28, 125, 212
Zolf, Larry: 263

Copyright Acknowledgements

The editor wishes to thank all the individuals and publishers for permission to reproduce material listed below. Every effort has been made to obtain applicable copyright information. Please notify publisher of any errors or omissions. All rights reserved.

Cartoon by Aislin reprinted with permission of the cartoonist and *The Gazette* (Montreal).

"The Beautiful Banks of Toronto" and "You Blanket Me Like Impending Doom" reprinted with permission of Al and George: Al Rae, George Westholm and Anthony Mancini.

Cartoons by Grahame Arnould reprinted with permission of the cartoonist.

"Simmering" and "Women's Novels" from *Murder in the Dark* Copyrigtht ©1983 Margaret Atwood reprinted with permission from Coach House Press.

Cartoon by Bado reprinted with permission of Guy Badeaux, *Le Droit*, Ottawa.

"If I Had $1000000" by Barenaked Ladies Copyright ©1991 words and music by Steven Page and Ed Robertson reprinted with permission.

"Turvey Is Enlisted" from *Turvey: A Military Picaresque* by Earle Birney used by permission of the Canadian Publishers McClelland & Stewart, Toronto.

"Carrying Th Torch" from *Beyond Even Faithful Legends* Copyright © Bill Bissett reprinted with permission of the author.

"It's a Girl (Father Expected to Live)" from *Arthur! Arthur!* Copyright ©1992 Arthur Black. Reprinted with permission of Stoddart Publishing Co. Limited, Don Mills, Ont.

"Bobby Clobber, Public Relater" by Dave Broadfoot taped at Massey Hall in Toronto, December 1991, reprinted with permission of the author.

"Glorious and Free" by Dave Broadfoot from *Member For Kicking Horse Pass*, performed for *Air Farce*, May 1990, reprinted with permission of author.

Excerpts from *Sex and Security: a Frank and Fearless Political Statement By the Honourable Member of Parliament for Kicking Horse Pass*. Copyright ©1974 Dave Broadfoot. Reprinted with permission of the author.

"Procrastination" by Bill Carr reprinted with permission of the author.

Excerpt from *Heartbreaks Along the Road* Copyright ©1987 Roch Carrier. Trans. by Sheila Fischman. Originally published by House of Anansi Press. Reproduced with permission of Stoddart Publishing Co. Limited, Don Mills, Ont.

Excerpt from *Moo* Copyright ©Sally Clark. Reprinted with the permission of **Playwrights Canada Press**, 54 Wolsley St., 2nd flr, Toronto, Ont. M5T 1A5, (416) 947-0701, fax (416) 947-0159.

"And the Warranty on His Shadow Has Expired" by Warren Clements originally appeared in *The Globe and Mail*, January 9, 1988. Reprinted with permission of *The Globe and Mail*.

"Nestlings" cartoons by Warren Clements Copyright © Warren Clements reproduced with permission of the cartoonist.

"SNAP" and "Vintage Misery" by CODCO: Cathy Jones, Greg Malone, Tommy Sexton, Mary Walsh and Andy Jones. Reprinted with permission of CODCO Ltd. and Salter Street Films.